BOSTON

STER

SLATERSVILLE

HODE

PROVIDENCE

ISLAND

NEWPORT

STERLY

MANTUNUCK

ISLAND SD.

ISLAND SD.

BLOCK ISLAND

"This Town Meeting Country is a complex land full of paradoxes valid only in New England, yet it has been created by a few basic principles of just and democratic government and at its core lies respect for the integrity of man's spirit."

TOWN MEETING COUNTRY

by

Clarence Webster

Self-reliant, independent, yet endowed with a fine community spirit, the people of New England have come to represent American tradition perhaps more completely than has any other regional group. Clarence Webster's book about the New England town, its early days and late, its customs and people, is a narrative packed with old truths and some mighty interesting surprises.

Town Meeting Country is done with a loving hand. Mr. Webster is writing of the region north and east of New London, Connecticut, and of the small towns which grew up in that region. This is his home base, and he does its traditions and its folk lore full, sound, and humorous Yankee justice.

Most Americans will get deep satisfaction, hours of thoughtful pleasure, and no little pride out of reading a book like this at a time like this. For, as the author points out, this book is the story of the New England town and to know that story is "to understand in part why the United States can be a democracy . . . and the best place to study this story is in *Town Meeting Country*."

UNTRY

AMERICAN FOLKWAYS

EDITED BY ERSKINE CALDWELL

In Preparation

AMERICAN
FOLKWAYS

EDITED BY ERSKINE CALDWELL

TOWN
MEETING
COUNTRY

by

CLARENCE M. WEBSTER

DUELL, SLOAN & PEARCE • NEW YORK

A WARTIME BOOK

THIS COMPLETE EDITION IS PRODUCED
IN FULL COMPLIANCE WITH THE GOVERN-
MENT'S REGULATIONS FOR CONSERVING
PAPER AND OTHER ESSENTIAL MATERIALS

MANUFACTURED IN THE UNITED STATES OF AMERICA
BY THE VAIL-BALLOU PRESS, INC., BINGHAMTON, N. Y.

To the memory of my mother
whose ancestors helped settle
the Town Meeting Country

Contents

Contents

TOWN MEETING COUNTRY

CHAPTER 1

Town Meeting Country

ALL over the United States there are "countries" of people, and in each there is a central force that has molded the thought and behavior of the people of the region. That force may be the newness of the land, or the difficulties imposed by nature, the physical contact with desert and plain, or a religious idea as impelling as that of the Mormons, but always some dominant power creates man's folkways.

In New England it is the town.

That complex unit of life, the New England town, is more than so many persons living in a rectangle seven miles one way and six another, with a charter from the state, and its own selectmen and the money they can spend. It is a concept of political philosophy and, also, a deeply satisfying spiritual reality. This town gives the New Englander exactly what he demands—a sensible and efficient form of government with freedom to be himself. Even though the town encloses us, it is not tyrannical. Sometimes the power that creates our folkways is jealous and demands of the individual a strict conformity in behavior. Witness the mores of the South. But the New England town is wiser. After we have obeyed its laws, it allows us to do as we please; in fact, it encourages us to act in ways that often disconcert our visitors.

This, then, is the story of the New England town. To know it is to understand in part why the United States can be a democracy, and the best place to study this story is in Town Meeting Country.

The limits of Town Meeting Country are sharply defined. That is as it should be, for boundaries mean a lot to New Englanders. For instance, we walk our town bounds every few years.

3

We never suspect another town of stealing some of our territory, but keeping the bounds straight is a sacred duty. Yankees like to know "where they stand." We distrust anything indefinite or muddled, or the casual or broad or sweeping estimate of material affairs; we must set sharp boundaries to our town, our farms, and our lot on the village street; and we are meticulous in details of business and demand exact accounting down to the last penny. We are not being fussy; we are making sure of the externals of life so we can settle down to enjoy it.

One cannot say with a fine generous gesture, "Oh, this country begins about here, or perhaps twenty miles farther east, and runs to, well, let's say to that range of hills or maybe the next one."

I am not out in the Desert Country or in the High Border Country. I am in a small segment of New England where a mile is something to reckon with. I am in Town Meeting Country.

Long Island and Block Island sounds are on the south of us. The western boundary begins at the mouth of the Connecticut River, follows it to East Haddam, and then goes north to Ludlow village in Massachusetts. Then the line runs due east to the southern limits of the city of Worcester. From there it goes southeast to the Rhode Island line at Slatersville; then it drops south to Block Island Sound at a point just west of Mantunuck.

Those boundaries enclose an area of about sixty by fifty square miles. Approximately two-thirds of it is in Connecticut. On the north is an irregular rectangle of Massachusetts about fifteen miles in width and thirty-five miles in length. On the east is a strip of Rhode Island ten miles wide and forty miles long. Down on Long Island Sound is our largest city, New London, with a population of twenty-five thousand. Due east eighteen miles is Westerly, the only Rhode Island city in this region. Along the Sound there is a narrow belt of low, open country; then it slowly rises until it reaches a general elevation of one thousand feet at the Massachusetts border. Still farther north the hills are lower, and in Rhode Island the highest one is only a little over eight hundred feet.

One large river, the Thames, which is almost a long, shallow bay, runs from New London to Norwich, the second largest city. Into the Thames flow the Yantic, Shetucket, and Quinebaug. Along these are a dozen or more small mill centers, and even the lesser rivers have their little industrial villages. In the jumbled mass of hills to the north, the rivers break up into brooks, and they in turn become tiny streams.

In the hills and on the irregular plateaus are the villages. A score of them are the tourist's dream of what rural New England is like—a slender-spired church, old houses with white clapboards and green blinds, all standing around a green or behind neat lawns that slope down to the road.

Between each village the roads wind up hill and down. Here and there is a narrow valley with a little brook running through it. In the valley are fine fields and meadow lands. The houses and barns on these farms are large and well kept, and herds of Guernseys or Holsteins feed in the open pastures. The hill roads are bordered by a few good farms, but more often than not the fields are stony and the pastures clogged with brush. And for miles the road may pass through woods, with only an occasional farm to show that people live in this country. Once in a while a dirt road runs crookedly up into the hills. On it is an old house that once was beautiful in a reserved, dignified way. Now it is falling to pieces, and the sheds and barns are in worse condition. A little farther along is a shack made of old boards and tar paper. A stovepipe juts from one window, and in the door stand two dirty children.

All sorts of people live in this country. The small cities are full of names strange to Anglo-Saxon ears and you hear other languages spoken in the stores. The mail boxes by the side of the country roads tell you that Allada, Lejeune, Somonski, Paletti, and Sincovitch live next to Moseley, Griffin, Tillinghast, and Utley. Every so often there is a place with flower gardens and a stone terrace and lawn chairs. Inevitably a sign proclaims that this is Meadow Acres or River View or Home Ground. You know that city folks live here, for they are the only ones who name their homes.

However, the visitor almost inevitably misses the significance of one thing he sees. Those signs beside the road—"Town of Hebron," "Entering Town of Dudley," "Scotland Town Line" —mean nothing to him. He didn't see any town. All there was near the sign were woods and pastures and mowing lots and maybe one lone house. But when he passed the town sign, he was going from one unit of life to another. Each are similar in basic design, but emphatically, proudly, and cussedly different in tax rates, budget, and other important ways. For Yankee towns are like Yankees; they are created and sustained by the same ideas as their fellows, but damned independent otherwise.

Of course, there are towns in most of the other regions of New England. Such urban areas as Boston, or the strip of cities from Newport to Woonsocket, or New Haven to Port Chester, have no time for such anachronisms, but all the rest of the Six States can show these baffling units of communal life. That northern wilderness of the State of Maine has not been made up into towns yet, but let a few more city sports invade it, and the guides will hold a town meeting in self-defense. Yes, there are these communities called towns all over New England, but the best region to study is this country of mine.

In the southwest corner of Connecticut the Lords and Ladies of the Manor have pretty well bought up the village houses and the outlying acres, and the townspeople have turned into forehead-knocking parasites. On Cape Cod the year-rounders are just as badly off; New Hampshire mountains are full of tourists and appreciators in the summer and snow fanatics in the winter; and the State of Maine is a glorified shore resort or sportsman's lodge. Of course, quite a few towns in those regions are holding out, but there are not enough of them to form a sharply defined unit of life. And although Vermont has plenty of strong communities, these are not as representative of the folkways that created them as are ours in Town Meeting Country. Up in the Republican Hills, those little cities and villages haven't had to fight the hard battles our towns have won. The Indians were pretty well subdued when much of Vermont was settled, and it has never had to combat industrialization and foreign conquest the way we have. Up there the town has lived without being tested; down in this land it has proved its strength; here it stands for more than age. It is old, and it deserves to be old.

There is another reason why Town Meeting Country best illustrates the way the New England town dominates its people. Here, as in no other region, we have the small mill city. At least, they are cities as far as numbers go—say, over six thousand, or some other arbitrary figure—and they are urban enough in schools, hospitals, hotels, and so on. But in folkways they are "towns built around a mill or two." It is hard enough nowadays for any community, no matter how remote, to preserve that identity of spirit that marks the true New England town, and when a polyglot mill city retains it—well, there you have something worth studying.

This Town Meeting Country was destined to be made up of just such towns and small cities. New London had a fine harbor, but the Thames did not reach far inland and did not tap a rich hinterland. None of the rivers that flowed into the Thames was large enough to be the home of a great industrial valley, but inevitably many little cities sprang up. And on the still smaller streams there were built mills around which a few hundred people lived. Up above the narrow valleys were the hills and woods. Here and there were sweeps of meadows or open land on a hilltop, and each was the site of a village.

It was inevitable that this region become a slowly developing structure of townships. A few settlers would come and take the good land beside a little river or on a hillside. When more people arrived there was no room for them, and they founded a settlement a few miles away. It was the same way with the small mill cities—there simply wasn't room on this or that stream for more than one industry, so the ambitious man said, "To hell with it! I'll find some water of my own." When a country develops that way, its people never concentrate in one favorable site or create one specialized way of making a living. But such a land does build a lot of hardy, self-sufficient communities.

Scores of ways of life built the Yankee towns and cities. Killing Indians efficiently, bundling, slave-running, peddling, working hard and late, rum drinking, breeding big families, marrying again when he or she passed on, preaching original sin, berating the heretics, teaching the three R's, being sure of your grants and bounds, respecting the dominie, going to church on Sunday, upholding the good old doctrine and discipline, demanding yours; being contrary, peevish, narrow; being a good neighbor and working for the good of the community. Those were some of the folkways that helped build the town; the same folkways, along with those created to fit new situations, still sustain us.

One of these folkways, brought down from the past and yet still strong, is the most significant of all. At least once every year the voters, or perhaps the voters and also the property owners, come together in more or less solemn conclave. Now and then they meet twice a year and, if suitable petitions are presented,

the citizens can assemble as often as they wish. They seldom misuse their right, so the New England town meeting has the dignity
of an event created by some deep-rooted desire in the people.
And that is just what it is—an assembly born of the spirit of the
people who come to it.

Once upon a time, in the very earliest months of the Massachusetts Bay colonies, all the town affairs were handled in
meeting. But almost immediately the Puritans saw that this plan
was altogether too cumbersome; therefore, the town meeting's
function was confined to approval of taxes, appropriations, and
other such annual problems. But while the people took away
the assembly's power, they knew that it must in another sense be
kept; in fact, should take on added dignity and worth in the eyes
of men. Today the same town meeting is held to prove to the
world that, if it wanted to, the New England town could run its
affairs by the yea and nay of popular vote. Of course, it doesn't
intend to do any such thing, but it wants it fully understood that
it is sworn to this principle.

Because each New England community has its meetings, and
there are towns everywhere in the Six Sacred States, it is obvious
that this particular Town Meeting Country of mine has no
monopoly on Yankee Witenagemots. But the meetings down this
way are more representative than those anywhere else. These
meetings are old, and they have survived many forces from
within and without which seemed about to destroy them. Not
only have they continued to live; they have made newcomers and
aliens bow to the principle they stand for. In no other region of
New England have these assemblies stood the tests they have in
my country.

Though Town Meeting Country is old, not very often does the
visitor smell the musty odor of dry rot that hangs over many
ancient towns and cities. It is beautiful, but never flamboyant or
seductive. It is a sober country that disdains gallant gestures and
the glorification of wild deeds. We rejoice that the turbulent
Miz-zou-rye does *not* flow through our pastures, and we would
put a Hatfield or McCoy or Wild Bill Hickock in the county jail
along with the vagrant ballad singer and the cowboy who disturbed the peace with his loud talking. It is a sensible land where
romance does not flourish, and the picturesque froofraw of life
is not appreciated. Scarlett O'Hara was not a neo-Puritan

maiden, and a Congregational Deacon would rent Tara Hall to the summer folks. Practicality is the motto of this country. We would drain a bayou and use all the Spanish moss for bed ticking.

Legend and lore are discouraged in these towns. Memories can be held in secret places of the heart, but to talk about them is not quite decent. This is a tolerant country where many different people and races live in the same town and grant each the same rights. It is a contrary, set, stubborn, and thoroughly cussed land that regards acts of dour conduct as nothing more than the way a sensible person behaves.

This Town Meeting Country is a complex land full of paradoxes valid only in New England, yet it has been created by a few basic principles of just and democratic government, and at its core lies respect for the integrity of each man's spirit.

CHAPTER 2

The Redskins and the Godly

OTHER sections of this dramatic and articulate land tell horrendous stories of Indian massacres and battles. The lone settler defending his cabin against the redskins; the covered wagons fighting off the whooping savages until the cavalry rides to the rescue; Custer's Last Stand, immortalized in song, in movies, and large paintings that hang behind the bar beside the one of the blonde nude. All these are part of the legend of how a stalwart race conquered a treacherous foe. To listen to this lore is to believe that the Indian did not begin to be a mean hombre until the first settlers invaded the regions west of the Hudson. The legend is that he became steadily more vicious and warlike as he was met farther west, and he reached the high point of diabolical cussedness on the plains of Montana and Wyoming where he had the audacity to best the sacrosanct U. S. Cavalry.

History devotes pages to the trouble with the Five Nations, a chapter to Tecumseh and Pontiac, and books to the Sioux, Comanches, Apaches, Blackfeet, and the other terrible western tribes. A few of these accounts tell of possible wrongs suffered by the Indians, and several admit that they worried the whites considerably, even in open battle, but on the whole the tales recite the glories of victory by the white man as he pushed west. All these accounts of warfare with Indians are based on fact. Covered-wagon trains were wiped out, and Custer's men fell fighting bravely. But before 1700 the New England colonists had suffered more, fought harder foes, and beaten them more thoroughly than all the other pioneers put together ever did.

The conflicts with the Iroquois in the Mohawk and Genesee Valleys come nearest to being as fierce and dangerous as those the Puritans waged, but even in New York the outcome was never in doubt, while my ancestors just missed being thrown out of the land they had appropriated. The western battles in the nineteenth century were bloody and hard, but if Custer was defeated there were more regiments to take his place. That is the real story back of all the later Indian battles. Individual settlers and groups and even towns might be conquered, but more people took their place; the westward push of a growing nation was irresistible. Pioneers in abundance, money, confidence, weapons, military training, an army, and a strong central government to support the whites gave the invaders an overwhelming advantage and made the defeat of the Indians inevitable.

It was a different story in New England in the seventeenth century. A few pioneers, hardly organized at all, ill-armed and poorly trained, unsupported by money or fresh recruits, had to fight for their existence, not only as individuals but as an experiment in colonization. Deerfield was a venture in settling the wilderness, and if it could not exist, the whole scheme of life in the new country would fail, or at the least be delayed for a long time. The early Puritans had settled in villages which were all within what seems to us now to be a very small area. Theoretically, these compact settlements could go to each other's aid, but the wilderness roads were poor, and before Brookfield could be rescued by Oxford, King Philip had done his work and was attacking Deerfield. These villages did fight hard and were of course harder to wipe out than a cabin in Kentucky, but when they fell the loss was greater in men and women and social consequences. And the tribes which fought the Puritans were as fierce and wily as any that ever took a scalp; furthermore, for a time at least some of them were led by one of the greatest of Indian strategists and fighters.

Town Meeting Country did not suffer quite as much from Indians as did the regions to the north and east, but its settlement and growth were dependent on the outcome of the conflict, and the two deciding battles were fought within its bounds. So the story of the Redskins and the Godly must be told first.

When the first settlers came to the region, the principal Indian tribes were the Narragansetts on the west shores of Narragansett Bay and the Pequots in the lands around the Thames River. The former were powerful and warlike, and held in subjection the Nyantics a little to the west and south. The Pequots were probably the bravest and most ferocious of all the New England tribes, and, therefore, about the toughest of any Indians the white man ever had to tackle. The Nipmucks to the north were less belligerent and, along with the Mohegans farther west, were dominated by the aggressive Pequots.

The first trouble came in 1633 when eight traders were killed by Indians subject to Sassacus, sachem of the Pequots. Three years later John Oldham was murdered near Block Island by Narragansett followers. From the very first the New England Indians displayed a great deal of skill in evading direct responsibility for a killing. A shrewd and crafty set, they were undoubtedly the equal of any Indians in guile, a fact that added considerably to the Puritans' task in subduing them. However, the whites had soon learned not to trust any protestations of innocence, and in revenge for Oldham's death they ravaged Block Island and killed as many Indians as they could find. Sassacus was very angry and immediately proposed to the Narragansetts that they join him in a war of extermination. If this proposal had been accepted, the struggling colonies might easily have been wiped out, but the Narragansetts hated the Pequots and also were friendly toward Roger Williams and his Plantation. So they refused the alliance and the Pequots went to war alone.

In the winter of 1636–1637 the Connecticut towns were attacked, and in Wethersfield ten people were killed and two girls stolen. The Puritans saw the danger that menaced the settlements and acted swiftly. In the spring of 1637, John Mason and John Underhill got together a small force of white men and persuaded about five hundred Mohegans, Nyantics, and Narragansetts to go with them to attack the Pequot fort near what is now Stonington, Connecticut. But when the fort was neared, the red allies slipped away, leaving seventy-seven Puritans to capture a camp covering three acres, surrounded by high palisades of wood with two very small openings at opposite ends, and defended by seven hundred good fighters. Think over those facts. The usual stories tell of a few whites besieged by hordes of yelling savages. Here the drama is in reverse: the Puritans, apparently in a hopeless minority, were carrying the fight to the enemy.

Mason took one opening, Underhill the other, and the Puritans began to fire into the Indian camp. The Pequots emerged, and those who escaped the whites were killed by the cowardly Indian allies who returned to the battle when they saw that the

dreaded Pequots were not invincible. In the end only five of the
enemy escaped, while the whites suffered two men killed and sixteen wounded. Early accounts of the affair do not tell very much
about details of fighting, but it is obvious that the Puritans must
have been very effective indeed with the musket and sword. Also
they followed up their victory most thoroughly. Those Pequots
who had not been in the fort were now destroyed in a running
fight to the west. Sassacus managed to escape to the Mohawks,
but those diplomats promptly killed him and sent his scalp to
Boston as proof of their good will.

All in all, this Pequot-Puritan battle was one of the most remarkable ever fought in this country. The whites had not waited
for more than one evidence of red menace before they went into
action. Then they had dared to assault a force almost ten times
superior in number. And, most astounding fact of all, they managed to win. To finish the miraculous campaign, they pushed
home their advantage ruthlessly and broke the Pequot nation
once and for all. The men who won this victory were not professional soldiers; neither did they have plentiful reserves behind them; they were sober, industrious pioneers who knew that
if they did not risk all on one battle they were lost.

After the Pequot massacre there was relative peace in the New
England colonies for almost forty years. The Puritans were in a
large measure responsible for this era of good feeling. More often
than not they bought land from the Indians, and efforts were
made to civilize the latter. John Eliot's work of christening was so
effective that by 1674 there were about four thousand converts,
fifteen hundred of whom lived in villages. One Indian even went
so far as to graduate from Harvard in 1665! But this happy period
was to end.

In 1660, Massasoit, sachem of the Wampanoags and ally of
Plymouth, died leaving two sons: Wamsutta or Alexander, and
Metacom or Philip. Soon after his father's death, Wamsutta died
under suspicious circumstances after a visit to Plymouth to answer charges of plotting mischief. Philip, now sachem of the
tribe, began to prepare to fight, but for some reason he waited
thirteen years before he struck. At various times he was reproved
for "showing a hostile spirit," and once an attempt was made to
disarm his tribe. John Mason and John Underhill would have
said sternly, "Wipe out the heathen before they make some real

trouble," but already the hard old spirit of the first settlers had
softened, not too much of course but enough so that watchful
waiting and appeasement could replace the swift thrust of the
sword.

At last a friendly, or treacherous, Indian went to Plymouth
with the story that Philip was plotting some real deviltry. Soon
after coming back from the white men, the talebearer was found
dead. For his murder three Wampanoags were tried, convicted,
and put to death. Incidentally, the jury that tried them was composed of both whites and Indians. No one knows now what that
gesture signifies. Were the Plymouth colonists giving even-
handed justice, or were they putting part of the blame for the
execution on Indian shoulders, so that there would be tribal
hatreds? The Wampanoags, however, were not impressed by fair
play or show of power. In June, 1675, King Philip's War began
with an attack on Swanzey. Troops were hurriedly called from
Boston, and Philip was driven from his headquarters in Mount
Hope, Rhode Island, but while this futile campaign was being
staged, the elusive Indians descended on Dartmouth.

The Puritans realized at once that they were fighting a superb
strategist whose men moved through the wilderness with almost
incredible swiftness and who seemed to anticipate each move of
the militia. In quick succession Middleborough, Taunton, and
Mendon were attacked and fearful atrocities committed. Now
the Nipmucks joined Philip and trouble flamed from the Connecticut River to Boston. Brookfield was besieged for three days,
and when it was rescued only one house stood unburned. It was
Deerfield's and Hadley's next turn. The latter settlement was
saved by the appearance of a mysterious stranger who rallied the
citizens. Perhaps he was Goffe, the regicide; perhaps one of those
strange men who lived hidden in the new country.

Philip struck at night, or in the morning, or at dusk; he smote
one town, and the next day he or his men attacked a hundred
miles away. Only a tough-minded people could have resisted
panic, and even they began to build up legends about the Indian
king who moved with such terrible swiftness. Here and there all
over eastern Massachusetts and Connecticut there are high cliffs
where Philip is supposed to have sat on some rocky throne and
plotted new raids or watched the rape of some settlement. But

the Puritans, even while they feared their enemy and almost gave him supernatural powers, fought on grimly.

For a while the struggle seemed to be going against the new settlers. For one defeat of the Indians, such as Hartford, there were half a dozen massacres that cut down the feeble Puritan forces. Probably the worst disaster of all occurred near harassed Deerfield. In September, 1675, eighteen wagons with laborers were sent to the abandoned town to finish threshing and bring in the grain. To escort them went Captain Lothrop and his train-band of ninety picked men. This was the Flower of Essex, and the best-drilled and equipped company in New England. After the work was finished, a night march was made, and at seven in the morning, as the company was crossing what is now called Bloody Brook, it was ambushed by the Nipmucks. Eight white men escaped.

Less than a month later Springfield was attacked and thirty houses burned. The colonists now faced a desperate situation. Such strong towns as Boston probably could survive any attack, but the other settlements seemed doomed, and certainly no pioneers could be persuaded to go into the wilderness. The Federal Commissioners met in daily session at Boston, and people began to say that the Lord had let loose these savages to punish New England for ceasing to come down hard on all heretics and especially the Quakers. Even the Puritan morale was obviously breaking.

And now there were well-founded rumors that more terrible warfare was impending. So far the stubborn, proud Narragansetts had refused to join King Philip, although he had done his best to persuade them. However, they harbored his men and were daily becoming more arrogant toward the whites. There was very good reason to believe the talk that this powerful tribe would soon go on the warpath. The Puritans had come to the crossroads. A quick decision was imperative, and it had to be right if they were to survive. If the Narragansetts joined the other Indians, even Boston and Providence and Newport were in grave danger. There was but one thing to do—strike the Narragansetts before they themselves could strike. With them out of the way, the Puritans might win the war, for every victory cost Philip many warriors. Of course, the Narragansetts were theoretically at peace with the whites, and there was also a treaty of friendship, but Puritans were ever pragmatists willing to forget theory if the end sought was a righteous one.

In December, 1675, a strong force marched against the Narragansetts, who were entrenched in lower Rhode Island in a fort even stronger than that which had been held by the Pequots. Situated in a dense swamp, it was surrounded by a palisade of stakes in which there was but one opening. The approach to this gate was over the slippery trunk of a felled tree, and a strong blockhouse guarded it. Inside this fortress were about two thousand men and many women and children.

The battle that ensued can be told as briefly as was the story of the Pequot massacre. The Puritans breached the palisades in more than one place and poured a heavy fire into the crowded fort. The Indians fought bravely but eventually fled, leaving behind them over one thousand dead and all their winter supply of corn. One quarter of the Puritans were killed or wounded, and many of the latter died in the snow as they tried to get through the swamp to a settlement. This became known as the Great Swamp Fight, perhaps the fiercest and most decisive battle ever fought in the United States between Indians and whites.

Victory over King Philip was now almost assured, but for a time he kept the upper hand; in fact, the settlements were hit harder than ever. Not only were the Wampanoags on the warpath, but the once docile Nipmucks had forgotten the Christian teachings of Eliot and others, and were enthusiastically burning and scalping.

In February, 1676, Lancaster, Massachusetts, was almost destroyed. From this town Mary Rowlandson, the minister's wife, was carried away and held until she was ransomed for twenty pounds. Apparently the Indians had learned sound business methods from the Puritans. Five other towns were destroyed that winter and spring, and the marauders once got within twelve miles of Boston. But this foray was almost the last serious threat. In April a force of seventy white men was surrounded by five hundred Nipmucks. Although fifty of the Puritans were killed and six burned alive, one hundred and twenty Indians also fell, and in May the power of this tribe was crippled by the loss of three hundred more warriors. Spurred to a last desperate resistance, the surviving Narragansetts and Wampanoags burned all the outlying houses in Warwick and many in Providence.

In passing, it should be noted that Roger Williams was rewarded by Massachusetts—for his work in keeping the Narragansetts quiet so long—by having his decree of banishment suspended for the duration of the Indian hostilities. A careful people, the citizens of Massachusetts!

The power of the Indians was broken, but they fought on. At Pawtucket fifty whites were killed, but they took with them three times as many of the enemy. Still more of the Narragansetts were accounted for in June, and on August 12, 1676, the war came to an end when King Philip was tracked down and killed. Ironically enough, he was shot by an Indian ally of the Puritans.

Once their leader was gone, the surviving Indians caused little further trouble and seemed to lapse into a fatalistic acceptance of their punishment. It was swiftly administered. Hundreds of the Indians were sold to the West Indies as slaves, where they promptly died.

So ended the fiercest Indian war this country has ever known. Fifty out of the existing ninety settlements had been attacked, and thirteen almost destroyed. Over six hundred houses were burned. The same number of men—one in every eleven able to bear arms—was killed and many women and children were massacred or taken captive. The war was also a severe financial strain on the new colonies. The cost to the Plymouth Colony alone was more than one hundred thousand pounds, a huge sum for those days and one very hard indeed to raise.

But New England was saved, and the Indians never again seriously threatened its existence. The colonies settled down to the serious business of making a living, supporting the right religious tenets, and creating a sound community life. There was no time to turn their recent troubles into picturesque legend. Storming Indian forts was not a brave adventure to the hard-bitten Puritan fighters; it was a necessary chore. I can hear a deacon remark after he had come back from the Great Swamp Fight: "The Sword of the Lord has fallen on the heathen. Praise the Lord! Give me that invoice of goods." And an unregenerate volunteer say: "Waal, them red scoundrels is done for. Got t' start workin' hard now t' make up for time lost."

Thus by the time the settlers began to spread their homesteads over the land, they were relatively safe from attack. The tribes still roamed their old grounds, but now they respected the white man's fighting power. He in turn was willing to forget and in a certain manner, forgive. For it is to the Puritan's credit that he never persecuted his defeated enemy. Wicked Indians should be promptly and effectively disposed of, but those who remained docile were to be tolerated. And so the pioneers were free to create the sort of life they wanted.

CHAPTER 3

Puritans in the Wilderness

THE very earliest Pilgrims and Puritans were like ordinary English citizens except for one strange failing—they wouldn't stay in England. No other definition can fit the motley boatloads which landed in Massachusetts. They believed in this or that religious doctrine, or none, although it was very unwise to admit that last fact. Some were tough, shrewd, and hard-working; others were weak and lazy. A few were learned; most had abundant common sense, and many looked to the Bible for daily guidance. If Inner Light ruled their conduct, they left hurriedly for the spiritual penal colonies of Providence and Newport. But almost all were of English blood, and indentured servant, artisan, or Cambridge graduate had a background of Magna Charta, the common law, and respect for some form of vested authority. They had grown up in the same land, and no matter how much they might quarrel among themselves, there would always be a broad common basis of agreement on certain very important ideas of how respectable people should act when they were running their own affairs. Such folk are the right ones to build towns and live in them as good citizens.

No one knows what would have happened in New England if the Celts of Ireland, Wales, and the Scottish Highlands had arrived just when Plymouth and the Massachusetts Bay Colony were being founded. Undoubtedly colonial history would have been livelier reading than it is now, but I wonder whether the town meeting, for example, would have developed into the efficient instrument of government that it was soon to be. Too much argument for its own sake would have ruined the quiet of taverns where, over glasses of hot rum, Puritans agreed on original sin; the Scarlet Whore of Rome would have lifted her skirts in the shadow of the meeting house, and hotheaded Campbells or MacGregors would have declared, "Down with this abortion you

call a town! We stand by our clan!" It was New England's salvation that for almost a century the majority of her people came
from England and were of Anglo-Saxon blood. You could tar
and feather a stiff-necked Royalist, and after all he had inherited
a few sensible ideas, but mad Celts would have been hard to fit
into the scheme of community life.

However, in spite of the unity of the people who settled New
England, any minor prophet would have declared that these
English were not going to live in complete harmony and broth-
erly love. They had come to the new land for a variety of reasons,
and men and women who dare risk much are likely to be strong
individuals who will stand up for their own peculiar ideas.

From the very first there were two potentialities in the character of the New England settlers. They were admirably fitted to
create an efficient community; they were also bound to be very
independent citizens. Our history is the story of how these two
inner forces were reconciled and made to work together.

The First People in Town Meeting Country

The first Europeans to visit this region were probably Dutch
traders who came to the Long Island shore to exchange as little
as possible for furs offered by the Indians, who were then more
guileless than they proved to be later on. Captain Adrian Block
explored the coast as early as 1614 and probably sailed up the
Thames River. But the Dutch were business men and not colo-
nizers, and no settlements were started by them in this region.

The English came here in a characteristic manner. In 1633,
John Oldham and Samuel Hull left Plymouth to do a little scout-
ing. History does not tell us what they were looking for, but it was
probably something more material than a wilderness sanctuary.
On their way west, the two scouts met Indians with faces black-
ened with graphite. Their curiosity aroused, Oldham and Hull
asked the redskins where they got the black stuff. The Indians
were obliging enough to take the two men to a crude mine at a
place near what is now Sturbridge, and which was called Tantuisque. Sure enough, there was lead here, and the two Pilgrims
hastened home to spread the good news. No special moral can be
drawn from this, but it is symbolic of Yankee tendencies.

In 1638, John Winthrop purchased a tract four miles square
around Tantuisque. Land was very cheap in those days, and he

wanted to make sure that he included any other deposits that might be in the neighborhood. But attempts to mine the lead were not successful, for the vein ran almost perpendicular. Yankees are a stubborn race, however, and for years new shafts and tunnels were sunk. Today they honeycomb the ground around the old mine, and discarded machinery rusts in the alders. But we never forget, and some day a new company will be formed to dig at Tantuisque. It has the loveliest of Indian names, but we are interested in that lead.

In 1635, a settlement was started at Saybrook, just across the river from my country, and in the same year fifty persons crossed the northeastern part of Connecticut and tramped southwest to the river valley at Hartford. Having very sensibly come up the river, the Hollanders were already established here, but the Puritans soon put these fur traders in their place. In 1636, Thomas Hooker and his rebelliously devout followers took the same route across Connecticut, but we hear of no one who halted by the way; in fact, the meager reports call this northeastern corner a wilderness of hills and woods.

The story of the 1637 expedition along the shore country to battle the Pequots at Mystic has already been told, but one proof that sound community life was soon to be established must not be omitted.

"A Christian minister, Rev. Samuel Stone, accompanied the expedition and served with remarkable efficiency. Hence from the bivouac of the soldier arose to heaven probably the first incense of intelligent prayer ever publicly offered on this soil to the living and true God. . . . With the break of day on the 26th occurred the terrible onset, with muskets, sword, and flame, that swept down six hundred Pequots, demolished the fort, and broke the life of the nation [Indian]." * The first intelligent prayer and the first Indian massacre—only two days apart. Already New Englanders had learned the secret of a well-ordered existence.

After the shores of Connecticut and Rhode Island were safe from the Pequots, a settlement was made. In 1646, John Winthrop the younger, the one who dabbled in mines, came over from Fisher's Island where he had already established himself. There were possibilities, he thought, in developing the area around the broad mouth of the Thames River. Within two years

* From *Westerly and Its Witnesses*, by Frederic Denison, Providence, 1878.

there were more than forty families in the village. Because it was to become a great commercial center, or so thought the new settlers, the first name of Pequot was changed to New London, and the Mohegan River became the Thames.

While New London was being developed as a second metropolis there were more sensational happenings a few miles to the east and northeast. In 1636 Roger Williams had come to Providence to escape the wrath of the Bay Colony. Three years later, Newport and Portsmouth were founded. Around these small villages was soon gathered as fine a collection of religious rebels as any country has ever seen. The first Friends arrived in Newport in 1657, and a year later fifteen families of Jews from Holland added to the spiritual confusion. It must be granted that the Narragansett Plantations, as they were called, allowed all comers to think as they pleased; in fact, the Plantations became famous as a place where any sort of idea was tolerated. Yet even a tolerated rebel feels rebellious at times and decides to move on. To the east was the very unsympathetic Massachusetts; so the adventurers had to go west.

Forthwith, began the first troubles of Town Meeting Country. Its aim was to create a solid and efficient colony, and sensible men saw no reason why they should worry about such questions as the source of inspiration or the meaning of an obscure text. They were pragmatists from the start. Uppermost in their minds was the practical value of an established church working smoothly with the civil government. There would be time later on to discuss theology. Of course, a man had the right to think as he pleased, but while he was doing so he ought to act like other people. But the rebels from the Plantations were prone to put matters of personal faith before civic expediency.

At least two of the refugees were blameless; in fact, their story is one of the few authentic Puritan idyls. John Babcock came to Newport from Plymouth—a stalwart lad with a bold heart and no great respect for the good old English idea that a man should be content with his lot. In Newport, John worked for Thomas Lawton and soon fell in love with Mary, his employer's daughter. In true story-book form the father objected to John's lowly station and forbade the courtship. But Mary was in love, and one day the couple sailed away from Newport in a small boat and braved the Sound until they came to what is now Westerly. There they landed and became the first white settlers in that region. Those are the bare facts, but the romance and adventure are told better in "The Pioneers."

> *The banns were said spite legal bar;*
> *When harshly shut from home,*
> *They planned their love-lit way afar,*
> *Nor recked of storm or gloom.*
>
> *Superior to the waves they met,*
> *They rode the billowy sea.*
> *Till, doubling Cape Misquamicut,*
> *They hailed a land-locked lea.*

After safely arriving the young couple set up housekeeping.

> *Thus lengthened months rolled by, while not*
> *The voice of kin or friend*
> *Was heard to cheer the lonely cot,*
> *Or Christian counsel lend.*

But at length other pioneers came.

> *So new settlers dared the wild to break,*
> *And build on neighboring height,*
> *Whose glowing hearth-fires joined to make*
> *The pagan region light.**

So was Westerly founded.

Norwich was settled not long after New London, and now the shore and deep Thames estuary were ready to fulfill the hope that this would some day be a great commercial and shipping center. As yet no settlement had been started in the wilderness north of Norwich. Even in the more hospitable low hills and meadows of central Massachusetts, Brookfield was not founded until 1664. Between that harassed outpost and the head of the Thames there was no village. Only the toughest people could be expected to venture into these lonely stretches. Down on the shore the settlements were close enough to be almost neighborly, and

* From *Westerly and Its Witnesses,* by Frederic Denison, Providence, 1878.

the river and the Sound made communication easy with Newport and Providence on one side and the New Haven and Saybrook colonies on the other. But up north there were nothing but rude Indian trails. When this interior country was opened, there came the real test of the New Englander as he sought to create a stable unit of life.

Hill Settlement

Any one of a dozen Connecticut, Massachusetts, or Rhode Island towns would illustrate how a Puritan community was started, and Woodstock, Connecticut, is a good example.

The settlement of Roxbury, Massachusetts, now a suburb of Boston, had for some time after 1650 been growing a bit crowded, and already several families were talking about pulling up stakes and starting a new town farther west. The traditional idea is that the Puritans moved here and there under the impulse of a fierce desire to worship as they pleased, and that each new exodus was another Holy Trek toward a Promised Land. True enough, some new colonies were founded because of dissatisfaction with the old community's spiritual ideas, but plenty of them owed their genesis to more material reasons. Very often the restless citizens had accepted gladly the religion of the group they left; and, furthermore, they established in their new home the same form of church doctrine and government. If this acceptance of traditional ideas had not existed, the New England town would have been little more than an ill-fated experiment.

In the case of the Roxburyites, there is a definite record of the reason for their discontent. The limits of the town "being so scanty and not capable of enlargement," several persons "not having received the same benefit of issuing forth as other towns have done, when it has pleased God to increase the inhabitants thereof in their posterity . . . were compelled to leave." It was all very simple. Already the bounds of that particular town were set, and the land therein distributed. However, Puritans bred little Puritans who, when they grew up, wanted their own houses and acres. Since they couldn't buy land, they moved. It should be noted carefully that a definite town had been established and could not be enlarged; furthermore, a group of individuals proposed to move en masse. They had lived in a neat, well-bounded unit; they proposed to create another much like it. Puritans did not pack up and leave one house they had happened to live in; they left a town. Neither did they trek blindly into the wilderness and set up life. From the very first, my people were town folks. They were individuals also, and appallingly set ones, but they instinctively realized that to carry their insistence on personal freedom too far was fatal. Very seldom do you hear of a lonely Puritan homesteader living miles away from anyone and obeying no community rules.

The citizens of the town of Roxbury, both those who wanted to leave and the ones who didn't, began in an orderly and sensible manner to arrange for the migration. Over in Rhode Island people got mad and cleared out unceremoniously; in Massachusetts they called a town meeting and observed the amenities of decent adventuring into the wilderness. They sought to achieve that happiest of all Yankee states of mind—knowing where you're at! They would meet tragedies and hardships as great as any endured by American pioneers, but these came from such forces as hostile Indians, hard winters, and heartbreaking labor, and such enemies could not be eliminated by the best plans.

So the Roxbury citizens held a meeting and voted that if at least thirty persons would agree to plant and settle new land they should have land and also a £100 loan to be paid back in five years and in equal portions. This money was to be used for public charges: i. e., meeting house, minister's house, mill, bridges, and so on. It was a characteristic decision. Pioneers should not venture forth without knowing that they could get good land; they must also carry along a little ready cash to be expended to the glory of God and the material welfare of the settlers. Of course, the money would be spent in Roxbury for articles to be taken with them, and so the new settlers and the ones who stayed behind were both benefited. And the money was not a gift; it was a loan, and there were definite instructions about paying it back. This new colony was expected to be solvent. Such caution and sound business policies are not much like the reckless spirit that opened the West, but they work, and that simple praise is enough for New England.

Plenty of Roxbury families were ready to accept the offer. The next task was to find land. So the selectmen petitioned the Massachusetts General Court for right to purchase a tract seven miles square. It is not necessary here to explain how the colony acquired its acreage; at least, the court could give a clear title. And that was needed, for there had been many quarrels already over disputed property. The pioneers might be going into an untracked wilderness, but they knew their fellow Puritans well enough to take every precaution against future trouble. No Yankee feels right unless he has an attested deed to his land.

The petition to purchase was made in 1683, but not until three years later did the first thirteen Roxburyites start to prepare a way for the others. Special church services were held for them, and they left in the firm conviction that they would encounter great danger. They were not disappointed, for, according to early accounts, the route they took was very hazardous, since they had to pass over one deep river four or five times. Puritans could storm an Indian fort but, unless impelled by necessity, they were a cautious race who did not enjoy adventure. At last the tract was reached, examined, and approved. Probably a messenger was sent back to Roxbury, for the records tell next of the selectmen buying the land from Major James Fitch, greatest of all American land agents.

In August, 1686, thirty families arrived at their new home. This tract was southwest by west of Roxbury and approximately sixty miles away as the crow flies. Hartford was about forty miles to the southwest and Norwich a little closer due south. Brookfield to the north was nearer, but it was a tiny settlement that had been almost destroyed by the Indians. The area was hilly and wooded, but there was some clear land and plenty of small streams. The worst danger was from Indians. Although King Philip's power had been broken, the memory of his war was still vivid in redskin as well as in white minds.

Exactly what the people were like who moved from Roxbury cannot be definitely stated. They were English by blood, and undoubtedly no one belonged even to the lesser county gentry by tradition. On the other hand, there seem to have been no indentured servants. Some differences in social standing and wealth must have existed, but on the whole the venture was made by thirty families so nearly equal that they can be thought of as forming a homogeneous group.

There was no time wasted in setting up an organized community. A saw mill had been erected by the earlier scouts, and now the land was distributed so that houses could be built. Ten acres were reserved for the future pastor, a quarry sequestered for hearthstones and flaggings, and a deposit of clay kept for making chimney bricks. The settlers were divided into three groups to occupy three specified localities, and then lots were drawn. The seven oldest men were in charge, and the distribution was completed within two days after the arrival of the main body of pioneers. Puritans work swiftly, especially when they want to get settled on their own places.

The first land drawings were for the home lots which were from ten to twenty acres in size. Later on the meadows, uplands, and woodlands were distributed. The settlers camped out or built rude shelters for the rest of August and during September and October. Religious services were held in the open air every Sabbath. The first house was completed in November and was undoubtedly a frame structure, for the saw mill was already in operation. Records show that some time during the autumn one man was told he would be given fifteen acres of home lot, fifteen of upland, thirty of meadow, and one hundred of woodland if he would build a grist mill and grind good meal "clear of grit." Another was subsidized to erect a second sawmill, and warned that there must be a convenient way provided to carry timber to the mill.

Within four years land had been broken, fences put up, orchards set out, roads built, and the houses made more comfortable. So far Woodstock, or New Roxbury as it was called then, was little more than three small groups of houses held together by a common purpose, a threatening danger from Indians, and, most important of all, inherited concepts of what a town ought to be like. This new community was modeled on an older mode of living. Each family held a home lot and also several outlying tracts. As yet the isolated farms later found in New England had not come into existence. No one dared to live too far away from neighbors; besides, they had always known a closely knit communal life. To this system of home lots we owe the beautiful village streets of Town Meeting Country, and it also explains why the present-day Yankee farmer may own land in half a dozen corners of the town.

In 1690, the new colony was granted the rights of a town by

the General Court, and the settlers began to build an efficient legal and political organization. The task was not too hard a one, for they had ample precedent to guide them.

SELECTMEN . . . CONSTABLES . . . TOWN MEETINGS

Historians disagree about the earliest models of the New England town system. Some trace it back to Teutonic customs; others say that it was based on English methods of government. However this may be, the fact remains that the people of Woodstock could look to other New England towns for guidance in the task of creating a good system of community life.

There was Dorchester, for example. At first it was under the control of clergymen who were aided by the advice of magistrates. Soon, however, the secular management was strengthened, for it seems that the clergy held wrong ideas about what a sensible town should be like. One strong-minded dominie urged his congregation to be more devout; otherwise, said he, they would contradict the main end of planting this wilderness.

Up rose a Puritan and shouted, "Sir, you are mistaken! Our main end was to catch fish!"

Of course, such a forthright statement was seldom made; most of the time the rebels kept quiet and did as they pleased. At any rate, the Dorchester ministers retained their high position and honors, but a town meeting was called, and on October 8, 1633, were formulated the first provisions for town government.

At first there was a general gathering at the meeting house every Monday at eight in the morning. Here were recorded "orders necessary for the good government of the community." Twelve men were selected as a sort of steering committee. Charlestown, Massachusetts, had much the same organization, although its first committee had only three men on it. This town soon found that "by reason of many men meeting, things were not so easily brought into a joynt issue." So an order was passed providing for a board of eleven selectmen serving for a year. It was to do all town business except elect officers and dispose of town land. All the acts of these selectmen must be approved by the town, but from the very start there was remarkably little interference with their control. Very soon, however, the increasing duties made other town officials necessary. Soon there was full staff of fence viewers, pound keepers, hog reeves, surveyors of highways, sealers, a town clerk, the bell ringer (also the grave-digger), and, of course, a constable. The constable had undoubt-edly been appointed before the selectmen or even the minister. A community must behave itself, no matter what else happens.

Of course, such a town was not entirely free to do as it pleased. Over it was the colony, and no laws could be passed in town meet-ing that were at variance with the General Statutes. The General Court was powerful, too, and in the early days was especially jealous of its right to dispose of lands. But on the whole the small communities were running their own strictly local affairs very smoothly within a short time after they had been settled.

The development of this form of local government illustrates several aspects of Puritan mentality. For instance, it was capable of creating a compromise between theory and working practice. At first a town meeting met every week, and every piece of busi-ness was voted on. Almost at once it was evident that this arrange-ment wasted time and undoubtedly fostered long, useless argu-ments. So the set-up was immediately changed, and very soon a small number of selectmen was running the town, with the entire citizen group meeting at irregular intervals to exercise a gen-eral control. A community of theorists and idealists would never have forsaken that first splendid concept of every man a town father. It would have clung to it regardless of proof of its in-efficiency. Confusion and muddled government would follow, and with them the inevitable quarrels and schisms. Soon the com-munity would break up into violently partisan groups, and an-other glorious experiment in living would have gone on the rocks. But from the very start the Puritan was a pragmatist, and when theory began to obstruct the orderly conduct of life, it was kicked upstairs into a dignified and revered upper chamber where meddling clerics were kept.

Speaking of clerics reminds us of another marked ability shown by the early settlers. This is the skill with which they struck a delicate balance between the religious and the secular affairs of life. At all times during the first century, the church and its au-thorized ministers had great power, but the apparently devout and humble flock never allowed doctrine, discipline, and holy men to interfere unduly with town government. This genius for compromise and neat distribution of separate worths and functions distinguishes the Puritan and his descendants from other less subtle statesmen. Any selectman from any small New England town could have come back from Munich victorious, and he might even be able to settle the Irish and Indian questions.

DEMOCRACY BE DAMNED!

These Puritans had no idea of building a pure democracy. In fact, they did their best not to have one, and the early New England town had the following classes of people: proprietors, householders, inhabitants, freemen, and a miserable fifth estate.

A proprietor was a resident or non-resident owner of land. If he did not live in the town he had no political rights. As a resident he was probably a freeman, but the owning of land did not put him in this class. A householder was the head of a household. Very naturally some women were so designated. The only qualification for the status of inhabitant was to be a male of "honest and peaceable conversation" and accepted by the major part of the town, or, in Massachusetts, certified by the General Court. In the Connecticut colony the freemen were "householders [male] that are 21, or have held office or have £30 estate." No unmarried man could vote for governor, magistrates, or deputies unless he had held office or had real estate valued at £30.

The identity of these classes might vary in different colonies, but in all of them the important person, the freeman, was a property owner and a member of the church. Inhabitants were respectable men who also went to church, but they had not acquired enough property to advance them beyond mere respectability. And a householder, if male, was undoubtedly a ribald spirit who made money enough to be a freeman but couldn't qualify as an honest and peaceable conversationalist.

Beneath these four classes was another composed of people who can be described in no better manner than by saying that they were present. No good account of these Puritan zombies who were alive and yet did not officially exist has come down to us. Undoubtedly they were a varied collection of gypsies, eccentrics, tramps, wandering artisans, idiots, low-lived degenerates, and certain plain, well-meaning people who, for one reason or another, could not acquire even a house of their own, but squatted in some miserable shack on land that no one took the trouble to claim. From such people came the later Jukes, and they were squatters who lived on Puritanism's Tobacco Road.

Another enemy of democracy was the insistence on religious orthodoxy. Freedom and tolerance of worship reigned in the town only when all men accepted the same doctrine. Mark that qualification. The early Puritans granted liberty when no one felt the need for it. But inevitably this complete harmony was broken. Schisms arose; misguided men were lured into antinomianism or caught strange ideas about the Sabbath or infant baptism; a few even followed a Quaker maiden into utter heresy. When such things happened, the town forgot all about men being equal and sternly insisted that only good Congregationalists could vote and hold office.

The power of the individual clergyman was helpful in establishing order and conformity. He was not expected to interfere with such matters as sales of land, tax rates, and new roads, but he kept a sharp eye on the conduct of his flock. Now and then he went too far and spoke publicly of the discreet rum drinking or fornication of solid citizens; then the deacons suggested that he quiet down. As a general rule, however, a tactful and firm minister could be a powerful help in administering sensible government. Because the church and the minister were so important in the early New England town, some historians have argued that it was ruled by a theocracy. The Congregational Church and its ministers were part of the complex structure of devout, orderly living, but they were not revered in their own right; they were the revered means to a greater end—the correct management of the town.

Woodstock Again

Backed by all the tradition of older towns, the new community began to run its own affairs. The first town meeting set the tax rate and gave the constable the job of collecting the money. It also decided to ask a man to settle in the ministry. What he should be paid was left to the selectmen's discretion "so as they exceed not what was formerly proposed . . . specially in the money part." From the very first the secular town held the religious purse, and here is proof that our towns were not theocracies, for all men know that religious control is based on more than religious authority. The final terms of ministerial payment were: after settlement £40 the first year; £50 the second, and £60 the third. Ten pounds were paid each year in quarterly installments; the remainder was in "current pay," another name for anything the poor man and his family could burn, eat, and wear. He was also given a twenty-acre home lot with other rights and divisions. On this land the town would build and furnish a house.

While the minister was being provided for, a town pound was erected and two watchhouses selected, as there was still danger from hostile Indians. Every man was ordered to get a ladder for his house or be fined five shillings. A man was also chosen to teach children and youths to write and cipher. A minister, a pound where stray cattle could be put, protection against Indians, a ladder to fight fire with, and ability to write and compute prices and interest were the necessary equipment of a town. It can be taken for granted that some one already had a license to sell rum.

During the next five years nothing of interest seems to have happened in Woodstock. Undoubtedly trips were made to Boston at irregular intervals for articles that could not be manufactured at home. Indian scares were frequent, but no trouble occurred. Houses were built, land cleared, and farming begun. In 1691 the meadows of the town were distributed among forty-five proprietors, each getting his share of good and bad land. During this year a meeting house was proposed. Until now the Sunday services had been held in private homes. Mark the name *meeting house* and not *church;* it was to serve for all kinds of meetings, both secular and religious. This building was to be thirty by twenty-six feet, with fourteen-foot studs. It was to have one gable on each side. That was the sort of meeting house the town built first, and never let any amateur historian tell you that a big, slender-spired edifice was "the first church erected in . . ."

Apparently at this time many citizens were staying away from town meeting, for a law was passed ordering all men to attend or be fined three shillings. Some settlers were dissatisfied with the distribution of land, and a committee of three was appointed to control this important matter. It was also voted that those who had complained should bear the cost of the meeting at which the committee was appointed. That's Puritan logic for you—make the complainants foot the bill, and there won't be so many complaints. By now there were deeds and mortgages to be recorded, and in 1693 a town clerk was appointed. The New England community knows that a sound economic life depends upon keeping all legal matters straight, and the clerk was a man of importance, a sort of permanent under-secretary who was undisturbed by political upheavals. Constables, selectmen, and, especially, ministers could be changed to satisfy fickle demands, but the town clerk kept the books, and a good one was too valuable to meddle with. Woodstock's recorder was duly appreciated, for he was given twenty acres of land, and a fee of twelve pence for each town meeting held and sixpence for each filing of a grant.

The first store in Woodstock was started in 1693 after being subsidized with twelve rods of land. The proprietors dealt largely in furs, but they also took the surplus produce of the town and exchanged it in Boston for liquor, ammunition, and other necessities. Part of the furs came from the Indians, and some liquor went back to them; at least, the records tell us their drunkenness "caused much grief to good men." However, we do not hear that the storekeepers, subsidized by the community, were admonished. Private enterprise could be condemned for some of its practices, but it should not be meddled with. From the very first, Puritans never made the mistake of confusing morality with good business.

By 1694, the meeting house was completed, and from then on all public gatherings were held in it. Now the church was organized by a "council assembled according to common usage of the churches in the Province of Massachusetts Bay," and the Cambridge Platform was adopted as a rule of discipline. These people were no radicals seeking freedom from restraining customs; they were men in search of new land and economic opportunities, and the old ideas of religion and law were good enough to be perpetuated.

But Woodstock was not prospering the way it should. In its eight years of life it had built a government of its own, a sound religious structure, and made some material progress. There was also a little interest shown in education. But new settlers did not come, and the original population was dwindling. All the land had been distributed, but not all the home lots had been developed, and the common lands were unfenced. Roads were overgrown with brush, bridges were falling, and the grain spoiled in the millhouse because there was a leak in the roof. Some of these details would not have worried a community of non-Puritans, but our ancestors demanded an orderly and neat existence.

However, the town gradually began to prosper a little. In 1703 the burying ground was fenced, and in 1710 the building of two schoolhouses was authorized. It strikes me as significant that one act preceded the other. Once in a while the Puritans could make a gesture of reverence before they went on with the business of life. The burying ground where the pioneers rested, God's Acre, should be kept in a seemly manner, even if all the children did not learn to read, write, and cipher.

About this time a fulling-mill began to operate; another citizen took to making coffins. A gravedigger was also appointed and, always careful about paying out good money, the town established a very practical system of payment. Digging the grave of a child five years old or less brought him in two shillings; for one five to twelve, three shillings was paid; for all others he got five shillings. He was also required to "find" his own tools, make the graves a suitable depth, and give "proper attendance." Other wilderness communities might leave burial to the family, but in New England death as well as life was a town affair.

That Woodstock was getting along fairly well, at least for some people, is proved by the fact that about this time a leading citizen died and left an estate of over five hundred pounds. A man could prosper, even in a struggling town, by being careful and shrewd. There were several ways of turning an honest penny, besides farming and storekeeping. Bounties on wolves were paid, and one year even the birds gave a profit. Like the famed people of Killingworth, the Woodstock settlers thought that the blackbirds were hurting their crops. To have paid a bounty at once would have been too costly, for there were a lot of blackbirds, so the selectmen decreed that before Michaelmas every person capable of voting must bring in twenty-four heads or be fined a penny for each one missing. Having thus decimated the flocks, the town began to pay a penny for each blackbird head. It also allowed sixpence for a dozen heads of some mysterious creature called a "yolo-bird."

In 1721 a new church was built, undoubtedly a bigger and more dignified one than the first. According to the undemocratic Puritan custom, pews were distributed according to social rank and wealth. In Woodstock the people seem to have built their own pews, but generally the town sold the completed seats of worship to the various bidders. At any rate, sixteen Woodstock families were seated in appropriate manner. What happened to the rest of the devout townspeople is not explained; probably they sat in the back part of the church and made critical remarks on the aristocrats up front. Some may also have commented that the cost of the new meeting house was so great that one schoolmaster was forced to alternate every four months between the two schoolhouses.

One of the greatest myths about Puritans is that they were more interested in democratic education than in anything else. Such a notion is quite false. The earliest settlers of New England were determined to create a stable and efficient system of community life, and in order to achieve that goal they paid their first attention to civic and ecclesiastical affairs. For by means of the town and the church, and only by them, could they build that desired unit of living. Selectmen and ministers held the people together and told them what to do; pounds, fence viewers, constables, deacons, and dominies worked to keep order and decorum, and a schoolmaster was a luxury. Puritans respected education for its commercial value, the power it gave men to read Holy Script, and its lifting of the individual out of defenseless ignorance; they also sacrificed much to create schools and colleges. They were far ahead of other colonies in this respect for education and active promotion of it, but the little red schoolhouse was built after the meeting house, the place where freemen came together to be molded by spiritual and legal precepts into good citizens.

By now Woodstock was acquiring a true town consciousness that thought of its acres and homes as dedicated to the use of Woodstock folk alone. For instance, chance residents and vagrants did not fit into a soundly built town. As early as 1723 these undesirables were so numerous that a law was passed saying that "If any person entertain or hire any stranger or transient person, except for nursing or other inevitable occasion, they shall give good security to the selectmen of the town that they shall not be burthened or charged with them, or forfeit 10 s. a week for 4 weeks and then 20 s." Puritans were not a hospitable people or given to keeping open cities of refuge, but they were less harsh than they seem. Vagrants and wandering artisans were a disrupting influence; therefore, they should be kept out of town. Probably many a good deacon gave a vagrant a good meal and some heartening rum, and then sternly ordered the fellow to leave. As a human being, the deacon was kindly and merciful; as a towns-man, he could enforce stern but practical decrees.

By the end of the first quarter of the eighteenth century, forty years after the first settlers came, Woodstock was almost a typical New England town. Only one thing was lacking to complete its similarity to other little communities. No minister had been dis-missed. However, this inevitable event soon happened.

As might be expected, the quarrel started over economic and not spiritual grievances. The town had been remiss in paying the minister's salary but, remembering that the best defense is attack, it now accused him of not improving the land granted him, and soon afterward took it away from him. While he continued to ask for more money to meet the increased cost of living, the poor man tried several ways of making a few extra dollars, and even went so far as to speculate in land in another town. The town, pleading dire poverty, finally raised his salary to £75 a year, but warned him "to devote himself more especially to his sacred func-tion that they may be encouraged by his vigorous performance for the future either to continue this said sum or to enlarge it."

But the minister, either from necessity or greed, kept on specu-lating and experimenting in secular affairs. He also introduced singing of "regular tunes." This innovation shocked the con-servatives; discontent and criticism increased, and finally a town meeting was called to decide "whether it will be for the Glory of God, the interest of religion, and the peace and comfort of the town that the labors of Mr. Dwight should be continued further among us." God, religion, and the town must approve of the dubious Mr. Dwight.

He was dismissed by a vote of sixty to one, with one cautious man staying neutral. So Mr. Dwight left after thirty-six years of being Woodstock's pastor, and at another town meeting his suc-cessor was called. Mark the fact that the town, and not the church members or Ecclesiastical Society, did the ousting and the later hiring of another minister. And do not forget that the "peace and comfort of the town" was considered when Mr. Dwight was tried. Very clearly there was no theocracy in that community. The church and its minister were servants of the town, and the citizens were determined that they should not begin to feel bigger than they actually were.

The story of the settlement of one New England hill town is that of dozens of others. About so much and no more could happen to pioneers. Woodstock was spared an Indian massacre, but otherwise it performed the usual tasks and met the same problems. But here and there the Yankees of southeast New England managed to inject a little variety into the hard and matter-of-fact business of setting up a tight and sensible little community.

MEN OF MYSTERY

Even if the region north of the shore and between Providence and Hartford was a wilderness when the first townspeople came, a few strange white men were already living there. One was John Cates. When he came from England or where he first lived in America, no one knows; but it is certain that for a year he lived in a cave near Windham, Connecticut, with a Negro slave. Cates was obviously a gentleman, and the tradition is that he was a political refugee, even a regicide. Apparently he had brought some money with him, for he bought land and built a house. When he died in 1697 he left a communion service to the Windham church, and two hundred acres to be held in trust for the town schools, and two hundred more for the town poor. Today Windham and the town later set off from it still draw interest from the funds given by John Cates, mysterious gentleman of England. Whatever else you say about them, you must admit that Puritans keep a trust.

Over in the remote western part of Rhode Island, in the Vacant Lands, lived another unexplained man. His name was Theophilus Whalley, but he is supposed to have really been Edward Whalley, one of the judges who tried Charles I. Whalley and his son-in-law William Goffe escaped to America, and after several adventures in Connecticut, they went to Hadley, Massachusetts. Here Whalley is said to have died in 1678, but the belief persisted that the story of his death was told to cover another flight. The mystery man of the Vacant Lands came to West Kingston in 1680. After the death of his wife he moved farther into the wilderness and lived there with his daughter until he died in 1720.

Edward Whalley the regicide was born in 1615; therefore, if he and Theophilus were the same man, he died at the rather incredible age of one hundred and five years. And where did he find his family after he left Hadley, and why did he live so openly in West

Kingston for a time? The answers will probably never be known, but at least we are sure that a gentleman lived in the Vacant Lands, just as John Cates did over in Windham.

The other men who came before the regular settlers were probably far more mysterious. Consorters with Indian squaws, fleeing criminals or indentured servants, eccentrics, and vagrants, they lived for a few months here or there and then passed on. Few had the ambition to clear land for themselves, and not one of these earliest Yankees seems to have become a freeman in any town.

EARLY REALTOR

All through the history of the early land sales of this region runs the name of Major James Fitch, Jr. A Puritan by birth, his was more the spirit of the gentleman adventurer than that of the sober, cautious pioneer who settled a town and then settled down in it. Of course, Major Fitch did enjoy a profit from a neat sale, but he could also spend that profit and not always in sensible ways.

James Fitch was the oldest son of the godly and honored first minister of Norwich, and as a very young man he was interested in land surveys and transfers. Realizing that he needed official position to support his activities, he played politics and was elected county treasurer. About the same time he somehow acquired the title of Major, but he had no thought of campaigning against Indians; he knew a better way to handle them and get a few square miles of their land. Soon he had the most influence over the Mohegans of any man in the colonies.

Owaneco, son of the great chief Uncas, was especially fond of the major. This noble Mohegan was a terrible sot, and the land speculators were always trying to catch him half-drunk and get his mark on a grant of land. So it was obviously Fitch's duty to save his friend from such unscrupulous men. He succeeded so well that in 1680 Owaneco signed a legal document which read in part: " . . . but finding that some, through their great importunity and others taking advantage of me when I am in drink by causing me to sign deeds, not only wronging myself but may spoil it ever being a plantation, for these and other reasons I make over my right and title of any and all of my lands and meadows unto my loving friend James Fitch Jun. for him to dispose of as he shall see cause."

Of course, less persuasive land agents resented the major's success with Owaneco, and a petition was made to the General Court to set aside the grant. But the major won the battle, and now he was the legal guardian of the drunken Owaneco and virtual owner of many square miles of land that could be settled. Probably he was never quite sure how much territory he did control. Every Indian sachem's idea of the extent of his control was hazy; Owaneco's imagination could be easily stimulated by rum, and the major's own surveys were more than a trifle elastic.

During the notorious administration of New England by Sir Edmund Andros, the pioneer realtor was forced to be very quiet, but with the deposition of James II Fitch became more prominent than ever in local and state affairs. At the first general election he was made a member of the Council. Now he was the most prominent person in eastern Connecticut and the most picturesque Puritan to be bred in this land of steady habits.

He made royal progresses through his domains. Clad in fine clothes and followed by a retinue of Indians, soldiers, and land-jobbers, the major surely brought color and romance to the wilderness and the little towns. He sold townships as if they were mere farms, surveyed disputed bounds, and held courts of inquiry; in short, he was Lord of the Marches, and a man who almost held the High and Low Justice. He controlled land, which was something far more important than legal power. I think that all of Major Fitch's political adventures were made with the aim of strengthening his position as the master of broad lands. From somewhere back in his ancestry this son of a pious minister had been given a great desire to rule over territory and help people develop it. His acres were never given away, but probably his greatest joy was in the fact that he was the man who had the acres to sell.

Such a man was sure to have enemies, and they were very articulate indeed. Branding him as a land-pirate, they declared that no one since William the Conqueror had ever taken so much that did not belong to him. At first these attacks were ineffective. Fitch did splendid work in controlling his Indian friends and keeping them from joining King Philip; in fact, it was probably his restraining influence that saved the southeastern shore towns from massacre. But after the Indian war was over, Fitch's enemies began to attack the validity of his land titles. Undoubtedly they realized that personal abuse stimulated the major, but to take away his beloved baronage would kill him.

The first rival claimants to cause real trouble were the Winthrop heirs. That astute Puritan family, first of acquisitive aristocrats, had collected land almost as successfully as Fitch himself, and now the later Winthrops claimed that practically all of Fitch's territory was theirs by an Indian grant earlier than Owaneco's. The General Court of Connecticut delayed its decision, and while it pondered Fitch and the Winthrops kept right on selling land and encouraging settlements. That was not all. Bounds and fences of disputed property were removed, crops were seized, and a brisk guerrilla warfare actually broke out. Little is said in local histories about this thoroughly unlawful episode, but undoubtedly a good time was had by many Puritans. It was just the sort of thing that would appeal to the exuberant Fitch, but even then a Winthrop was supposed to be a very sober and law-abiding citizen.

But there was a tragic side to this minor war. Good money had been paid out for the land in dispute, and now the titles might be found worthless. Nothing disturbs a Yankee more than trouble over a deed, and while the rougher inhabitants brawled and tore up fences, sober men met in solemn meeting. There is no record that Major Fitch attended any of these; in fact, we are told that he rode here and there, drinking and singing with his retinue, selling more land, rallying his friends, and doing a little political logrolling. And his efforts were rewarded, for every one of his claims were upheld. Soon after this victory he became head of the council. No one will ever know the complete details of that legal battle, but I am willing to bet that the court came to the sensible conclusion that since both Fitch and the Winthrops were holding lands without clear title to them, those lands might as well go to a native son. Or it may be that even in those days a Boston aristocrat had the power to irritate the people out in the provinces. And an even more powerful argument in favor of Fitch would be the fact that he actively encouraged settlements and was willing to help a man get a few acres for a farm. When no one has a right to a grant, why not give it to the one who will do the most with it? Even a high court of Puritans can be pragmatic.

For many years Major Fitch was one of Connecticut's best-known citizens and certainly the most vivid and colorful. He was a public benefactor and the first layman to aid Yale materially; a friend of the people, he was an advocate of popular rights and sided with the Connecticut Lower House when it clashed with the Upper. Half the time he was under church censure and suspension for "excessive conviviality," but he continued to help each new town build a meeting house, and like all good Puritans he gave to preaching. For the major was dual in nature as are all true New Englanders; he could act like a throwback to the gaudy Elizabethans, but he also knew the worth of a strong church and the help it could give in building a town.

Such a man as Major James Fitch ought to die at the moment of his greatest triumph, but the truth is that his last years were embittered by quarrels and money troubles. His political power had waned, and the governor forbade plantations to be started in any of Fitch's remaining territory until the titles were once more examined. The major, full of gout and injured pride, was exceedingly angry and, like the border baron he was in part, issued a proclamation asserting his right to every acre he claimed and, furthermore, his contempt for the governor's edict. The language of the document was Puritanical in its decorum, but the spirit was that of a feudal lord telling the pettifoggers of the Inns of Court to be silent. A very wroth governor and council ordered Fitch's appearance before them to answer charges of "false and seditious expressions." Unable to ride because of the gout and thoroughly unsubdued in any case, the accused man refused with great insolence to budge a step.

This time he had gone too far. A sensible court might uphold a dubious claim, because to do so would help colonization, but no man, not even Major James Fitch, could defy authority and get away with it. So the General Court of 1717 issued a warrant for the rebel. But before it was executed, he humbly confessed his fault and asked forgiveness. The fiery major might be proud and haughty, but he was enough of a Yankee to know when to retreat. But he did not give up any of his land claims and, after all, what is a confession made under duress as compared with many square miles retained?

Having won a public victory over the major, the Upper House let him go free after slapping on a fine of £20. But the Lower House, loyal to the friend of the common man, declared that

Fitch's apology was enough. In the end the major paid no fine, did not ride to Hartford, and kept his lands. That confession of guilt and the plea for mercy were not proof of defeat; it was merely the gesture of a sensible man who can bow the knee in order to rise and fight another day.

But this was the baron's last battle. Seventy years old when he defied authority, for ten years more he quietly managed his complex affairs and undoubtedly took part in as much excessive conviviality as his age permitted. The manner of his death is not recorded, but I hope it was attended by that same motley retinue of Indians, vagrants, and land-jobbers which had followed their master over his lands.

Everybody takes it for granted that other sections of this country bred men who lived with flamboyant vigor, but here in the land of steady habits our ancestors are supposed to have all been sober men who downed their rum dourly and forswore the froo-fraw of life. Yet we had our Major James Fitch, minister's son, giver of aid to churches and a college, excessively convivial, friend of the common man and his red brother, and a man who loved land and got hold of it the easiest way, and then did as he pleased with it. But the major was even more than all that; he was one of the men who did his share, in his own way, of course, to build a strong civilization in the wilderness.

BLACK JAMES

One Indian learned how to handle real estate like the shrewdest of the white men, despite the fact that he probably never met Major Fitch or observed his business methods. He was called Black James, and we hear of him first as a constable appointed by the Massachusetts Colony to help the white magistrates bring justice and peace to the Praying Indians. Black James was a Christian and a very devout one indeed. The next step for the constable was to claim part of certain lands. What his arguments were I do not know, but at least he was given £20 in money and a reservation five miles square for himself and his followers.

Probably that little deal was the best one any Indian ever made in these United States. But Black James was not through; he immediately sold half of his land for £10 more. Then he did the wisest thing of all; he passed out of colonial annals, apparently with land and £30 intact. If carefully expended that much money could supply a small tribe with rum for a long time, and there must have been great rejoicing among Black James's Christian followers.

PRAISE THE LORD!

Until 1708 the Connecticut towns had little or no trouble about religious doctrine and discipline. Each church was in a way a separate organization with full powers to administer its own affairs, but all agreed as to articles of faith. If Woodstock got rid of its pastor, or Windham kept theirs, the two towns did so for purely local reasons which did not affect the general structure of Congregationalism.

By 1700, however, the happy first years of complete unity were no more; parishes got queer notions and the sound tenets of belief were rejected. According to the conservatives, all the trouble was caused by emigrants from what was soon to be called the "State of Resentment." Left alone, the Connecticut churches could have got along nicely, but these malcontents from the Plantations over east stirred up trouble wherever they went. Kicked out of their first home, or leaving in a burst of wrath, they descended on peaceful shore or inland settlements and immediately began to find fault and incite weak-minded people to rebellion.

Some of the first trouble-makers were Sabbatarians, later to be known as Seventh Day Baptists. Seceding from the Newport Baptist Church in 1671 and having built their own place of worship, they promptly quarreled among themselves, and the losers moved to the infant colony of Westerly. Soon the western reaches of Rhode Island had numerous groups, and Connecticut began to complain. Of the movement one of its historians writes, "It was a large and strong centre of moral power. Direct and far cast its sacred light. Its members held high and consistent ground against al forms of sin, and valiantly wielded the 'sword of the spirit' for the overthrow of public and private wrongs." In brief, the newcomers were energetic reformers who meddled with private lives, disturbed quiet towns with loud cries about salvation and reform, and in general broke up the unity of secular and religious life. For they asserted vehemently that the laws of man were not those of the Lord and that His decrees, as interpreted by the Sabbatarians, were of prime importance. The same doctrines were accepted in theory by the Congregationalists, but at least they used their sense about the whole matter.

Quakers also came to the settlements along the Sound. For some reason the religious radicals avoided the hard life of the hill towns, preferring the more or less established existence farther south. An especially violent Friend was one James Rogers who gathered followers in New London and Groton, and moved back a few miles into the low hills. The Rogerenes, as they were called, believed in direct action and thought nothing of trying to break up regular church meetings. Sad to relate, such activities appealed to some Puritans; at least the new movement flourished too much to please the Old Guard.

Other small groups of strangely dissenting Puritans took up residence from time to time in Connecticut, and at last the Congregationalists realized that something must be done. As I have said, up until now the churches, each a separate unit, had been held together by unanimity of belief and folkways. Now it was apparent that some definite and legal church government was needed if the heretics were to be dealt with. In 1708, the General Court called delegates to a synod at Saybrook. These twelve clergymen and four laymen drew up the famous Saybrook Platform. This called for "biennial meetings of the ministers of each county in consociations to consider matters of common interest and exercise certain control over the ministry."

That was the way the Congregational Church in Connecticut forsook its old belief in the individual parish and began to create a system of government. Mark the fact that no one had wanted this platform before its adoption became necessary if the churches were to be protected against the new heretics. One parish could not withstand strange notions perhaps, but supported by a strong consociation of county ministers, it might be able to put the trouble-makers in their place. Such reasoning is thoroughly Puritan in character. Situations demand a certain form of action or of legal organization; forthwith, they are adopted, not because they are theoretically defensible, but because the given situation demands them. Folkways created in that manner are strong and lasting.

By 1725

New London was founded in 1646 and eighty years later most of the Town Meeting Country that is now Connecticut and Massachusetts had been split up into townships. Population was scanty in many places, but almost everyone was living in a town. However, some of west-central Rhode Island was still an unorganized Vacant Land, and it was common knowledge that those folks spent more time thinking up new ideas than they did building strong towns.

The first pioneers had died, and so had many of their children and grandchildren; the third and fourth generations of Puritans were running the communities. They were different men and women in some ways. In the very earliest days families had to work together or perish, but now that economic life was easier and the danger from Indians was over, a man could branch out for himself. That latent capacity for individuality that was always in the Puritan had begun to assert itself. And yet at times these men-by-themselves had to organize in order to defend their traditional ways of life. That is the way the duality of the Yankee developed. The individual was released in part; he was also brought closer to other individuals because union was necessary. Out of that blending of two desires came the ability of the New England townsman to remain himself and yet also be part of the community.

CHAPTER 4

The Town Grows

RUNNING THEIR OWN AFFAIRS

BY THE middle of the eighteenth century the little communities of Town Meeting Country had become efficient units of self-government. Of course, the idea of separate identity was not carried beyond the bounds of good common sense. No town set itself up as wholly apart from its neighbors. It traded with larger centers, accepted the authority of the General Court and the two Houses, and conformed willingly to extra-legal principles. But Woodstock or Hampton or Brookfield knew exactly when its obligations to the colony ended and just how many rights it had as a separate town.

The selectmen were the rulers of the community and had enough varied duties to frighten anyone but a practical Yankee. Builders, diplomats, lawyers, accountants, financiers, social welfare agents, and often stern critics of public morality, they seldom bothered with set principles and fixed precedents; in fact, they were happily ignorant of them and, instead, fitted their decision to the given situation. The problem came up of what should be done about that bridge over the Little River the folks up in the North District are protesting about. The three Town Fathers go to look at the bridge and decide to put in two new planks and shore up the underpinning. That way they'll satisfy the fault-finding North District voters and, at the same time, the rest of the citizens who are always howling about high taxes.

That was an easy problem, and so was the dispute between Andrew Rindge and Lyman Baker over the bounds of a wood-lot. In that case the records were searched; then the selectmen turned from law to surveying and ran a line which, they declared, ought to satisfy both parties. This done, the Fathers told Andrew and Lyman to stop squawking and let other people get on with their spring planting. Of course, the costs of record searching and surveying were split between the two disputants. But the insistent demand of the South Valley citizens for a new road was a more complex affair.

The harassed selectmen argued that this was no time to be spending a lot of money (it never is in a New England town) and why couldn't the complainants be reasonable! After all, going to the store and church by way of the Ridge Road wasn't much farther. "Tell ye what we'll do. We'll fix up that Ridge Road, an' mebbe in a year or two we can see our way clear to give ye what ye want. But right now money's scarce, an' lots of folks is kickin' about the taxes."

But the South Valley was stubborn. It wanted a new road and was going to have it or know the reason why.

The selectmen moved to their second line of defense, that of designated power.

"Who's runnin' this town, you folks or us?" they demanded. "We're th' legally constituted authorities, an' we're doin' our best t' keep things on a sound footin' an' expenses down, but we can't get nowhere if you fellers keep interferin'. Now shet up!"

Such a stern order worked frequently, for Puritans respected official authority, especially if the officers speaking had been elected by the town. Anybody sent from outside to govern was in for a bad time, but the home boys ought to be supported unless they were obviously in the wrong.

This time, the South Valley voters decided that the selectmen could be defied.

"Th' hell you're runnin' th' town!" they declared. "Th' people elected ye, an' they've got some voice in sayin' what ye can an' can't do. We'll have a town meetin' an' thresh this matter out."

Now the Town Fathers spoke fervently. Town meetings cost good money, they pointed out. The clerk had to write out warnings and post them, and then he got fifty cents for taking down the minutes. Besides, it was foolish to call a meeting; folks was busy making a living and oughtn't to be bothered. Just be reasonable and you'll get your road some time. The rebels were not impressed.

"Do we get that town meetin' without fuss, or do we have to carry around a petition for one?" they asked insolently.

The selectmen swore, moaned piteously, and finally called a town meeting. It was the privilege of the South Valleyites to appeal to the town as a whole, and even the most bullheaded selectman respected such inviolable rights. He might put up a bluff of refusal, but in the end he yielded. So the voters of the town met in more or less solemn session, talked over the whole matter, voted on the motion, and decided that the South Valley didn't need a new road. The defeated citizens went back to their farms speaking bitter words, but they did not pack up and leave town as a lot of unreasonable people in other states would have done. They had tried their best, and their defeat had come at the hands of something greater than mere humans, the Town Meeting. For very early in their career as free people the Puritans accepted the one basic rule of self-government that forty men taken separately may be wise, foolish, honest, or knavish, just as all individuals may be; but when they come together in legal assembly and debate on town affairs, they constitute as nearly a sacred, omnipotent, and all-wise conclave as any this side of the Judgment Throne.

These town meetings were conducted in a very seemly manner. Always a dignified little town, Hampton, Connecticut, formulated one of the most famous sets of rules for procedure:

"1. Choose moderator.

2. Annual meeting to be opened with prayer.

3. Every member to be seated with his hat on, and no member to leave his seat unnecessarily, and if necessary, to do it with as little noise as possible.

4. Members, while speaking, shall address the moderator and him only and speak with hat off.

5. No member to speak more than twice upon one subject without leave of meeting, and but once until each member has had opportunity to speak.

6. As soon as a member has done speaking, he will take his seat and not speak after he is seated.

7. Every member must speak directly to the question before the meeting.

8. No persons have any right to do private business in any part of the house."

Hampton folk were not so unruly that they needed this meticulous code to keep them within bounds; they were merely Puritans

who believed in orderly conduct, and the best way to get it was
to draw up a definite set of rules. If they had that, any one who
raised a rumpus would be violating a voted ordinance and could
be dealt with in a legal manner.

Of course, each town had a full complement of minor officers.
Fence viewers, pound-keepers, a brander for casks and hogsheads
(and he "found" his own branding iron), assessors, constables,
hog reeves, and as many more as could be thought of. None of
these men were overworked, but their combined efforts did keep
the town in good running order and gave the citizens the comfortable feeling that there was a law and an officer to cope with
every situation. No regular police system was needed. The constable served writs and hailed offenders before the courts and
looked after the very rare fellow who fought and brawled. The
church was ever ready to help the secular officers deal with cases
of heresy, dipsomania, assault and battery, disrespect to the cloth,
and bad debts. Only when murder had been committed was the
sheriff called in from the county. Such intervention was accepted
as legal, but it was also considered more or less of a disgrace. The
town folks ought to limit their anti-social conduct to acts which
could be handled by their neighbors.

Those little towns managed their affairs remarkably well and
achieved a surprising amount of independence without getting
out of step with the state authority. That is ever our way of
behaving—run your own life just as much as you can while you
remember that you are also part of a greater unit of government.

Manors Aren't for Yankees

Every so often some one in New England tried to establish
a system of community life not modeled on the township. One
such experiment was in part of what is now Pomfret and Brooklyn, Connecticut.

Captain John Blackwell bought 5750 acres from that greatest
of all realtors, Major James Fitch, Jr. With his usual disregard
for precedent and a kindly desire to please a good customer, the
major handed the captain a remarkable grant of rights. It stated
that the purchased land "shall be accounted a separate tract by
and of itself, to hold to him [Blackwell] and his heirs and assigns,
so neither the rest of the purchasers, nor their survivors or heirs
shall challenge to have, hold, or enjoy, any joynt or separate

interest, title, power or jurisdiction or privelege of a township, or otherwise, howsoever, within the same form from henceforth for ever." In other words, the tract was not a town and never could be, and Blackwell and his heirs and assigns could do with it and the people on it as they pleased. They were Lords of the Manor, lacking only the *droit de seigneur,* and perhaps Fitch took that too for granted.

This remarkable document was completely at variance with every Puritan principle of land settlement, but, and here is supreme proof of his greatness as a man of affairs, the major persuaded the General Court of Connecticut to declare it valid in every detail. He had pulled off his best real-estate deal; he had created a manor in a land of democratic towns.

Captain Blackwell does not seem to have lived on his baronial acres; at least, no record is left of residence or improvement of the land. In 1713 this tract, now known as Mortlake Manor, was sold to Jonathan Belcher. This land speculator was to become Governor of Massachusetts and then of New Jersey, and later founder of Princeton. In those days the turning of an honest penny in a real-estate transaction was considered very good form indeed. Soon after this transfer, the barony began to give trouble.

First of all, Belcher or his agents found one Jabez Utter squatting on the domain. Undoubtedly these undeveloped tracts were often frequented by queer people, but Utter was more than a recluse. He was a professional horse thief. While away on business his wife, Mary, guarded the home. When Belcher's men ordered her to move, she flatly refused. Persuasion and threats did not work, and at last what is described as a "crowd of boisterous men" was assembled from nearby towns. But Mary Utter was not cowed, and she barricaded the doors and windows so well that at last three men had to crawl down the chimney. In the end the valiant matron was ejected from her house, but the record states that she fought to the last.

The Utters were not the only illegal residents of Mortlake, and it soon got the name of being a very lawless region. Belcher would not employ men to supervise his manor, and at last the neighboring towns appealed to the courts to have this nuisance abated. But the General Court reaffirmed the right of Belcher to govern his land as an individual. For a time it looked as if Mortlake would continue to be a haven of refuge for all kinds of

undesirable people, but before long even the most conservative
court began to realize that manors were not for Yankees.

The downfall of Mortlake began in a characteristically Puritan manner. Another low-lived family had been squatting in the
manor, a man and woman and their idiot son, Peter. After the
husband died, the woman appealed for aid for herself and boy.
But the neighbors were just as poor, and—here is the crux of
the whole affair—there was no town to go to for legal assistance.
Belcher was Lord of the Manor it is true, but he was in Massachusetts or New Jersey. So the widow applied to the next regularly established settlement, Pomfret, for help. That cautious
town thought hard, and soon realized that here was a fine opportunity to demonstrate that a town was a far better institution
than any manor. Besides, no community wants to be paying for
the support of people who do not belong to it. So the Pomfret
town meeting handed down this decision: "That we are not
obliged by law nor conscience to take ye charge upon ourselves,
and desire the selectmen to make due return unto her [the
widow], and if, after this, she do offer to impose the same [Peter
the idiot] upon the town we desire the selectmen to follow her
in the law as a trespasser, at the town's charge."

There you have a fine example of town logic. Peter and his
mother were not citizens of Pomfret; therefore, they could not
be helped. If she became too insistent, she must be treated as a
trespasser on soil on which she had no right to tread. And, lastly,
the town would pay the selectmen for carrying out the ejection
or arrest. That would teach her to live in a regular town like a
sensible person and not go squatting in some manor where there
were no selectmen or taxes or any other sensible adjuncts to decent living.

Rebuffed by Pomfret, the widow somehow managed to go to
Peter's birthplace, Norwich, with him and there asked to have
him taken care of. Norwich officials promptly said he did not
belong to them and ordered him back to Mortlake. But this was
going too far even for those practical days, and the court of New
London county committed Peter to the care of a tenant of the
Lord of the Mortlake Manor. It also summoned Norwich and
Pomfret to appear and show reason why they should not provide
for Peter. The two towns sent representatives who flatly refused
to accept the charge. The court delayed action and finally ap-

pointed three justices to be temporary guardians of the bothersome boy.

By now the court seems to have determined to get to the bottom of this affair. So Pomfret was again brought up for questioning. She sent two men to defend her rights, and we are told that their expenses were paid from rates previously granted for schools and meeting-house repairs. Here is final proof of what were first things in the Puritan scheme of affairs. Pomfret was determined to evade responsibility for Peter, but she would never have spent many pounds if there had not been a deeper principle involved. And that principle was this: that the rights, privileges, and benefits enjoyed by the inhabitants of one town cannot be summarily demanded by anybody who is in trouble. Town citizenship was a well-nigh sacred thing, much like the prized Roman right Paul invoked, and only bona-fide residents could claim its protection. So, when its own identity was at stake, Pomfret was willing to use money allotted to school and church.

Pomfret pleaded its case so well that the New London court was forced to compromise. It did so by handing Peter over to Windham County officials. And one year later he was back in Norwich, politely deposited there by Windham County which said, in effect, "You bred this nuisance; now please take care of him." No further mention is made of the distressed widow and her boy, so I suppose that Norwich resigned itself to the inevitable and kept them.

In the towns around Mortlake Manor there were many angry remarks. A lot of money had been spent and more time wasted just because the tract was not a town. A movement was started to render void the grant of rights that Mortlake held. But Belcher had powerful friends and, furthermore, the manor inhabitants objected to being put in a town. With the exception of such unfortunates as Peter and his mother, most of them were having a fine time with no one to look after them. So Mortlake Manor kept on being a thorn in the flesh of Windham County until its inhabitants made their great mistake. Some inherited instinct told them that they needed a church, so they set about building one and finding a minister. The neighboring towns heard and rejoiced. At last Belcher's Tract was settling down to respectability. But the joy was short-lived. Independent as ever, the

Mortlakers refused to choose a minister duly approved by the Windham County Consociation of Congregational Churches; instead, they picked one who suited their own tastes. Colonial records do not tell who this dominie was, but the odds are good that he was a Baptist, and probably from Rhode Island.

Now the towns knew that they must do something about this annoying manor. Idiot paupers were bad enough, but defiance of church rules was infinitely worse. The means by which the enraged communities persuaded Belcher, the Lord of the Manor, to give up his claim are not clear, but a little while after the ordination of the undesirable minister, the tract was sold for the goodly sum of £10,500.

One of the purchasers was a Tory and an Episcopalian, Colonel Godfrey Malbone, and he was later to be a thorn in the county's flesh, but at least he believed in town government. So ended the only eastern Connecticut experiment in baronial and manorial government. That sort of thing was all right in England, but here things didn't get run right if there weren't a few town meetings every year, and if selectmen, and assessors, and constables, all duly elected, were not in charge.

GETTING A LIVING

Most of the Yankees lived off the land. Along the Sound there was fishing, and some men built small ships and began to carry goods to Boston and Providence and New York, while bolder spirits started a southern coastwide trade and went as far as the West Indies. Of course, a few thought nothing of crossing the ocean and, as early as 1647, an ambitious Mr. Whitney was granted a franchise for the killing of whales in local waters. Down along the shore, men were getting restless. Soon they would be in Bering Straits or at the Antarctic ice barrier or trading with the Chinese.

Farming might be the backbone of economic existence in the hill villages, but many citizens found other methods of turning a dollar. Some ran taverns where the infrequent travelers could eat and sleep and the local citizens buy a drink of rum. From the very first a few merchants had bought up farm produce and taken it laboriously to the larger towns where it was exchanged for cloth goods, notions, ammunition, salt, spices, and hard liquor. Then there were the saw and grist mills and later the fulling mill and all the little home shops a growing town can support.

All these men lived on a home lot and probably had some acres of meadow and woodland in other parts of the town. Even the minister, spiritual and intellectual aristocrat, had his own acres and was supposed to work them. For existence was not possible unless the lands and the animals on them contributed most of the necessities of life. A merchant got his ready cash by shrewd barter; a blacksmith and a minister and a doctor had their special trade or profession, but all of these townspeople were bound to the soil. Each house was a miniature collection of many industries. In it the women folk cooked, brewed, preserved, carded, spun, wove, made candles, braided rugs, and, of course, reared children and tried to keep them alive. Every farmer was an amateur machinist, carpenter, and blacksmith, and took pride in wasting half a day in patching up a broken shaft. For a shilling the blacksmith would have done a good job but, no, the farmer wanted to save that shilling; furthermore, he enjoyed the good feeling of doing things for himself.

"Independent as a hog on ice" was what they called the Yankee townsman from the very first. Few obligations outside those in his own household were recognized. One of the few was the support of the church, and also the minister as long as that consecrated man behaved himself. Another duty was of sober, thoughtful consideration of all town problems and, if elected to office, of honest attempts to handle these problems. There was a third obligation, recognized by all save the most low-lived and cussed Puritans, of the need for being a good neighbor. That meant keeping your fences up, helping out in an emergency, and, in general, giving the other fellow a hand if he needed one. Gracious hospitality, genial humor, or even reasonably good temper, were not required; some of the best neighbors were, and still are, the most profane and cantankerous of men.

Having fulfilled these obligations to society, the Yankee townsman tried his best to live for and by himself and his family. As a result of this desire, his methods of getting a living were from the very start quite individualistic and, therefore, productive of new ideas, startling innovations, and of the industrial era that was to make America great. Out of the blacksmiths, carders, mill owners, and odd-job men of the Yankee lands came our factory barons; from the soil came the men who knew how to make a living for themselves without asking favors.

THE THREE R'S

The Puritan religion demanded that each man read the Bible for himself. It was taken for granted that sensible people would agree with Congregational doctrines, but they must read and meditate nonetheless. Thus they helped insure their spiritual future and, only by knowing Scripture and theology could they become church members. Only church members were voters, so there were material as well as spiritual reasons for acquiring more than casual book learning such as satisfied the majority of citizens in other states. Puritans were at an early date convinced that the man who couldn't read, write, and cipher well was the one most likely to come out the little end of the horn in a bargain. And always there was the genuine desire of many Yankees to know what was going on in the world of politics and decisive happenings.

But the practical leaders realized that such motives for learning were not enough to stir all people. So, in 1650, Connecticut passed a law requiring the establishment of elementary schools in all townships of fifty families or more, and of Latin grammar schools in towns of one hundred or more families. Parents were fined if they did not send their children to school; furthermore, some towns voted themselves the right to take boys from such recalcitrant families and apprentice them to a trade. The state fixed the minimum provision for maintenance of schools and attendance; after that, each town handled its own problems, the greatest of which was always the raising of funds. Gradually, however, the state of Connecticut began to assume greater charge of the town schools. In 1795, it sold the three million acres in the Western Reserve which the original charter had given it, and the money received was turned into a trust fund, the income of which should be used to support all schools in the state.

Over in the Vacant Lands, schools were not considered important. Not until 1800 did Rhode Island pass the first free public school law embracing the entire state. Private schools were numerous in Providence and Newport, but over to the west the squatters and poor farmers were not provided for. When exasperated citizens remarked, "Those Plantations!" they included the sin of anti-democracy along with that of strange religious beliefs.

But in eastern Connecticut and that part of Massachusetts that lies in the Town Meeting Country, the lower schools were by now far better than one would expect to find in a new land, and even the secondary schools showed promise of splendid development. Most of the famous academies were started after the Revolution, but one of them was famous much earlier. At Columbia, Connecticut, Eleazar Wheelock started an Indian school. Here Samson Occum, famous Mohegan preacher, studied, was ordained, and served as a missionary. In 1766 he was sent to England to raise money for the continuance of the work. When he came back, he had all of fifty thousand dollars, much of which had been given by the Earl of Dartmouth. Wheelock's school was now prosperous, and plenty of bright Indian boys came there to study. Then the principal suddenly accepted the offer of Governor Winthrop of land on the Connecticut River, and the school was moved up to Hanover, New Hampshire, there to become Dartmouth College and to have Eleazar Wheelock as its first president.

An old story tells that the school need never have been moved; that Darthmouth College came near being now in Columbia, Connecticut. But the early citizens of that town had fine orchards that brought in quite a bit of income, and they were bothered by young redskin depredations. So the danger to thrifty living was removed, and now Columbia is serene and untroubled.

Of course, not every Yankee got even the rudiments of an education. There were always the idiots and those "not quite all there," and every town had several low-life families who asserted that their rights were being tampered with if their kids were hauled off to school when they'd rather be trapping muskrats. This extreme spirit of independence survived for almost two centuries. As late as 1910, a descendant of Puritans boasted that all he could do was scratch his name and read "big print"; furthermore, he insisted that in a long and honorable career as a good hired man he had never felt handicapped by his lack of education.

"Jammin' a lot of nonsense into a boy's head don't learn him t' swing a scythe nor a naxe nor lay a load of hay nor milk a cow clean," was his opinion.

On the whole, however, most little Puritans learned to read, write, declaim, and cipher. All ages went to school, and tales are told of bearded brothers carrying a three-year-old so that the latter might start his education. The teacher for the infrequent spring session could be a woman, but the winter months demanded a strong arm if discipline was to be kept. The schoolmaster might be a semi-professional who ran a small farm on the side, or he was a college youth picking up a few dollars so that he could study another semester. If he came from out of town he was boarded around. The length of his stay at each house depended upon the number of pupils it sent to school, and the diaries of those days are full of laments that a prosperous farm where there was warmth and good food couldn't be enjoyed more than a week, while seven long ones had to be endured in the squalor of those poor but prolific folks up Bear Hill way.

The rural school system of New England was exceptionally efficient in every respect, if we take into consideration the poverty of the people and the lack of a tradition of popular education. Out of the little schoolhouses came men, and women too, who read the Bible and also the dodgers put out by those rebels in Boston and the Committees of Correspondence. These same men and women, because they could read and write as well as the next person, weren't taking anything from anyone; they were standing on their own rights. Out of the three R's of the town school came contrary folks who had thought and read for themselves and were willing to fight at Bunker Hill, or speak in Congress for the Union.

Churches and Church Folk

Good Sensible Congregational Religion. The early Puritans had two reasons for clinging to the Congregational church. First, it preached the correct religious doctrines and conducted a seemly and dignified service that did not smack of Popery and yet was less crude than the shouts of Baptists and other uncivilized sects; second, it worked with the town and state in the very important task of creating and preserving a sound, moral community life. The church did not rule the town; neither did it stand aloof in holy and theological state; it was, instead, an agent of the people as well as of the Lord. That sort of religion was the only sensible one, said the early settlers; one where the Lord, through His minister, took an active hand in helping out a hard-worked select-man or constable, and was in turn supported by the town officers.

For example, in 1729, an indiscreet Hampton, Connecticut, man said of the current pastor, "I had rather hear my dog bark than Mr. Billings preach."

Today such a statement would be nothing more than a vigor-ous comment on a strictly ecclesiastical situation, but in Hamp-ton it was a civic crime as well as blasphemy. The unnamed pro-faner was brought before the town magistrates and lectured. Either truly repentant or just scared, he promptly confessed his sin and told of deep repentance. The really interesting part of this case is that the comment on Mr. Billings was apparently not an original one. For as early as 1643 a Mr. H. Walton of Lynn was presented to court for saying that "he has a Leeve to hear a Dogg Barke as to heare Mr. Cobbett Preach." This rebel was acquitted, and his estimate of preaching caught the popular fancy and was passed around until it became part of the folk lore of Puritanism. Eighty years later it was repeated down in Connec-ticut, and once again the critic was brought before the civil au-thority to answer for his defiance of a minister who was an integral part of the government of the town as well as of the Divine Scheme.

Now and then a revered minister became too much of a leader who wanted others to obey him. Then the bolder spirits of the congregation protested. For no Apostolic Succession gave the Puritan minister supernatural powers; he was hired by the peo-ple, and responsible to them fully as much as he was to Higher Powers. One of the men who forgot his mundane origin was the Reverend Mr. Moseley, pastor of the Hampton, Connecticut, church for fifty-eight years, and not one without excitement.

For some time, Reverend Moseley had been feeling his power quite a bit. He passed out hard sentences for casual indulgences in rum and love, he refused church membership right and left, and he ran the church affairs to suit himself. For a decade Hamp-ton deacons and solid citizens demanded, "Who does he think he is? Don't he know we've got some say in matters?" At last the rebellious church members asked their preacher for a more ex-plicit explanation of his idea of discipline; they also asked that a body of elders be allowed to assist him in running church affairs. A meeting was called, but Mr. Moseley, as moderator, dismissed it when the troublesome demands were made. Another meeting was held, and at this one the vigorous preacher scared most of the members into silence. But an unabashed minority drew up a withering remonstrance which denounced the minister for dissolving meetings or talking too much himself at them. He also admitted church members who had no "grace in their heart" or did not have the approval of other members.

At this point the rebels asked, "Sir, are you wiser than Christ?"

After this, the paper of indictment descended to such trivial matters as lack of access to church records, too few ministerial calls on some people, and the burning question of why the Moseley slaves, a man and wife, had been parted. The indignant dominie struck back; there were meetings and more meetings, and at last one exasperated citizen cried in public, "That he saw the Pope's horns begin to bud out some years ago, and now they were grown out." Mr. Moseley demanded his reviler's excommunication; the latter continued to talk about Pope-Moseley, and the town was split into two parties. The details of the battle are interesting, but I am most concerned with the way it ended and how peace was brought.

In any other community, save a Puritan one, there would have been a complete split between warring groups; a protesting church would be built, and general disruption reign. But my people knew that even the question of Popery should not be allowed to ruin the efficiency of a sound church, so the formidable County Consociation of Churches met and passed judgment. Its verdict was as sensible as its act of taking charge of this dangerous quarrel. The Reverend Mr. Moseley was commanded to examine himself and labor after greater perfection of gentleness and circumspection, and his mocker was told to be more peaceable in the future and not talk about Pope's horns.

Do not get the idea that Puritans were compromisers because they feared a battle. By no means. A halt was called in the Moseley controversy, because continuing it would have hurt the church, and hurting the church would affect that complex organism called town life. Puritans were genuinely interested in religious doctrines, in church discipline, and in ecclesiastical questions, but if needs be they could say to rash controversialists, "Now that's enough! Forget it, for you're putting the church in danger, and no doctrine is worth that."

The Puritans had a good, sensible religion. The church was of God and of the town; the minister was His emissary and could also speak harshly to a brother who had been overtaken with drink on the highway. Both church and minister enjoyed divine sanction, but quite often they were tested by their ability to work smoothly with the several units of community life.

Most significant of all is that out of this concept of the sensible nature of religion and its servants and practices there will never develop bigots, fanatics, and pulpit-thumpers. Mystic truths may never be revealed to neo-Puritans, but their folkways are tolerant and there are no brandings in the name of the One True Religion. For the Puritan town demanded a good sensible religion, and having developed one, it handed that inestimable gift on to future generations. Puritan theology and discipline is supposed to have been harsh and dogmatic, but out of them came the spirit that has allowed all creeds and races to live together. The wilderness town created a religion that would work, and it still remains vital and sensible.

The Lord's Day. Calvin played bowls in Geneva on Sunday, and the first English Dissenters did not think of this seventh day as one of morose inaction. But in 1595, a Dr. Bound proclaimed that the Scriptures enjoined that Sunday must be observed like the Jewish Sabbath. And, since the evening and the morning were the first day, this Sabbath was from sundown on Saturday until sundown the next day. These principles were promptly accepted by the next generation, and the Lord's Day began its career.

New England Puritans followed their English teachers and, in most cases, went them one better in making the Sabbath holy. A legend has it that a Connecticut tithing man went so far as to stop General George Washington and ask why he was riding on the Lord's Day. The Father of his Country promptly answered that he was journeying to the nearest divine service. And as late as 1831, a Lebanon, Connecticut, woman was arrested on her way to her father's house on Sunday for "unnecessary traveling." However, this act was undoubtedly one of spite and cussedness, for after long litigation, the woman was given damages for false imprisonment. A case like this is fine proof of the interrelations of the New England church and state. You violate Holy Writ when you desecrate the Holy Day, but a constable arrests you, and if he does so wrongly you appeal to a temporal court and get temporal damages for being imprisoned for a spiritual sin.

The truth about the early New England Sabbath observance is that the Puritans were strict in enforcing the very laws other people made and then neglected. Probably the edict against traveling was the only absurd regulation of Sabbath conduct, and after all even that one is not very cruel.

The famous Connecticut Blue Laws are a fiction of the resentful mind of a Reverend Samuel Peters who was kicked out of Hebron, Connecticut, for being a Tory. In his *General History of Connecticut* he declared that there were statutes that "no one shall travel, cook victuals, make beds, sweep house, cut hair, or shave on the Sabbath day. No woman shall kiss her child on the Sabbath or Fasting days." Such laws never existed, but a 1676 edict was thoroughly in keeping with Puritan custom. It forbade all work and business on Sunday, "works of necessity or charity excepted."

Surplice and Cross. Until Revolutionary War hatreds branded many of them as Tories, Episcopalians were regarded by sensible, orthodox Puritans as people given to silly and useless display in church service and altogether too much dominated by their rectors and curates who, it was claimed, were very arrogant and conceited. However, kindly mercy was shown these yearners after mummery. For example, as early as 1727, Connecticut passed an act of toleration of Episcopalians and permitted them to pay their ecclesiastical dues to their own church if there was one in their town. Of course, if this were not the case, the orphan worshiper supported the local Congregational church or went to jail.

This state of affairs caused stray Anglicans much anguish. Forgetting that they had been given toleration, they wailed that they should not be made to pay dues for a church they despised. But only a few of the lonely devotees of surplice and incense could change matters. One of these men of iron will gave Windham County its first Episcopal church and now lives in history as a great colonial patron of Anglicanism.

Colonel Godfrey Malbone, of King's College, had traveled much in Europe, but he found Newport's society most delightful; furthermore, his father had built up a fine business there with ships and warehouses which may have harbored several cargoes of

black ivory. So the young man settled down in the city which
even then was not quite Puritan. On his father's death he inherited a large estate, but before long the merchant prince began
to be bothered by the colonial rebellion. Privateers seized his
ships and goods, and the courts could give him no protection.
Then his new home, called "the most splendid edifice in all the
colonies," burned.

Thoroughly disgusted, and apparently much in the spirit of
the spoiled youth who cannot have his way, Godfrey Malbone left
Newport and went to Brooklyn, Connecticut. Here he bought
three thousand acres, built a house, and stocked his farm with
animals aplenty and Negro slaves. Up here in the sticks he would
be left alone to live as he pleased. To the north was the ungov-
erned Belcher's Tract. In nearby Brooklyn village were only un-
couth yokels who could undoubtedly be made to fear a man of
quality, even though they might resent him.

For a few years Godfrey Malbone did live undisturbed. He received gentlemen, and them only, politely; gave alms to the
worthy poor; and paid his town and church rates without question. But he attended no meetings and was not in the least interested in local affairs. However, since the earliest days Puritans
have had the ability to force people to notice them.

In 1768, the Brooklyn Congregational Church was in such bad
condition that it was decided to build a new one. A meeting was
called to discuss means of raising money, and Malbone was put
down as the man to be taxed the most. He was openly, even
blatantly, an Anglican, but that made no difference; he owned
property in Brooklyn and must, therefore, be taxed to support
Brooklyn's official church. If he rebelled, why then, let him turn
Congregational and get some good out of his taxes.

Godfrey Malbone heard nothing of the church meeting until a
loyal tenant came running with the news of the intended levy.
Then the colonel, as he was now called, went to Mr. Whitney, the
minister, and protested strongly. The diplomatic minister led the
colonel to the church and pointed out the needed repairs. Malbone scoffed, said that a few clapboards would do the job, and
more than intimated that a tumbledown edifice was good enough
for Dissenters. Such an attitude did not please the Brooklyn citizens, for those were the days when rebellion was in the air, and
aristocrats and Tories were especially irritating. So the town went

ahead with the plans to have a new church and let Colonel Malbone pay the largest assessment.

That incensed gentleman did not at first believe that Dissenters
and yokels could make him support their scheme, but before long
he began to worry. He consulted a Tory lawyer about how to
evade the church levy. The lawyer shook his head and stated that
it must be paid unless Malbone got an English court dispensation
or had in Brooklyn a church of his own sect to which he paid
rates. The colonel was incredulous. Go to all the bother of an
English court appeal just to get out of a tax? He'd be damned
first! If he spoke sharply enough to these people he had once
described as being full of "cant, cunning, hypocrisy and lowness
of manners" they would probably remember their station in life
and let him go tax-free.

But at a hot meeting the colonel was defeated and faced the legal
necessity of paying one-eighth of the entire cost of a church edifice he would never attend. A scared if not humbled man, he now
remembered that his lawyer had said that having an Episcopal
church in Brooklyn would solve the problem. The colonel saw the
light. He would introduce Anglicanism into Windham County.

Colonel Malbone proved to be an able organizer and collector
of funds, and on April 12, 1771, lovely and dignified Trinity
Church was publicly opened. Never once did the unwilling missionary pretend that he had built his church for religious motives
only. As he said, to have done so would "border very near upon
that damnable sin of hypocrisy and falsehood from the schools of
which he was endeavoring to bring over as many as he should be
able." But no matter what his reasons, the strong-minded colonel
did bring Surplice and Cross to Windham County.

The Great Awakening. Even sensible Puritans yield now and
then to spiritual urges and fervors, and during the first half of the
eighteenth century only the most resolutely orthodox escaped
untouched. The Great Awakening, or the Quickening of the
Spirit, as some called it, began about 1740 and did not abate its
vigorous proselyting until at least twenty years later. Its own
historians say, "Through the intervention of the Spirit of God
it was a new birthday to our land; formalism fell before the truth,
and ecclesiasticism gave way to the Spirit." * However, the Old

* From *Westerly and Its Witnesses,* by Frederic Denison, Providence, 1878.

Guard Congregationalists of that day speak of the Awakening in terms reminiscent of an Archbishop Laud harrying an upstart and loud-mouthed meeting of Dissenters. Somewhere between the two estimates lies the truth. This outburst of religious liberalism was inevitable; on the other hand, it most certainly did menace the security of the towns and hinder their development.

There is no doubt that the zeal and devotion shown by the earlier Puritans was not found in the eighteenth-century churches. Having the task before them of firmly establishing the one correct system of belief, and having in large measure accomplished their aim, it was only natural that ministers and laymen alike should turn their attention to matters of organization and discipline. For instance, the Windham County churches, in solemn meeting, were asked to decide "whether a person refusing to sit in the place where he has been regularly seated in the house of God, and publicly jostling and interrupting others from sitting in the place where they be seated, be a censurable fault." It was voted that refusal was not censurable but jostling was. Another question debated was: Should confessions of public scandal be made before the whole congregation or members in full communion only. The decision was that the entire body of worshipers should enjoy the revelations.

But in spite of such ecclesiastical fussiness and interest in petty details, the great majority of Congregationalists seemed to have been satisfied with the way their churches were run in the early decades of the eighteenth century. Of course, the Baptists and Quakers were always objecting to things, but no one paid any attention to them! And when thoughtful ministers whispered that the Congregational churches might be a little more spiritual, the parishioners hastened to add that such reforms took time and nothing was ever gained by stirring up folks.

But Puritan desires for a sedate and peaceful religious life were shattered by the fervent preaching of Edwards and Whitefield. At first, the orthodox clergy saw little harm in a rebirth of zeal; but they soon changed their minds and began to revile this awakening. For all sorts of new members were joining the churches, and men and women shouted strange and disturbing words about purifying the Temple. Unqualified and unordained preachers went from town to town, exciting the people to frenzied enthusiasm. Religious meetings were loud with groans, shrieks, and shouts, while the more zealous fainted or had fits. Some lay prostrate for hours; others complained loudly that they were possessed by devils. The more enthusiastic people south and west of the Alleghenies would have understood that such actions were nothing more than the natural and pleasant ways of proclaiming your salvation, but the Puritans who did not shout looked at the weaker vessels with profound misgivings. As one horrified man wrote, "So terrible and affecting were the outcries at some of the meetings that the noise therof was heard for more than a mile, seeming more like the infernal regions than the place of worshipping the God of Heaven."

But the noise and strange actions that went with the new salvation did not disturb the more thoughtful conservatives as much as did the ideas these zealots were expounding. For a century, the Puritans had been carefully building a social structure in which the church and the civil authorities worked together. Tolerance was granted the beliefs of Baptists, Anglicans, and even Quakers, and all that was asked of them was seemly behavior and support of the town. So far, the communities had thrived and were slowly and surely creating a stable, democratic, and efficient scheme of life, and the Congregationalists felt that at least some of the praise should go to their church which had so sensibly realized that it must work with the state.

Now these Separatists—Inner Light disciples they called themselves—were insisting that the Church and its religion should stand apart from the secular community. And man himself was to obey the church first and the state second. Furthermore, he could not be a good church member simply by observing the rules and paying his rates; he must be saved anew and, once saved, continue to be a positive force for good. As final judge of each citizen's worthiness to be called a Christian there were certain very personal tests and obligations. No longer could piety be defined in terms of correct community behavior; it depended upon how much the would-be pious had accepted salvation, been "washed in the blood of the Lamb," "born again," and experienced many other strange phenomena. It was all very disconcerting to sensible ministers and deacons, this separation of the spiritual life of man from his daily existence, this insistence that the only thing that mattered was his spiritual rebirth.

At first the conservatives did little to combat the new ideas and actions, but very soon they realized that they must take notice of them. So stiff laws were passed. Liberty of speech was restricted to settled pastors of churches. Pastors alone could not talk as they wished; they must be settled in a regularly organized church. And any unlicensed person who should exhort or preach without permission of the pastor of the town should be bound to his peaceable and good behavior until next county court for one hundred pounds. Since few exhorters ever had that much money, or friends who had it, arrest for illegal exhorting meant a long jail term. It was also enacted that it should be considered disorderly conduct for a minister, even if ordained, to enter another minister's parish and preach or administer the seals of the covenant without the consent of, or in opposition to, the settled minister or the major part of the church members.

After passing these laws and a few others, the conservatives sighed with relief. They had put the upstart exhorters in their place and had done so in a seemly and legal manner. But the new rebels were also Puritans and, therefore, very determined to have their own way. They chose to begin their defense by doing the one thing that would damn them forever in the eyes of the godly. They started a brisk campaign to purify the Congregational Church itself. To have left the church would have been bad enough but understandable in a way, and such an act could be forgiven, for, after all, Baptists and Quakers and Episcopalians were granted tolerance. But to stay in the congregation and try to make it conform to new and erratic ideas was unbelievable. A shouting Quaker was probably queer by nature and might be pardoned, but an Inner Light Congregationalist was simply perverse and cussed. No mercy should be shown him. The battles raged in almost every town. What happened in one of them illustrates the tragicomedy that was being enacted everywhere.

Canterbury, Connecticut, had been one of Major Fitch's favorite developments, and its people may have caught some of his restless spirit. At any rate, they had enjoyed the excitement of the Great Awakening days. The stiff decorum of religious services had been forgotten; new preachers had exhorted them, and they had met in the intimacy of each other's houses for prayer and exhortation. And now these pleasures were forbidden. The only one who could preach the word of God was the ordained minister, or some person approved of by him. The Inner Lights mourned, pondered, met in solemn deliberation, and voted to fight for their freedom.

Within a few months Canterbury was, as the records say, "in great confusion." On the side of authority were the solid, conservative citizens, theoretically headed by the minister, but turning for advice to some rich and influential layman. With him stood the town officials, for the shrewd and intuitive Yankee mind had told many that sound town government was threatened by these proposed changes just as much as was the Congregational Church.

Canterbury's Inner Lights were not very well organized, but their leading spirit was Elisha Paine. A year before he had heard a divine call, but after being approved by a ministerial board, for he was a serious and learned young man, he refused to subscribe to the Saybrook Platform, saying that it claimed powers not granted by Scripture. These Liberals were annoying when they argued like that. Couldn't they see, asked the orthodox, that the platform supported a strong church and a strong town? And if it did say that, why bring up the question of scriptural sanction? But Elisha Paine persisted, and very soon came to the further conclusion that his call was a far more valid permit to preach than any license given by mere men, even if met together in solemn consociation.

The Inner Light leader began to preach from house to house, and later, as his fame spread, from town to town. The orthodox waited and forgave often, but at last they could do no other thing. In February, 1743, Paine was arrested and sent to jail. Friends offered to give bail, but his conscience forbade such compromise, and in jail he stayed until May when he was discharged. Back in Canterbury he was welcomed as a martyr, and many Inner Lights prepared to follow him in his crusade for a purified church, to clean and make more spiritual the church of their fathers. As yet there was no desire to break away and start another parish.

It must be said to the credit of the orthodox church members that they tried even now to bring peace to the turbulent congregation and town. Instead of putting Paine back in jail they went so far as to call a new minister in the hope that he would please the Inner Light leader and his disciples and persuade them to come back to the fold. But the hope was a vain one. When the Reverend Mr. Cogswell arrived in Canterbury, he was forthwith examined by the rebels themselves. To their horror he admitted that the state and town had power over a church body; furthermore, he did not ask for satisfactory evidence of regeneration before granting full church membership. Of these two defects in the dominie's ideology, one ecclesiastical, the other theological, the former seems to have shocked the Inner Lighters the most. They were loud in their declaration that their battle was for a purified creed, but any attempt to exercise civil authority over the church was in their minds the deepest form of tyranny. The orthodox were just as firm in their determination that church and state and town should work together.

The Reverend Mr. Cogswell was rejected by Elisha Paine and his brothers and sisters. This unreasonable attitude and insolent rejection of the overture of peace killed all chance for compromise. The old guard called Mr. Cogswell; it also threw another brother into jail. Whereupon the rebels fasted and then met in prayerful deliberation. The idea born of the conference was a very logical one. Why not have a church of their own? It would still be Congregational in name, but it would hold higher spiritual standards for full church membership, and no state or town would interfere with the running of it, for Scripture alone would be the guide. So the rebels withdrew from the regular church and met in a private house.

The orthodox members prepared for a real battle. Inner Light notions could be forgiven; departure from the church to Baptistry or Quakerdom might be forgotten; but no small town could support two official churches, and if that town was to be a strong, unified body of people there was no place in it for division and quarreling. There could be but one church and it must be given equal authority with the civil government, not because of Scripture or theological reasoning, but because the exigencies of community life demanded that giving of power.

The old guard began the attack by bringing Elisha Paine once more before the county court for exhorting. Again he was convicted, bail was offered and refused, and he was lodged in jail. But by this time the sheriff himself had become an Inner Lighter, and Elisha was allowed to preach in the jailyard; in fact, his friends used boards and timbers that belonged to the county to build bleachers to seat the listeners. Having won this first skirmish, the Inner Lights felt so confident that they actually proposed that if they were given back their share of the expense of building the old church, and were not asked to contribute further to it, they would retire peacefully to their new congregation. I suppose that this compromise included the unwritten clause that the obnoxious Elisha Paine would be kept at home.

The conservatives never hesitated; they refused the peace proposal. This was no mere inter-church quarrel, it was organized society versus anarchism. They went ahead with their plans to ordain the Reverend Mr. Cogswell, who had not met with Inner Light approval. Now the rebels made their great mistake. If they had merely gone their way and established a new church they might well have won their battle, for they were far more numerous than the conservatives. But instead they appealed to ecclesiastical law.

"You cannot ordain the Reverend Cogswell," they declared. "It takes a majority of church members to call a minister, and we are the majority. Furthermore, for the same reason, we are the true Canterbury church, and you are nothing at all."

The minority wasted no time in futile argument. They took the case to the Council of Churches. That body, ever ready to support law and order, handed down a decision worthy of the most subtle medieval scholar.

"Yes, the majority of church members is the ruling body," it said, "but unfortunately you Inner Lighters are not church members. For anyone who does not accept the Saybrook Platform loses his ecclesiastical standing and also his legal privileges. The sixteen orthodox members still remain the only true Church of Canterbury, and you are less in the eyes of the Town and Church than the lowest Quaker."

"But the Saybrook Platform must be accepted by a majority of the members of a church before it is binding on that church," argued the unhappy rebels.

"Ah, no," answered the Council. "If you do not accept the Saybrook Platform you are not a member of a church."

Confronted with this double-edged logic, the new church that was not a church—in fact, did not exist at all—this church sighed deeply, held a session of solemn fasting, confession of sin, and prayer, and started to act like the real and purified Congregational Church of Canterbury. It had one hundred and twenty members; they were pious and sincere folk who strove to create a better religious life in their town, but from the very first this new church was doomed. It had a few years of strength and good works; then it began to lose members. The fervor of earlier days was forgotten by some, and a new generation was growing up, and then too most Puritans are greatly disturbed if they are not legally sanctioned in what they do. They can be fierce rebels if the situation demands such rebellion, but until desperate they prefer to be protected by the approved order. Many Canterbury Inner Lighters began to feel uneasy about their position outside the pale of ecclesiastical law. There was still another reason why the new liberal movement failed. Men and women who had been moved by religious fervor and a sincere desire to purify the church had already seen that the community could not exist if it were not unified in all its organized existence; that two churches could not live together, and especially when one of them was bitterly opposed to full cooperation with the civil power. These thoughtful Puritans reluctantly abandoned the church that was near to their hearts and went back to formality and order. They sacrificed a dream of a better church so that the town might be strong.

That was the way the Inner Light church was born and died in Canterbury. In dozens of other little towns the same struggle and defeat took place. To know the folkways of this region, you must know, among many other things, why sincere seekers after freedom and righteousness were legislated against and thrown into jail and could not keep a church of their own.

The New England town was built on strength, and tragedy inevitably follows in the path of the strong. The killing of the liberal religious movement was a tragedy, but it had to be.

Miracle Girl. Right in the middle of all the religious upheaval in Canterbury, that most un-Puritan of things, an authentic miracle, occurred. When twenty-year-old Mercy Wheeler was stricken with the burning ague and wasted to a skeleton, doctors saved her life, but she lay speechless and helpless for several years, unable to take bread or meat. Her mind was clear, however, and she was "greatly wrought upon by spiritual impressions." She pondered much upon the fact that liberty of speech was denied the Inner Light exhorters, and all at once, after six years of silence, she began to talk and before long had dictated "An Address to Young People or Warning to them from one among them that may be called a Warning from the Dead." But after forty-eight hours of busy speech, Mercy lapsed into a silence that lasted two years. Then she once again began to talk. There was also such great physical improvement in other ways that she was able to sit up in bed and feed herself. However, the use of the lower part of her body was still denied her.

All the Inner Lighters of Canterbury were interested in Mercy Wheeler, but as a very pious young woman only, and certainly not as one supernaturally inspired. Fasts and lectures were held in her room, and her influence on young people was great; still, however, she remained strictly of this world until May 25, 1743. On that day she heard a voice saying, "If you wilt believe thou shalt see the glory of God now."

Then came a series of "queer feelings"; after them a thrill and a shaking, and Mercy Wheeler felt so strong and well that she rose and walked for the first time in sixteen years. That Sunday she rode horseback three miles to church. The story of her miraculous cure spread and "was blessed to the awakening and strengthening of many." In nearby Plainfield a public thanksgiving service was held for her, and soon a "Discourse" on her cure was published, "together with the full medical details and affidavits to these facts." This book or pamphlet ran through two editions and was popular even in England.

Great was Mercy Wheeler's fame in quiet Windham County, and among another people it would have spread far. But today her story is hidden in old tracts and histories; certainly no shrine honors her, and young people do not know of her pious example. That forgetting was inevitable, for Mercy Wheeler was a Puritan maid, and she was also a disturbing reminder that now and then even the elect do not act in a sensible way. Puritans are always pushing some facts and memories back into secret rooms. Some are grim and terrible or obscenely revolting; but all are suppressed because Puritan life was "reasonable," and there was no place in it for those moments when the spirit of the flesh or of God moved men and women.

King Abbe. A man of substance in North Windham, Connecticut, Joshua or "King" Abbe seems to have joined the Inner Light movement more as a protest against the curbing of free speech than as a religious expression. For this Puritan was a

vigorous champion of people and causes. Not only did he help
build the bleachers in the jailyard so Elisha Paine's audience
could hear in comfort, but he often invited the persecuted to
exhort in his house. Reprimanded by the conservative church-
men and town officials, King Abbe became so defiant that in the
1740's he was often arrested and imprisoned as a person "of evil
name and fame and vile and profane discourse, guilty of high-
handed misdemeanours against common law and rights of man-
kind."

It is easy enough to see why King Abbe might have been a
thorn in the flesh of the established order. For instance, he did
not have orthodox ideas about sensible charity and how the poor
should be treated. When asked to help a poor man who had lost
his only cow, he shouted, "Away with your subscription paper!
Go into my herd and take your pick among the cows, and be
sure you get a good one."

Careful Puritans would certainly not approve of such flamboyant generosity. The King seems also to have been a loud,
cursing, and generally vigorous person, one not much like the
average sober man of lands and substance. But he could have
avoided the final disapproval of his class if there had not come
over him a most strange metamorphosis.

This profane and high-handed citizen got religion; at least,
he started a church of his own. Perhaps King Abbe's desire to
give the persecuted a chance to worship in freedom had much
to do with this new act of generosity, but there is also proof
that he was actually converted to his own creed. The Abbe-ites
were launched and soon had a church of their own in a valley
south of Hampton Hill. Probably the Abbe-ites lasted a few
years; then they went back to orthodoxy or shook the dust of
New England and started west. The King himself leaves no
further record. Perhaps he repented and became a drab and
orthodox deacon as were so many men of substance; maybe he
roared some good curses and left in search of a more generous
spirit. The second end is the one I wish for a Puritan who could
give away a whole cow.

Yale Is Angry. As serious, thoughtful students at that stronghold of sound Congregationalism, Yale College, and as loyal natives of Canterbury, it was inevitable that during the summer va-

cation of 1745, John and Ebenezer Cleveland should search their souls. Ought they to cleave unto the tenets of their college, or should they accept the joyous message of Inner Light salvation? They pondered and read the Scriptures, and they also attended Sunday services held in the home of a rebel.

Yale's espionage system may have been good, or perhaps the Cleveland boys talked of their soul struggles when they went back to college in the fall; at any rate, President Clap summoned the two before him in November. Did they not know that attendance at unauthorized religious meetings was forbidden? The youths pleaded that they were not actual Inner Light converts. They said they had merely listened to the sermon. That was no excuse, declared President Clap, and he suspended the two.

For a year there were petitions from liberals and answers by Yale. At last a period of reflection was granted to the culprits before final sentence was passed. The truth was, of course, that Yale had acted hastily and was now hoping that the Clevelands would come through with some sort of nominal apology and declaration of orthodoxy so the whole matter could be forgotten. Back to Canterbury went the Cleveland boys, there to pray and seek divine guidance. They were told, or they decided for themselves, that too high a price could be paid for a college education. Back to New Haven they went and told President Clap that it was the inalienable right of all men to worship in any seemly manner, and they, John and Ebenezer Cleveland, must help defend that right. Yale's austere head did not hesitate longer; he expelled the Canterbury heretics. Probably he liked those two unworldly youths, but Yale, like the Congregational Church and every town, must be kept unified and strong.

The Inner Light Cracks Down. The rebels who arose after the Great Awakening were legislated against and mildly persecuted, but they themselves were none too gentle when they got a little power. For when people strive fiercely for personal freedom in belief, they do so because they believe that the tenets they defend are the only true ones.

A very characteristic vote in sacred assembly was the one registered in Canterbury in 1745 by the liberals:

"Whereas our covenant obliges us to oppose sin and error in

ourselves and others, we do understand it to mean not only such things as worldly moral men condemn, but all such as the Word of God to [*sic*], viz; foolish talking and jesting, vain company, spending time idly at the taverns, evil whispering, carnal and unnecessary discourses about worldly things, especially on the Sabbath . . . and all other sins forbidden by the Word of God, both of omission and commission."

Such admonitions came from the rebellion against orthodox Puritanism and not from that supposedly grim and tyrannical force itself. Deacons taking their quotas of rum in the taverns shook their heads at the Canterbury pronouncement and others like it. This was going too far, they said. It was all right to make folks pay their rates and hold to the Saybrook Platform and go to church and back up the minister, unless of course he got to feeling his oats too much; but that was about as much as you could reasonably expect of anybody. Raising all this rumpus about carnal talk and tavern haunting and vain company was plain downright foolishness and ought to be put an end to. So spoke Puritans when their more excitable brothers and sisters tried to purify the Puritan land. We have always believed in moderation; that is, unless Indians drive us too far.

The Deacon and the Widow. The best way to get out of the consequences of breaking one law is to invoke the protection of another. This is especially true when you are a Puritan, and both statutes are from Holy Writ.

In South Killingly, Connecticut, an "excellent deacon" was excluded from Inner Light church fellowship on the charge that, although he had lately buried his wife, he "had backslidden from God and kept company with a carnal young woman and courted her and on that account went on Sabbath day night." Such circumstances, continued the charge, "gave grate greaf to many and ye turning of ye lame out of the way." And so for the Deacon's sins the church "with uplifted hands to Heaven, declared him to be to them as an heathen and a publican."

The deacon was embarrassed by this condemnation and went to a noted Inner Lighter. After very tactfully calling the pious vessel "an imbassinder of Jesus and his father in the Gospel," the accused man explained that this woman he'd been courting was all right; in fact, he believed that she had been converted. And as for looking after a wife so soon after the passing on of the first one, Scripture taught that if the husband was dead the woman was loosed by law, and he figured it worked both ways and let him free, too. And besides, didn't the Good Book say that it wasn't good for man to be alone? Maybe he hadn't done right in going to see that woman on Sabbath night, and he was willing to confess to that error, even if he had a clear conscience in the matter. The deacon ended his defense by saying that all this fuss about a simple little personal affair was "surprising."

There you have the various Puritans as they believed and supported the churches of their choice. Colonel Godfrey Malbone, once of Newport, gentleman, slaveholder, refusing to help the despised louts around him build a seemly place to worship, starting a church of his own to get out of hated church assessments; Elisha Paine, sincere believer, going to jail for his faith, preaching out of the jail window, arrested time and again, forgotten when his old disciples lost their fervor. "King" Abbe, blustering, profane, generous, hater of sensible, cautious Puritans: "Give him my best cow if he needs it. Why in God's name shouldn't Lish Paine preach if he wants to? By God, I'll have a church of my own, and it'll be free to everybody!" But even the "King" cannot win; he loses his church, and that is the last we hear of him. It is the same with Mercy Wheeler who heard a Voice and rose up and walked after sixteen years in bed. She was the Bernadette of the Inner Light movement, but all that commemorates her are a few dry, noncommittal paragraphs in an old county history. Puritan girls weren't supposed to hear voices and rise up and testify; they died sensibly of what ailed them. "Them Wheelers always was sorta queer. Mercy's Ma had flighty ideas before she married." The Cleveland boys came back to work on the farm. They were going to be ministers, but they worshiped outside the church, and Yale could not forgive.

CRIME AND PUNISHMENT

Murder Most Foul. Elizabeth Shaw's family lived in Canada Parish, which was later to be called Hampton. The neighbors said she wasn't quite all there, but she was pretty enough and liked to joke and giggle with men. When she was seventeen she went out in the woods once too often with one of them. It is hard to explain how she hid her pregnancy. Perhaps her mother took pity on her and helped. For Jared Shaw was a hard man who believed that sinners should be punished; yes, all of them, even the ones who weren't bright.

Not only did Elizabeth Shaw conceal her condition from her father, but she bore the child, and apparently he still suspected nothing. But she knew that she couldn't keep a baby hidden for long in the house, so she took it to the grim Cowhantic rocks half a mile away and left it there. Again there is a mysterious break in the story. Perhaps Mrs. Shaw told her husband about Elizabeth; perhaps he knew more than the girl thought; at any rate, he too went to the Cowhantic ledges and found a dead body.

Elizabeth Shaw was arrested, tried, and condemned to be hanged. No mercy was shown, or asked, for a girl who wasn't bright. Her execution was the first public occasion of its kind in Windham County, and many people attended.

During the early years of the eighteenth century Joshua Hempstead of New London wrote down interesting bits of local news. Now and then he reported having seen justice meted out.

". . . in the aftern I rid up to the Cross Highway above Jno. Bolles to see Sarah Bramble Executed for the Murdering her Bastard child in March last. . . . She was hanged at 3 clock. A crowd of Spectators of all Sexes and nations yet are among us from the neighbouring Towns as well as this: Judged to be Ten Thousand. It rained moderately most of the day."

In the Brookfield, Massachusetts, cemetery is the grave of Joshua Spooner, who was murdered in 1778 by three Revolutionary soldiers, urged to the deed by Joshua's wife, Bathseba. All four culprits were apprehended and tried. Their hanging was a gala event for Worcester County. It is recorded that during the long sermon on the inevitable fate in hell fire of murderers, a terrific thunderstorm broke over the multitude. After the sermon and the heavenly affirmation were over, the hanging took place to the "great edification of all present."

There you have three murders and the swift final punishment of all the guilty people except, of course, the fathers of the bastards. But murder was punished without mawkish concern or delay. Today the reader of these three accounts will probably be most impressed by the fact that the executions were public and, furthermore, attended by a large, probably quite jolly holiday throng. Undoubtedly our ancestors were a tough-minded lot, but that quality of spirit revealed itself in more than one way. It enabled them to turn a hanging into an illustrated sermon or a family picnic; it also told them to string up the guilty person promptly. Of course, they now and then included a feeble-minded girl among the convicted, but the injunction "Thou shalt not kill" makes no exceptions.

Once in a great while, however, Puritan justice failed, and for apparently the same reasons we discover today if we poke into these malodorous affairs. In 1747, the quiet town of Pomfret, Connecticut, gave its county a famous and long-remembered scandal. In April a popular and beautiful young woman, daughter of one of the town's best families, had died, declared Dr. John Hallowell, the attending physician, of natural causes. But three months later, an older sister came to the Pomfret authorities with a terrible story. The other girl, she said, had died because Dr. Hallowell had performed an illegal operation. She herself had known all about her sister's shame; in fact, she had helped her conceal it and also persuade Dr. Hallowell to do what he did. Right here the story is embellished by the folk tale that the repentant sister whispered of a small body, still breathing, that was thrown into the blazing fire. This, however, she did add: that she knew the father of the child, and she named the son of another prominent Pomfret family.

It was a drama of colonial high life, and undoubtedly the humbler Pomfret citizens predicted that the whole affair would be hushed up. "There's one law for rich folks and another for folks like us." At first, such cynics seemed to be wrong. For the doctor was tried and sentenced to sit in the gallows in public for two hours with a rope around his neck and then receive twenty-nine lashes on his naked body. After that he was to be remanded back to prison to wait for another court session where final judgment, foretold by the rope around his neck, would be passed. But soon the dirty work began, and the skeptics were vindicated.

Either the Windham County jail was flimsy, or a jailer was corrupt; in any case, Hallowell escaped and fled to Rhode Island. Nor was he taken back to Pomfret. That is not the only proof that Dr. Hallowell felt relatively immune from serious punishment. Not long after his flight he asked that his sentence be remitted so he could return to his wife and children. Rhode Island citizens added their plea, testifying to the good doctor's medical skill. The request was never granted, and John Hallowell remained in exile.

Here was a case where Puritan justice apparently failed. Money and influence may have saved the doctor, or perhaps a skeptical court decided that he was less guilty than some others and, therefore, should be allowed to escape. The whole affair lacks the forthright, vigorous touch of the ordinary criminal trial of those days. If there had not been some reason why the abortionist should be treated leniently, he would have stretched a rope to the edification of a large crowd.

Some other misdemeanors or actual crimes were punished very effectively by the early eighteenth-century towns. In June, 1743, Joshua Hempstead records:

"Nathll. Richards of Norwich was convicted of Adultery with Samuel Leffingwell's wife last Feb.

"Nathll. Richards of Norwich, aged 50, 50 stripes and Branded on ye forehead with A on a hot Iron and a Halter put about his neck and Sarah Leffingwell aged 50 had the Same punishment and excepting but 23 stripes."

Again from Joshua's lively account:

September, 1713. "I was in Town in ye forenoon to See a man Branded on ye forehead for breaking open a house in Lebanon and stealing Sundrys, etc."

When the foreigners pulled such tricks, they got more than was handed out to local criminals.

Hempstead records in March, 1727: "Mr. Watkins, an Irishman, was Branded in ye forehead and had his Right Ear Cut off or Cropt for Burglary. . . ."

Misdemeanors, and Sometimes Punishment. According to the laws of every Puritan state or colony, counterfeiting was a serious legal offense, but many people looked upon this activity much as did Kentucky mountaineers upon excise avoidance. A man turned out a reasonable facsimile of Old Garge's coins, or of the Republic's, and kited it around. Some people were fooled by it; others saved it until a more credulous fellow came along

In that way, they thought, no very great harm was done; at least the town was not hurt too much.

There was one especially famous gang of counterfeiters in the Town Meeting Country. In the northwest corner of Rhode Island was a desolate and heavily timbered area that merged farther north into the Douglas Woods. Up here all sorts of criminals and refugees from justice were supposed to hide. Even today old people can remember hearing of the reputation of this section, and it is still sparsely settled. At any rate, the gang of forgers lived in Forgers' Cave on Buck Hill and turned out Spanish milled dollars which were taken to the city by unknown persons and passed off as legal currency.

At last the law tracked down this band and captured them all. Then a strange thing happened. The criminals were set at large. People in those parts whispered that the forgers had threatened to tell who was taking the milled dollars and passing them off; and the talk went that some of the "first families" in town would be greatly put out if such disclosures were made.

Down in Wakefield there was the same lack of realization that counterfeiting was a real crime. In that town lived John Potter, a fine lusty Yankee squire, a foxhunter, a clever politician, and a lover of good food and wine, the sort of bon vivant no one ever thinks this land could produce, but who, nevertheless, was of and from us. Squire Potter throve and was admired by most of the town; in fact, he was so well thought of that one day he and some friends were warned that they were to be visited soon. So they took several armloads of heavy articles wrapped in burlap and put them in a rowboat on the shore of Potter's Pond. Then the jovial squire rowed out to the deepest waters and dropped the heavy bundles. When the officers arrived, the honest man was having a drink with a few old cronies. "Me a counterfeiter?" he ejaculated in deep surprise. "If ye don't take my word that I ain't mixed up in such things, jest search the premises. Ye won't find a thing that ain't up and above board." The law officers found nothing suspicious and went away, demanding bitterly how they could be expected to do their duty when these yokels always told the criminals that a raid was about to be pulled off.

There was another misdemeanor which, although officially condemned, was seldom punished too severely. Fornication was, very naturally, preached against often and loudly, but just as inevitably the couple was not branded with an F. At the most they were reprimanded before the assembled congregation. This seeming tolerance was in reality less the result of tempered mercy for human frailty than it was reluctance to interfere with any-one's private life unless the welfare of the community demanded interference. Adultery and murder were crimes which en-dangered the family and the town. If a man consorted with an-other fellow's wife, trouble of some sort was pretty sure to fol-low; killing was not only forbidden by the Bible, but it was an act which rejected the sound theory that punishment should be administered by legal authorities and not by the individual. But fornication was a private misdemeanor. The culprits were more than likely to settle down after a while and turn into sensible housewives and husbands; and, besides, there weren't jails big enough to hold all of them if any constable should carry out the letter of the statutes.

There were stern reproofs from the clergy and righteous in-dignation from many pious Yankees, but even these pure citizens were often forced to agree to a compromise with sin. For exam-ple, in 1765 the church at Groton, Connecticut, voted that "those parents that have not a child till seven months after marriage, are subjects of our Christian charity . . . and shall have the privilege of Baptism for these infants without being questioned as to their honesty." Such tolerance was in keeping with Puri-tan reasoning; it was also an almost inevitable concession if any church were to survive. For in town during the years from 1761 to 1775, of the two hundred persons owning the baptismal covenant, sixty-six confessed to fornication. In another period, this time of only two years, sixteen couples were admitted to full communion, and of these seven confessed to having made the two-backed animal. If this number of young people, orthodox enough to confess sin publicly, had cause for that confession, it is easy to imagine how the scoffers and low-lived Puritans were acting.

One serious crime was never punished by the people. Plenty of witches lived here, but all except one seem to have had amia-ble dispositions. For instance, East Haddam was full of broom-riders, but they were content to fly over to the Devil's Hop Yard north of Hamburg and brew vile messes in the potholes be-

neath the falls while Satan fiddled for them. No record is left
of their ever having used these magic potions on innocent beasts
or people; apparently they brewed for the love of doing so. In
other towns the old hag suspected of witchcraft (and there seems
to have been one in every community) was a harmless creature
who went through the conventional gestures and was at heart
a staunch conservative. In fact, I suspect that the Puritan town
had heard so much about witches from English folklore and
American superstition that it felt called upon to create these
witches at any cost. So the oldest and queerest woman who lived
alone was elevated to the rank of supernatural attendant. She
was mildly pleased and honored and tried to live up to the
witchly traditions. The town felt that it was not missing anything, and witch and town had a happy break from the dull
monotony of life.

But of course things were not so sensibly arranged in Rhode
Island. Over there people were not amenable to convention, and
the witches were no exception. On Hopkins Hill in Hopkinton,
up north of Westerly, Granny Mott lived in a shack with her
daughter. Nearby was an open field with a huge rock in its
center. Apparently this boulder was the altar for the local coven,
and Granny its custodian, for she never allowed the owner of
the field to plow too near it. When the line was passed, snap
went the plowshare. Such interference with the sacred process
of making a living was too much to be tolerated, and Granny
was at last driven out of town. But she returned and was killed
in true orthodox manner. A hunter who was out after heath
hens became angry because he missed one bird so often. So he
took a silver button from his coat and rammed it into his gun.
This time the bird fell, but its body could not be found. Next
day people heard that Granny Mott was dead. Of course, her
daughter refused to let anyone help prepare the body for burial.
As far as I know, that case is the nearest to a witch-tragedy that
this country had. It is significant that Granny Mott came to her
end because she interfered, by order of His Satanic Majesty, true
enough, but nevertheless interfered, with a Yankee farmer's
right to plow where he wanted on his own land.

Sarah Spencer of Colchester, Connecticut, may or may not
have been a witch, but she certainly knew her law. When Elizabeth Ackly accused her of riding and pricking, and James

Ackly made threats, Sarah promptly sued the libelous couple for £500 damage. And in the very days when witches were being hung in other parts of New England, judgment was given her for £25 and costs. The Acklys appealed, and all that Sarah finally got was one shilling. The jury also stated that it found the Acklys not insane, a comment which reveals what some Puritans thought of witch-hunters.

BUNDLING, RUM, AND OTHER AMUSEMENTS

No other early New England custom, or at least no relatively innocent one, is as famous as bundling. As most people know, this practice was nothing more than a man and woman, both fully clothed, getting into bed together, and sometimes they had an admonitory board between them. Winter nights were cold, so why not save wood and still be warm while you conversed sedately? This habit was generally confined to private homes, but one account states, "Parties of men and girls spend the night together at inns, both sexes sleeping together. Such great control have the females acquired, that several who have bundled for years, it is said, have never permitted any improper liberties. Indeed, it is considered as not in the least indelicate."

This opinion was not shared by the author of "A New Bundling Song: or a Reproof to those Young Country Women, who follow that reproachful practice and to their Mothers for upholding them therein."

Most other evidence seems to show that bundling was far from a completely innocent pastime, but these comments are from people who could scarcely be expected to forgive a brisk maid and her lover. It is my personal belief, however, that bundling started as a very conventional practice. Probably a pious young couple, talking in a cold room with a large bed in one corner, decided that they were strong enough to resist carnal temptation. So under the quilts they crawled and went on with their edifying conversations. The experiment was such a success that the two young Christians told their friends about it. The other boys and girls immediately saw the possibilities in this new way of enjoying an hour of serious talk, and before the winter was over, the town was full of couples bent on saving fuel and demonstrating their modesty. By the first snappy days of the next fall, all rural New England knew about bundling.

Why the custom died out is more of a mystery than its birth. No great improvement in rural morality was found in the years after we hear the last of bundling, and there does not seem to have been any serious church campaign against the practice. Perhaps it was just too much bother to keep bluffing about the innocent nature of bundling. At any rate, a pleasant custom died. There are wistful legends heard now and then that tell how a few conservatives up in the hills still cherish the old ways but, as a local skeptic remarked, "It ain't likely such folks would go t' th' bother o' thinkin' up a fancy excuse for doin' it."

Every debunker of Puritans always presents evidence that all male inhabitants of early New England swigged huge quantities of rum and cider, and the women folk took the same, or tippled on such exotic drinks as Health Beer, "pine chips, pine bark, hemlock needles, roasted corn, dried apple skins, sassafras roots and bran mixed with hops and a little malt." This evidence cannot be refuted, and anyone who knows anything about the Six States will never try to do so.

One county association of ministers sorrowfully warned and pleaded with one of their number, but at last he was suspended for drunkenness and breaking the Sabbath with vain and obscene discourse. A deacon was convicted of "excessive drinking," and a mere church member reproved for "being overtaken by drink on ye highway." In one store in a small town, twenty-five gallons of West India rum were sold in one week on charge account, and some customers paid cash or bought it by the tumbler for immediate consumption. One of the gallons went to the local dominie. At the raising of the Westford church, the workers were provided with one barrel of rum and one-fourth barrel of sugar. People drank in homes, taverns, at baptisms, weddings, funerals, and ordinations. As late as 1825, at the installation of a Connecticut minister, free drinks were served at a nearby bar to all clergy and laity, and the church paid the bill.

The Plymouth Colony's definition of drunkenness was as follows: "And by Drunkenness is understood a person that either lisps or faulters in his speech by reason of overmuch drink, or that staggers in his going, or that vomits by reason of excessive drinking, or *cannot follow his calling.*" [Italics mine.] In other words, Puritans began to worry about a man's drinking too much when he could not do his usual work and when he ceased to function as a useful member of society. A minister took home a gallon of rum; all well and good, as long as it did not keep him from preaching and being a pillar of strength in church and town affairs. A cooper drank a quart or two of hard cider every day of his life, but he made good barrels. And the man who was reproved for being overtaken with drink on the highway was a road worker who had downed so much that he could not earn his shilling a day. Drinking *per se* did not bother the average Puritan; he became indignant when rum or cider kept a man from following his calling.

SOME STRANGE PURITANS

There were three kinds of townspeople. First came the minister, the doctor, the deacons, and the other solid citizens. These last were of all degrees of wealth although none lacked good farms or shops. Second, there were the poorer farmers and the laborers, and, at the far extreme, the people "on the town." Some of these latter unfortunates had their own shiftlessness to thank for their disgrace; others were feeble in body or had suffered losses. Many of the citizens in the two main groups were far from moral or even honest; some were scoffers and ribald haunters of taverns. Their prosperity ranged from the fertile acres and big barns of a good farmer to the fifty cents a day of a hired man or the utter indigence of the pauper. Some of the poorest were most regular in church attendance; often a prosperous farmer gave only lip service to the Saybrook Platform. The two classes continually merged and were often indistinguishable save when one applied the test of wealth. And all, respectable, fornicator, drunkard, poor, rich, pious, or skeptic, were part of the town. They went to town meeting together and talked back and disputed—the hired man as good as the tavernkeeper. Probably a day laborer never got to be a selectman, and paupers were not assessors, but every one was a townsman and proud of it. The minister called on his parishioners in the poor farms as well as in the big houses on the village street. There were all sorts of gradations of respectability and wealth among such people, but none was outside the community.

Yet there was a third group of Puritans in the town. Beneath the others and below the quiet surface of life were people who lived in Hampton, or Brookfield, or Kingstown, or Woodstock and yet were not of those places and never could be. Their exclusion was not formal nor expressed in word or gesture; they were given every legal right and all forms of justice; nevertheless, these people were pariahs.

Every community in the Town Meeting Country had such families, and if you knew one you knew them all. Of course, a few added bizarre refinements to their sins, and one clan was noted for having a religious fanatic in each generation. This irrational man or woman was tolerated by his sinful relatives, and the town itself did the best it could to be liberal. Generally it was no more than mildly amused by the thought of godliness in "them critters," but on one occasion its sense of the fitness of things was sorely tried. That was when Abe asked to be admitted to the church. He argued with simple logic that he was a sinner; therefore, he needed Christ's help, and what better place was there to find it than in the Congregational Church? The dominie, deacons, and Ecclesiastical Committee met in solemn session. Abe had theology on his side, and the Bible and all of Christ's teachings as well, but how about the common-sense principles of running a church? But at last it was decided to give the right hand of fellowship and full membership to sinful and dirty Abe. To be sure, he was seated in the back pew, but he took communion along with the others, the deacon having a clean cloth in his pocket with which to wipe the edge of the cup surreptitiously after Abe had drunk from it. But, except for such rare exceptions to normal degeneracy, all these people were more or less the same.

The tribe that lived in my town was called the Gulls. (It isn't their right name, but the Jukes were given mercy, so why shouldn't others?) They must have come to that region back in the earliest days, perhaps as part of the regular settlement, but more likely as squatters without legal rights at first to any land, for the section where they had their first homestead was too remote and forbidding to have been chosen by any buyer. The road into Gull Hollow, for that is still its name, winds down half a mile to the northern end of a narrow valley. High wooded hills slope back behind a small farmhouse; to the south are alder swamps before more hills crowd in together. This valley is not more than a quarter of a mile wide and a mile long, but it is spacious when compared with the real Hollow.

Follow the narrow road down hill for a short distance, and suddenly you come out of the woods and are in the Gull homestead. Just one field of not more than four acres; forest and rocks border it on three sides; on the other a swamp like one in the upper valley. An old house is falling down in the field. The road climbs the eastern hills for a mile, and halfway up there is an old cellar hole. When you come to the top you find open fields and cleared pastures. You are back again in the New England you know. But you have seen one of the hidden places of our land; places where strange, unnatural lives are led by Puritans or their descendants.

The Gulls began to multiply in the house deep in the Hollow, and before long they filled it and the two houses that were built on the upper slopes. The men cultivated a few acres, but they were happier fishing and hunting and trapping or weaving baskets. At first these people bred among themselves. They had a strong English name, and one can guess at a better heritage a century before in the Mother Country, but from the time they came to New England in the seventeenth century they began to live apart. Perhaps a reluctant sense of guilt made them keep to themselves; more likely, however, they simply wanted to be alone to live as they wished.

This isolation would have proven fatal to the Gulls if it had continued long. Without new blood they would have bred more and more idiots. But Puritan boys were reckless, and more than one ventured down to the three houses to see the lusty, black-haired wenches there. The children which came had some of the strength of the purer strains in them, even though they were almost inevitably Gulls in appearance and character. A few of these halfbreeds did seem to have some desire to lead normal, decent lives, and they married young men or women from the respectable hired-man or day-laborer class. But more often than not the Gull blood was too strong, and the town began to say that Bill's oldest boy was queer, or another man's youngest child couldn't walk or talk yet and it was going on seven, or the girl was going out with men already. The listeners shook their heads and agreed that it was too bad, but what more could you expect of folks that was half-Gull?

That was the way the Hollow spread out and made its imprint on the towns around it. Down in the three houses lived a few patriarchs of pure Gull blood, but by the beginning of the nineteenth century a great many of the tribe had mingled in some measure with other people. Most of the time these alliances were with poor, ignorant people, or at least the legal marriages were, for of course any young fellow even of a good family might be tempted by an olive-skinned Hollow girl. As far as I know, the Gulls never bred with the occasional Negro family in town, or the still rarer Indians; in fact, miscegenation seems to have been the one and only sexual digression they did not indulge in.

So it happened that up the back roads were half a dozen shacks or old farmhouses which had been abandoned by other Puritans. In these places lived the Gulls or the families in which their blood was dominant. The men were always farmers in name, but as in the old days they lived mainly by hunting and trapping. There was never much cultivation of the rocky acres, and only a cow and horse and a hog and a few hens for livestock. The women were generally expert makers of hooked or braided rugs or weavers of carpets, and the best baskets made in town came out of those houses. Almost always there were eight to ten children and, in a day when infant mortality was high, a surprising number of the babies grew up. The young Gull boys might hire out on some farm, but they preferred to go into the woods to chop. That way they could live with some wench in a little cabin and do as they pleased. Besides, they were quick to take offense at any reproof and too liable to walk off in the middle of haying. Most of the girls lived at home until they married or went to live with someone, but every now and then one went to work out in some prosperous family. She was seldom kept long. Once in a while a Gull woman went to a nearby city and turned orthodox prostitute.

There was nothing primitively idyllic about these Gulls who lived in the Hollow or in the old shacks and refused to conform to ordinary standards. Disease, filth, incest, idiots, whores, poverty, laziness, illiteracy, all these were Gull attributes. On the credit side was little save the fact that the tribe seldom committed crimes of violence and wanted nothing more than to be let alone.

As far as I know, decent folk never tried to explain why a strong, healthy, God-fearing community could have people like the Gulls in it. The older generation may have thought that the Hollow was an awful example of man's original sin sent to cure vainglorious people of any false notions about their despicable nature, but later Puritans accepted the Gulls. Of course, there was always some talk about how such people lived, but no one ever did anything about their conditions until in later years the worst idiots were sent to county institutions. This indifference was a victory for the Gulls, and by the same reasoning a gross violation of all Puritan codes. Here these degenerates were, unmolested members of a social group which demanded that each person in it contribute to its maintenance and progress; yet they were allowed to remain useless and even dangerous. The Gulls not only lived in filth and degeneracy; they polluted good Puritan families. The town could not have imagined that these people gave anything of value save a few dollars in taxes; nevertheless, they were accepted as casually as the poison ivy on the stone walls.

There was one characteristically Puritan reason for this indifference; namely, the Gulls "behaved themselves" most of the time. Only a native New England townsman can interpret those two words as applied to a tribe of degenerates. That phrase means that the Gulls seldom stole from other people; were never boisterous in public; drank heavily only at home, and even there hardly ever fought and brawled. In fact, the average Gull was outwardly a very quiet and peaceful citizen. Furthermore, these people lived up to another part of the Puritan code. They paid their debts eventually and their taxes much more promptly; and they kept their fences repaired fairly well and their few cattle at home. In other words, the Gulls were not guilty of those misdemeanors which make a man a nuisance to have around. In the words of a twentieth-century Puritan diagnosing a Gull family which lived near his home:

"Them low-lived bitches ain't human in some respects. Filthy 'n' dirty don't half tell how they pig it together, an' as for decency, well, as likely as not a man's kids are his own uncles 'n' brothers, an' he's forgot who she had 'em by. But for all that they ain't much of any nuisance t' have round; in fact, they stay at home an' mind their own business more'n some other folks that are supposed to be a hull lot better. I ain't got no kick comin' on havin' them Gulls as neighbors."

The whole problem of the town and the Gulls was, and still is, about as complex as any the critic of New England ever tried to solve. When the Puritans tolerated degeneracy and did not try to tear it out of the social structure, they admitted that certain human forces could not be conquered and made to work for the common good. That is the way in which the Gulls were stronger than the town. Yet the town made an inherently vicious and moronic tribe "behave." The defeat of Puritanism was a moral one; its victory, a triumph of practical discipline. Perhaps that is as much as can be expected in any struggle with the powers of evil.

I have written of Puritanism and Puritans as apart from the Gulls and set over against them. I did so to make it easier to contrast one set of folkways with another. But the Gulls were Puritans and came out of Puritanism, out of the secret lower chambers all people build. These people have lived in the Puritan towns for centuries; there is no hope that we will ever be rid of them; their blood taints far too many a family; they exist because we are a complex folk out of whom come many manifestations.

Two Other Kinds of Puritans

My ancestors had never heard of the science of eugenics, but they did know that the Gulls were the sort who were likely to have undesirable offspring. It was a bit more puzzling, however, to find such proof of man's weak nature in other homes. There was apparently not much that could be done about it, so the off-balance members of decent families were merely kept out of sight as much as possible. No disgrace was involved when a maiden aunt became queer; the collapse was an act of God, but, on the other hand, there was no reason why she should be a nuisance. The Gulls and other low-lived folks weren't very careful about such matters, so their idiots and insane were on open display if they could walk or weren't in the state of one unfortunate cousin who was described by an ordinarily tough-minded Gull, "He don't look like anybody I ever see before, an' my meals don't set right after I've taken more'n one look at him." Solid, prosperous, church-going people disapproved of such callous treatment of unusual members of the family and did all they could to keep them hidden.

In most country towns there are tales of barred windows in the attic or over an ell kitchen. Now and then a dim figure was seen or a voice heard in obscene vituperation or frenzied prayer. There is no doubt that such rooms existed. In the earliest days no public asylums existed, and until well along in the last century a family was really merciful when it kept its afflicted members at home.

I have never accepted the legend of the "crazy house." This bit of folk lore told that a man, and sometimes it was a woman, was kept in a one-room building away off in the fields. The family carried food and water every day and in winter tried to keep a fire going in a stove, but sometimes a stiff body was found in the morning. I believe I am right in assuming that such brutality was not possible in a Puritan town.

So far I have been talking about out-and-out cases of mental disorders—the ones where the victims were violent or incoherent. To be "queer" was a euphemism for such a state of frenzy or delusion; milder cases were described as "odd," "a trifle off," or "not quite like other folks." Such middle of the road people were merely kept in good order and not allowed to become too noticeable. One or two "odd" women attended church when my great-aunt was a little girl, and she told of the one's gaudy bonnet ribbons and the other's quiet but steady weeping all through the service.

Of course, the men and boys who "were not quite all there," but were more or less presentable and harmless, were allowed to do just about as they pleased. Every community had one or two amiable half-wits who hung around the store and refused to learn how to work, and there were several others who had let themselves in for a hard life by mastering the use of an axe or hoe or pitchfork. It was generally conceded by the village wits that the slothful morons were far brighter than their industrious brothers. The dull women were generally kept at home by any family which wasn't low or hadn't Gull blood in it, and there was good reason for this precaution. One lusty and moronic damsel can raise a lot of trouble, even in a Puritan village.

THE SLAVERY PROBLEM

Negro slaves, as we know, were held by the Puritans. As early as 1641, Massachusetts passed this statute: "There shall never be any bond slaverie, villinage, or captivities amongst us unless it be lawfull captives taken in just warres, and such strangers as willingly selle themselves or are sold to us. And these shall have all the liberties and Christian usages which the law of God established in Israell concerning such persons doth morally require. This exempt none from servitude who shall be judged thereto by authorities."

This was one of the neatest bits of legal and spiritual compromise ever devised. There was to be no servitude save as commanded by authority, and no captives except as captured in just wars or sold to Puritans. It was sinful to sell slaves, but to buy them was another matter. The result of such reasoning and legislation was to allow the colonies to keep slaves, including captured Indians, with an easy conscience, and they proceeded to do so.

The experiment in labor was not a success. New England winters killed off many a high-priced Negro slave, and many of the others were reluctant to buckle down and work hard. Gradually the rural districts lost the blacks unless a large landowner like Colonel Godfrey Malbone could afford to keep the supply replenished. Now and then a rich villager, and sometimes he was the minister, kept a house servant. Generally this man lived in the cellar and cooked over one of the fireplaces so often found down there in old houses.

Most of the slaves in Town Meeting Country were kept by the merchants of New London and Norwich or the other coastal towns. Down in these busy and cosmopolitan centers the Negroes seem to have had a very easy and happy existence. Each group of slaves had its mock organization and its governor, duly elected. In Norwich Sam Hunton held office longer than his master, Samuel Huntington, who was Governor of Connecticut from 1786 to 1796.

The early practice was to hold an Indian in slavery if he were taken in a just war, and what war with the redskins wasn't a just one? However, there are very few records of such slaves. When the Reverend Mr. Billings of Hampton died in the first half of the eighteenth century, he left one Indian girl worth all of twenty pounds, but that is one of the last mentions made of such chattels. The reason for this lack of free Indian labor is obvious. There were no more wars, and the captives taken in the

earlier ones had died or escaped. It is also very probable that the
Puritans were glad to see the last of the Pequot or Narragansett
servants, for they were probably a sullen crew and hard to manage.

Southern historians may argue that slavery would have continued in New England if it had been a profitable venture, but
that statement tells only half the truth. Black ivory did corrode
in the cold air, and pious investors were keenly hurt, but it is
also evident that Puritans were never intended to be owners of
slaves. They understood an indentured servant, for he was a fellow who was theoretically at least struggling toward a definite
goal; he wanted to make something of himself. That sort of ambition pleased the hard-working master but, although he might
laugh at a Negro's jest, the latter's indolence and irresponsibility
of manner were puzzling and even stirred honest men to anger.
No Puritan owner of slaves was willing to adopt the Southern
planter's attitude and accept his property as so many simple-
minded charges who must be taken care of even while they were
kept in their place. This New Englander was used to dealing with
free men.

There was also a deep and instinctive fear of slavery in the
Puritan mind. He knew that he was not building a slave-master
civilization, but one based on the freedom of the individual and
that free man's voluntary participation in the affairs of his community. The slave did not fit into this scheme of life; he was at
best a nuisance, at worst a positive menace. Climate, shiftlessness, and abolition ideals helped free the Negro in New England,
but most important of all was the Puritan's realization that he
must stand by the work of free men.

So slavery died in New England. A colonial shipper or merchant never lost his standing or church membership if he did a
bit of trading on the Gold Coast, but all Puritans were glad when
the slaves died or were freed. They were not good townspeople.

LEGEND AND LORE

New England has always been a sensible and matter-of-fact
land. A Virginia with its feudal, almost knightly gestures, and a
gaudily wicked New Orleans were as alien to the sober Six States
as was Poictesme. No, color and splendor were not for us! We
laughed loud enough, we sang after a few hot buttered rums, and

we bundled and made love in every accepted and illicit way, but we saw no reason why such forthright pleasures needed embellishment with fancy language or invention. In fact, we were definitely not the kind of people who create romantic myths out of plain bare facts that ought to satisfy anyone.

My folks, however, did cherish a few useless and even colorful memories.

They kept alive the story of Matthew Griswold, first settler in what is now Old Lyme, and his eight lovely daughters. The Misses Griswold laughed and played jokes as if they weren't Puritan maidens, and each of them was courted by many men. Phoebe married a minister, but she never lost her delight in tormenting him. Once she took a leaf from his Bible so that on Sunday he read to his congregation, "And the wicked shall flourish like a green bay"—he turned a page—"mare," he continued. And Phoebe sat in the pew with a demure look in her eyes.

The Griswold girls may have come in for a lot of reproof from some people, but the way they were remembered makes me think that their town rejoiced to see so much beauty and high spirits. Phoebe and her sisters did nothing spectacular. They had many suitors, and finally married and settled down and raised children, and still kept on laughing and playing jokes.

Then there was the Pied Piper of Norwich who charmed rattlesnakes with the sweet music of his violin. Once he marched into town from Wawcekus Hill with a line of snakes, goats, and "varmints" trailing after him. Who the Piper really was or what he did I do not know. Perhaps he was a half-cracked squatter up on the hill where the land was so poor that they had to keep goats because cows starved on the pastures; or he may have been one of those wandering musicians who walked the roads of lower New England. At any rate, some sort of fiddler did something strange down in Norwich!

The poor Acadians came in large numbers to Norwich in 1753, but only one legend remains of their stay. It relates a typically Puritan act. For fourteen years the town endured the foreigners and their strange ways; then it rounded up two hundred and forty of them, packed them on a boat and sent them to Quebec. *Evangeline* was written by a descendant of Puritans, but he was a poet and had strange, romantic ideas about Acadians.

The witches who brewed in the Devil's Hop Yard did not

worry the respectable Yankees down along the Connecticut River, but the Moodus Noises were disturbing. Mount Tom, a large hill in Moodus, rumbled and groaned at irregular intervals and, according to Indian legend, had behaved like that ever since the evil spirits began to live in those parts. The early settlers were undecided as to the cause of the noises. One group inclined to the belief that strange, black-magic witches from other parts were quarreling with the local *white*-magic broomriders. Another school of thought spoke of Machimoodus who sat on a sapphire throne and shook Mount Tom whenever he waved his wand.

The theory that an immense jewel was at the bottom of the trouble, or at least connected with it somehow, was supported by a Dr. Steele who came to investigate in the 1750's. Building a home on the side of the troublesome hill, he plunged into his research. One night a white light led him to Rocky Moodus cave, from whose mouth he rolled a great stone. Then the whole Connecticut sky was lit up by a blood-red gleam. The next morning, frightened Moodus villagers found an empty house where Dr. Steele had lived, but he left word that he had taken with him two of the pearls which were causing all the trouble. However, he added that there were still some smaller pearls left in the cave, so there might be more noises in later years.

Sure enough, in 1791, there were heard loud explosions inside Mount Tom and under most of Moodus township; then came two violent shocks which broke chimneys and opened fissures in the ground. Ever since, there have been Moodus noises. Geologists have come, investigated, and talked learnedly of faults, and so on, but twentieth-century Yankees still get a mild thrill out of asserting, "There's something mighty queer about them sounds." We really believe the men of science, but it also amuses us to play with the idea that maybe, after all, there is some queer explanation of what we hear.

One of the most famous stories of this region recounts the Battle of the Frogs.

On a June night in 1754, the little village of Windham, Connecticut, had lost its characteristic calm. Its usual spiritual calm had been destroyed by the Inner Light movement; the French and Indians might invade the town at any hour, and besides, the weather was too hot and sultry for that time of year. So Windham was ready to listen and lend credence to the tale of a frightened Negro who had heard something terrible out in the fields. Now the rest of the town heard a mounting din and roar and tumult. The French and Indians had descended, or perhaps it was the Day of Judgment. Guttural voices shouted from the dark fields, "We'll have Colonel Dyer," and the answer came, "Elderkin, too." Since these two men were the chief Windham patriots, it was now evident that the affair was political and not supernatural. Undoubtedly the French and Indians were nearby.

All night long the uproar continued, and the cries for Dyer and Elderkin were fierce, but no hostilities began. When the dawn came, the fearful Windham people investigated the field. They found that, in a small mill pond, the frogs were very excited, and on the shore were thousands of dead bodies of frogs. The news of the night terror spread all over New England, and poor Windham was mercilessly ridiculed in song and story until the Battle of the Frogs became one of the best-known of all rural episodes.

A few years before the Revolution, a wolf harried the sheep flocks in Windham County. The man who was hardest hit was a brash, quick-tempered young farmer called Israel Putnam. He'd "get that varmint," he swore. But he had to wait two seasons before there came a snow just on the night of a marauding trip. Half of Brooklyn and Pomfret helped track the wolf to a rocky slope at the foot of which are hidden the narrow fields on which the notorious Gulls lived. The hunters looked at the dark mouth of the cave and decided that they would try smoking the brute out before they asked anyone to crawl in. But no fire brought out the wolf, and Ike Putnam began to get impatient. He tied a rope around his waist and crawled into the long passage.

Now the stories vary. One version says that he spotted the wolf by the glare of her eyes as he held up a lighted pine splinter; then he crawled back to the outside, got his gun, and made a second trip to shoot the wolf. At any rate, the future hero got his enemy, the last wolf to be killed in eastern Connecticut, and the grisly founder of a long line of stories about Old Put, who was our most colorful man of war.

In the corner of a field beside the Gilead Road in Andover is a solitary headstone that marks a grave like no other in New England. Down that road Captain Simon Smith was riding home to New London from the French and Indian War when he became so ill from smallpox fever that he fell from his horse. Nearby farmers saw the fall and came to help Captain Smith, but he died before a doctor could be called. When it was discovered that the dead man had smallpox, his grave was dug nearby, and into it was put the dead soldier, his equipment, and his horse. On the headstone was carved: "Loved, yet unattended. All alone. Sweetly repose beneath this humble stone ye last remains." The people of Andover still remember who was buried in that lonely grave.

Inevitably, the early Puritans had their quota of ghosts and haunted houses; in fact, every town in this country seems to have harbored at least one supernatural visitor. Now and then one of the peddlers who were always getting murdered returned to haunt his last bedroom. Over in North Scituate the only Indian ghost with a sense of humor kept up his activities for years and was really quite a personage. When alive, he had been a barfly at the Pine Tree Tavern, and after death his loyalty persisted. So, as a faithful shade, he descended on the rival tavern, the Black Horse, and went to work giving it a bad name. Any sleeper in one of the chambers was likely to be awakened by a hand grasping his hair and lifting his head from the pillow. The startled guest then saw a ferocious Indian, tomahawk in hand, standing over him. As a side issue, the redskin ghost played dirty tricks on North Scituate residents, probably those who did not buy their rum at the Pine Tree. Once he told a man that a treasure was buried under a fine apple tree. Up came the tree but no gold was found. The Indian spirit, presumably in a dream, then pointed out other trees, and the digging went on until a splendid orchard had been ruined. Even the ghosts were practical in Yankee Land, and, even more surprising, the best haunting was done in the taverns!

In 1660 the Massachusetts legislature passed this law: "If any person be wilfully guilty of their own death, every such person shall be denied the privileges of being buried in the common burying place of christians, but shall be buried in some common highway and a cart load of stones laid upon the grave as a brand of infamy."

Sewell's *Diary* for 1688 tells of such a burial, and adds that a stake was driven through the suicide's heart.

Even now in some towns a very old woman may tell you that "in the old days folks that did away with themselves wasn't put in the regular burying grounds. No, I couldn't say where nor how they was buried, but I remember my grandmother telling about it, and she got it from the old folks of her day. It seems to me she said that so far as she could remember they told her the body of one man that hanged hisself was taken away from his family at night by the authorities, and they never did know what happened to it, except that they heard a few days after there was signs of somebody having dug a hole in a crossroads down in the south part of town."

Our legends are like that. They are legends of secret, hidden deeds and sometimes of strange acts of justice or revenge. Many of them are whispered from one old person to another, and only by chance do they live for more than a few generations. If they do live, we who are genuine Yankees feel queer about telling them to other folks, especially strangers.

CHAPTER 5

To Hell with Parliament!

WHEN the English began to realize that their American colonies were growing wealthy and, therefore, should contribute more to the Mother Country's support, they set about collecting this just tribute with awkward and tactless methods. Immediately the Revolutionary War became inevitable.

Since 1620, the Old Country had been growing less and less of a reality to the Puritans. Their great-grandparents had come from there, and it was remembered in story and legend as a place of beauty, but it no longer actively stirred men's spirits. And of course these descendants of Englishmen put their own problems before those of a faraway, quasi-alien home land. For instance, the pioneers were ready to fight in such wars as the French and Indian, for they saw that their own safety was menaced. However, they could not be convinced that their hard-earned tax money should by some divine right go over the water; it ought to stay right at home and help the people who earned it.

Even the most practical Yankee and democratic Quaker still cherished a bit of sentiment for the king anointed and the fields of some shire or the old streets of a city, but such mental luxuries were indulged in but seldom and never when the question of levies, taxation, and wasted shillings came up. If the king and the mother land could not restrain the Puritans from rebellion, even less powerful was the English Parliament. When shocked Tories told their rebellious neighbors that they shouldn't speak so bitterly of the vested authority on the Thames, the ingrates had their answer ready, "What has Parliament done for us, and why aren't we represented?" The implications were obvious.

The churches, the state governments, and, especially, the separate towns were institutions that had helped the people create a sound civilization; in fact, they were nothing more than or-

98

ganized and practical expressions of these people's spiritual and political creeds. As coming from the people and as useful to the people, these three symbols of self-government should be obeyed before any parliament that was not of the people of the new world and did little to help them.

The English bungled the job of handling these folk who had acquired such strange and disconcerting ideas and, furthermore, they seemed inclined to use them as an inspiration for direct action. Although Englishmen loved freedom and would fight for it, they were not restive under the same restrictions that galled their provincial cousins. And all the time the latter grew more independent, less inclined to pay out good money without returns.

The years of preparation for war passed quickly, and the conflict came.

Town Meeting Country had been, from the first, right in the middle of the fray. It was especially angry about the taxation question. Connecticut had always insisted upon the close relationship of levies and representation. For example, no town sent deputies until it could pay its public charges. And now this wellnigh sacred principle of sound government was being violated. Worse still, the English did not seem to realize that a fundamental concept was involved. The Yankee farmers and shopkeepers shook their heads and realized fully that they and the English were two entirely different breeds. That being true, why not act toward the aliens as you would toward any foreigner? And that is what this region proceeded to do.

In 1765 Windham, Connecticut, organized its Sons of Liberty, and soon after that appointed a Corresponding Committee to spread news and propaganda. The town proudy claims that this committee was the first of its kind; certainly it was one of the earliest. Its citizens also believed in direct action, and the deputy stamp master appointed to it was forced to flee the town when he tried to carry out his functions.

Over in Lebanon the citizens, enraged by the Boston Massacre, drafted, in 1770, a declaration of rights and liberties that preceded the Declaration of Independence by six years. And in Mansfield, in 1774, a declaration of freedom was drawn up. Yankees wanted it fully understood what they were fighting for; they also felt much better if they held a meeting and passed a resolution. Such cautious procedure made the business of rebellion seem familiar, just like an ordinary town-meeting quarrel. Other people seldom understand us as we get ready to fight. We do not hop up and down and shout and sing; we call a meeting and debate the problem in correct parliamentary fashion; then a vote is taken, and the results read by the proper clerk. After that a motion to adjourn is made, and we go out and fight just as recklessly and hard as the gay Southern hellcats who spent the pre-battle hours getting tight or saying romantic farewells to lovely maidens under the jasmine and magnolia.

Look out for Puritans when they have properly voted to raise hell; they are legally and morally protected from all blame and are pretty liable to go the limit. They are still more to be feared if the vote is also accompanied by a long prayer by the duly appointed chaplain of the assembly. Fortified by the support of religion and social sanction, the absolved warriors have few scruples and descend upon the enemy with righteous wrath.

When war with England came, the men of this section were ready for it. Israel Putnam, wolf-killer and veteran fighter, was plowing in his fields in Brooklyn when the news of Lexington and Concord arrived. "This is it! Now let's go get them!" shouted Ike. According to legend, he unhitched the horses, jumped on the fastest one, and rode hell on hot leather to Massachusetts. One additional item in the myth says he did not stop for a drink until he pulled up in front of a Duxbury tavern. But, at any rate, Israel Putnam got to the debated ground as fast as he could, and right on his heels were many deacons, shrewd storekeepers, farmers, drunkards, Inner Light fanatics left over from an earlier era, degenerates like the Gulls, quite a few rich merchants, more hired men, and the inevitable crowd of teen-age boys with at least one mere infant who protested in alternate bass and tenor that he could hit a squirrel in the eye at fifty paces.

Six miles away from Brooklyn, over in Hampton, every man and boy capable of fighting left for the front. Down on the Sound tough old skippers got together just as tough crews and sailed out to catch themselves a British boat. The Yankees were on the warpath!

Two battles were fought on the soil of this country, one at Stonington in 1775, the other the tragedy of New London and Groton in 1781. At Stonington a small number of British landed from a ship and were repulsed by the local militia, which suffered but one casualty. But New London was another matter. Here the British forces were led by a native son, Benedict Arnold, once the hero of Connecticut and leader of its men at Quebec. While New London was sacked and many houses burned, Arnold stood on a hill and watched the destruction of the town he knew so well. Then he waited for his men to cross the river and take Fort Groswold in Groton. Here Lieutenant Colonel William Ledyard had 150 militia men to oppose a regiment of British regulars and a battalion of New York volunteers. Before the fort fell the Yankees had lost 85 of their number, but they accounted for 193 British. Lieutenant Colonel Ledyard gave up his sword to a British officer, who promptly thrust it into his prisoner's body. Then hell broke loose. Wounded and prisoners were mistreated, looting started, and finally the town was burned.

The shore communities took their revenge on the British when they sent their ships out to raid and harry. Captain Dudley Saltonstall of New London raised the colonial flag for the first time on any ocean; then his four ships sailed down to Nassau and stormed and captured New Providence. Another Sound craft, the Spry, was such a tiny schooner that it slipped through the whole enemy fleet as it lay at anchor in the English Channel. No one suspected it of being a privateer from across the ocean, and it went on to carry out more raids. Then there was the other New London ship that was sailed across to Long Island, and there put on wheels and pulled overland to Southampton. Back in the water again it sailed to Fire Island and captured five British ships.

New London, Groton, Westerly, Stonington, and all the other shore towns had a great time sailing circles around the Limeys, capturing their vessels, and bringing home many a fine prize. It was just the sort of war the Yankees on the Sound liked; one where a man made his own rules and fought as the situation demanded, and with more than an even chance that he could make patriotism pay a dividend.

The British never invaded the back country, but its men fought from Bunker Hill to Quebec to Saratoga and to Yorktown. At home the Yankees had been sober and dull and limited citizens who respected authority and believed that getting ahead in life was one of the chief aims of man. But in the field these same men were Puritans in the wilderness once more; pioneers fighting to make a new home for themselves, and this time a spiritual and economic one. Led by the fiery Arnold of his splendid first years and the hard-boiled, blustering Old Put they fought the British and retreated and fought again.

But as they fought they did not forget other loyalties. In the very earliest days of the seventeenth century there had been a genuine folk consciousnss in New England; in fact, the people were as nearly national in feeling as they were ever to be. But the Puritan fighter in the Revolution had divided his allegiance. As a member of this or that regiment in a general's army he did not forget that he came from some very definite town; he was also probably part owner in a farm or a small business. Most important of all, even though he might be a Gull or a near-pauper, he was a member and perhaps the head of a family. His town, his business affairs, and his own folks demanded part of his loyalties. He was pretty likely to take time out from fighting to get in the crops or do some other home job. Probably he went back to the army again, but he always kept his deep consciousness of himself as a private citizen.

This very independent and unmilitary spirit came near losing the war for us, but probably the Revolutionary soldiers were wise in clinging to their separate identities. A wave of indignation can unite a people and turn them into a crusading army; but when the end comes the conquerors may return to an empty land. The Puritans who fought England knew that such a tragedy could more than offset any military victory, so they kept alive the town and the family. As ever, the Puritan was a dual character, but unlike most such men of divided allegiance he did the two jobs he began; he licked the British, and he also remembered his greater destiny as a citizen.

LEGENDS OF WAR DAYS

Because the Town Meeting Country fighters were sober, practical men, the story of what they did in the Revolutionary War is apt to be a dull one. Arnold and Putnam were of heroic stature, but the men they led were not the stuff of which saga and myth are made. Arnold came home to New London to witness an awful revenge; Ledyard killed with his own sword;

privateers at sea; Hale dying a martyr; those are the highlights of this country in rebellion.

But let me tell of what one man did from a small office in a little town. Under the leadership of Jonathan Trumbull, the War Office of Lebanon Common was the northern business headquarters of the Continental forces. Here all the great leaders met in conference; here ways and means were discussed. Once when Washington asked for food for starving troops, Trumbull collected and dispatched by ox-sled train 1500 barrels of beef and 3000 barrels of pork. This quiet, efficient business man of Lebanon was a hero of the war.

Sometimes the women are the ones who are remembered for their deeds. In Hampton the frame of a house was ready to be raised when the call to Boston came. Only old and crippled men were left, but the women told each other that maybe they could manage. They did, and up went the heavy timbers. The family and the community it helps to make up must go on, even while the men are away at war. For they will return and they must not be disappointed. Hampton, and it might have been any town, sent away strength and yet had strength left. The House the Women Built still stands, and so does the town it stands in.

Mrs. John Loomis of Chaplin had given up hope of ever seeing her husband again. Two of the Chaplin men in his company had come back, and they told her that John had been wounded, and the last they'd seen of him he was being lugged to a house where a surgeon was working. Of course, John might have pulled through, but there was no denying the fact that many wounded never did show up again. Lucy Loomis nodded and said she'd heard as much. Next Sunday she asked the minister if he wouldn't hold some sort of a service in memory of her husband. He had been a deacon, just like his father and grandfather before him, and all the Loomises from way back had been good church members. The minister said he would be glad to pay respect to Deacon Loomis; in fact, he would preach a sermon next Sabbath from some appropriate text.

When the day came, Lucy Loomis put on her best clothes and dressed up the children and started for church. The baby was in her arms, and the other three walked beside her. She had gone half a mile when she saw a man in a ragged uniform coming slowly toward her. His head was bowed as if he were too tired to raise it, and it was not until he was very near that Lucy Loomis knew her husband had come back to her.

My grandmother's cousin, Rowena Loomis, used to tell the rest of the story as she had heard it from her mother who, as a young girl, had been in Chaplin church that Sunday: "The minister waited as long as he could for Lucy Loomis to show up for her husband's funeral service, but when she didn't come he began. He'd just given out the text when the door opened and down the aisle walked the whole Loomis family. Lucy had the baby on one arm, and the other was around John's shoulder. Behind them straggled the three other children. The minister stopped talking and waited until all the Loomises were seated; then he looked down at his sermon and then at the congregation. He was a man by the name of Upton and not any too up and coming and energetic, although people liked him well. Anyhow, he wasn't the kind to write a good sermon and see his work wasted, so what did he do but spot Mrs. Abiel Black in the audience! She was a Gull from over east of Chaplin, and Abiel didn't come from a much better family, but he had been killed in battle, and she came to church now and then. When the Reverend Upton saw the Widow Black, he knew he didn't need to talk without notes or have his funeral sermon wasted. So he preached a real eloquent service over Abiel Black instead of Deacon John Loomis. My mother said that the widow looked mighty surprised at first, but towards the end she was crying. And my father always said that any sermon that could make Liz Gull cry must have been a corker.

"Lucy Loomis paid more or less attention to the sermon, but John slept all through it with his head on her shoulder. My mother always said that, of course, he wasn't the first man to sleep through a sermon in Chaplin church, but she guessed he was the only one whose wife didn't poke him to keep him awake."

Romance and glamour of another land came once to this country. From Providence the French troops marched through our roads, and what is more, two hundred Hussars were quartered on Lebanon Common. Later in the winter, General Rochambeau arrived with five regiments and stayed until June. It was springtime in Connecticut, with French officers for country belles, and Hussars and soldiers for lowlier maidens.

A little way from the common and on the slope of a field

beside the road is a heap of stones that marks what Lebanon still calls The French Deserter's Grave. The man who is buried there was a private in the Duc de Lauzon's Hussars, and, inevitably, legend has it that he was really a nobleman who enlisted to fight for the brave new world. During the winter, the foraging of the Hussars bothered the Lebanon farmers so much that they appealed to the duke. So orders were issued making absence from camp between sunset and sunrise punishable as desertion. But the noble and private Hussar had fallen in love with a rural maid, Prudence Strong by name, and was willing to risk all to see her. Then one night he was caught as he tried to slip back into camp. He was tried and sentenced to death. Apparently the Duc de Lauzon did not share a Connecticut winter with his Hussars, for the story tells that Mistress Prudence Strong hastened to him and pleaded for her lover's life. She obtained mercy, and a messenger was sent to Lebanon with a reprieve. But, alas, he did not arrive before the Hussar had been executed.

That march of the French troops through the quiet New England countryside is still recalled by stories telling that they camped here for a night, or used that spring, or Rochambeau slept in this tavern. For once, my sober land had romance on its roads and commons.

But up in Wales, just across the Connecticut border in Massachusetts, is a different reminder that other foreign soldiers knew this land. Here are the cellar holes of a village established by a man named Veincke for fellow Hessians who were taken prisoners at the surrender of Burgoyne's army and, after the war was over, wanted to stay in this new country. No one seems to remember whether these refugees failed to make a living on the rocky land or whether they gradually mingled their blood with that of the old Yankee families.

The Yankees fought and went home to work and came back to shoot more British or be killed. They grumbled and swore and brawled as even Puritan soldiers must. Abijah Fuller of Hampton carried a wounded comrade across a battlefield on his back. Colonel Thomas Knowlton of Ashford organized his Rangers, one of whom was Nathan Hale. Before that Knowlton and his platoon of seventy-eight men had hurried to Boston and got there in time to fight behind the rail fence on Bunker Hill. The colonel fell at the Battle of Harlem Heights.

Then there was that Ranger of his, Nathan Hale, born in Coventry, and a schoolteacher in New London. A quiet, rather sober fellow, in the last moment of his life, he was somehow able to break the bonds of Puritan reserve and express what other men felt.

That was the way these Yankees helped build a nation. To most of the soldiers, those Revolutionary War years were nothing more than a break in the real business of life, a break that had been ordered by some strange law they did not quite understand even while they obeyed it. But they knew that a better civilization would come out of victory, so they kept on fighting. Then after they had done their part they took up the tasks they understood, raising a family, making a living for it, going to church, and being good citizens in their towns.

CHAPTER 6

Yankees Branch Out

AFTER the Revolution, the people of Town Meeting Country
tried to settle down in the good old ways. They would send their
best men to Hartford or Philadelphia or New York to help create
a new state and nation, but after all the home town and the
home place had first claim on folks' time and energy, and, of
course, they were the same as before!

But it was soon clear that no one could go back to the familiar
routine of life. There was a strange spirit of unrest, even of
rebellion in the air. Men argued in the taverns and got excited
about politics; others bought a few extra gallons of rum; more
citizens than ever took willing girls up into the haymows; and
fewer listened to long sermons on the Sabbath. Even righteous
men began to wonder if maybe they hadn't been a little bit too
cautious.

Inevitably the orthodox men and women preached about backsliders and heathens and said that the new crop of indifferent
and downright sinners was denying its ancient heritage. But the
truth was that the restless Puritans were merely obeying the demands of their own natures. They had always been dual in character. As townsmen they had been conforming members of the
social order; as individuals there was in them the capacity for
revolt and change. For over a century they had suppressed the
rebellious part of them so that the town could grow strong.
Community life had demanded that they respect the Saybrook
Platform and the ordained minister; obey the selectmen and
justices; uphold in every way the vested, legal authority of
church and state. Out of this conformity had come a stable, firm
life, not perhaps of the Union of States, but of the town, and
to the practical Yankee that unit of existence was the all-
important one. And now that his town was established, he could
be himself, and at the same time satisfy that other half of his
nature.

When some Yankees realized that they were free, they forthwith packed up their goods and started west to Ohio or Illinois, there to build another New England town and again be slave to its demands as it grew. Bolder spirits sailed out of Stonington or New London to China or the Antarctic; they bought a pack and filled it with trinkets and were the first of those half-mythical characters, the Yankee peddlers. A good many young men stayed at home and built those little shops from which grew the great New England industries.

But the majority of the new generation was content to go on with the old life. At first glance these folk seemed just like their fathers and grandfathers, but in fact they were troubled by new ideas, and out of their spiritual unrest came new folkways, greater tolerance and mercy, and the first real democracy that this country had known.

In the early years a stern rule by a few strong leaders had been necessary, but now that the struggle for existence had been won, more people could take part in the community life. There had been town meetings before, but you should also remember what I said about inhabitants, freemen, and others. If you lived in a town in 1700, you got a grim justice, no matter who you were, but you didn't vote or hold office unless you were a certain kind of man. Now that very practical system could be changed, and ribald hired men who never went to church and held no property could vote.

The Yankee was also free to do as he pleased in his private life. His folks before him had known the value and need for decent conformity to the social mores, although they, too, had been a bit set in their own ways. But now every man could let other people know that he was a man who had his own ideas about life and how to do things. It was the birth of an era of such staunch individualists that the rest of the nation has ever since been confounded by their capacity for being different.

DOMINIES AND DEACONS

The years after the Revolution were trying ones for the Congregational churches in this corner of New England. Drinking, immorality, profanity, and Sabbath-breaking increased. The spiritual leaders had always expected such evidences of man's carnal nature, but until now most of the sinners had been at least outwardly repentant when brought to judgment. This admission of its power was all the church knew it could expect from some toughened reprobates, and it was satisfied. But now the guilty citizens refused even to appear and be reprimanded; furthermore, they openly stated that it was about time the church woke up to the fact that it didn't have any legal power over them. If they'd done anything that they needed punishment for, let the sheriff come and get them.

The ministers and the conservative laymen met in angry session to think of a way to regain their old power. Some shrewd men said that it was unwise to protest and perhaps stir up dangerous emotions. Why not wait and see what was going to happen? If this spirit of rebellion died soon, the church was safe and had not stirred up a lot of trouble for nothing; if it continued and grew, the only thing to do would be to compromise and salvage as much power as possible. We realize now that such a decision would have been a wise one. For the day of the powerful state religion was over, even though the official disestablishment of the Congregational Church did not come until 1818. In the place of an organized religious body there was the parish or town church which was a law unto itself. But all the lords of the church were not wise or even discreet. They had enjoyed power too long; besides, many were sincerely convinced that the common people must be sternly held to righteousness. So these men resolved to fight for the old order. Inevitably they had plenty of trouble on their hands, because Yankees were beginning to branch out.

First of all, there were the queer sects which appeared regularly even among supposedly sensible people. Most vigorous of all leaders of these heretical groups was Jemima Wilkinson of Ledyard. But at last, after years of ruling her own private sect, she died, or at least the finite world supposed she had. Congregationalists rejoiced, and even her humble followers were a bit relieved, but the latter gathered virtuously around the dead leader and lifted up their voices in loud cries of grief. Suddenly the recumbent Jemima rose from the coffin and announced firmly that from now on she would do all the preaching, and they had better listen and obey for she had gone to Heaven and been sent back to earth as a Second Redeemer.

There were gossip and argument in Ledyard and the surrounding towns. No one could deny the fact that Jemima Wilkinson had looked and acted dead for more than a day and a night; it was also evident that now she was very much alive. The skeptical spoke of faking; the tolerant voted for fits and comatose states; but the devout flocked to hear the Woman Redeemer.

But Jemima could not quite convince the Yankees of Ledyard that she should be obeyed. Apparently there was full agreement among her congregation that something supernatural had happened to her; in fact, she might well be a second Lazarus, but even such believers did not like being bossed around by the Heavenly Visitor. Yankees are hard to convince of the truth of any story, and they are far more reluctant to take orders. So there was much passive resistance to the Redeemer's commands, and at last she announced that she would shake the dust of Ledyard from her shoes. And off she went with a few selected followers to Pennsylvania. For some reason she was not happy in her first resting place and moved on to New York. Legend says that her still worshipful people carried her through the woods in a resplendent chariot. At any rate, she settled down in a community she called The City of Jerusalem, a name which lasted until some practical post office official demanded a shorter one. Then Jemima struck on Penn Yan. We Connecticut people started a lot of cities west of the Hudson, but only one had a Woman Christ as its first citizen.

When Jemima Wilkinson left Ledyard, the orthodox sighed with relief, but the Rogerenes were left. For years those restless zealots had been sternly controlled by Puritans who demanded a seemly worship of Him, but weaker men were now in control, and the brothers and sisters went into action again. Above all things else the dignified service of the Congregationalists annoyed their rebellious spirits; so the men made loud noises under the church windows during services, and the woman carried spinning wheels into the aisles and there worked and talked loudly. Ejected and sent away by horrified tithing men, the Quakers lifted their voices in condemnation of the unsanctified and, of course, in protest against oppression, tyranny, and discrimination. The records do not tell how the Rogerenes were finally subdued, but I suspect that authority, spiritual and secular, was conveniently blind while angry Congregationalists did a little unofficial persuasion. At least the uproar stopped, although the Quakers of this sect lived on; in fact, there are still traces of them up in the country back of New London.

The conservatives had little trouble in defeating the enthusiastic Baptists, Quakers, and all the minor sects. Most Yankees, whether of the holy Saybrook Platform church or not, thought of non-Congregationalists as queer and irresponsible, and, believing so, were not likely to defend them against conservative attack. But plenty of men and women were eager to accept a newer and fresher creed if they could find it in the old church. They found it, but the end of the search was often tragedy.

Perhaps you remember that John Wyclif's Lollards were called Babblers. Connecticut had "Dodge the Babbler" and he was as sharp a thorn in the side of orthodoxy as any English priest.

In the last years of the eighteenth century, Pomfret, Connecticut, held a high place among the county towns. It was not as large as some, but it was wealthy and influential, and its people had a reputation for culture. As early as 1739 a subscription library had been started there, and more boys went to Yale and Harvard from Pomfret than from any other town in Windham County. But the community was proudest of all of its church. The meeting house was large and pretentious; the ministers who served it were men of parts and high character.

For years the Reverend Mr. Putnam had been the faithful Pomfret minister, but now he asked to be given a colleague. When his request was granted, the old man wrote to his Alma Mater, Harvard, to send a candidate. The man who came was Oliver Dodge. It is said that he had "lively and agreeable manners" and pleased all with his "fresh and animated discourse." Undoubtedly young Mr. Dodge was a pleasant relief from saintly but dull Mr. Putnam, and the town promptly called him to a colleague pastorate.

Soon the town began to realize that a new sort of preacher was among them, one who told of a kindly, tolerant faith in words anyone could understand. What was more, he called on all sorts of people, poor as well as rich, sinners and publicans, and he joked and laughed with them all and now and then even took a good stiff drink. Most Pomfret folks welcomed Oliver Dodge; it was a good thing, they said, to have new ideas and a human being to give them to you. There had been too much of gloomy hellfire stuff and sour faces.

But when it came time to ordain the new minister, the ordaining council was confronted by a small number of aggrieved citizens who brought charges against the candidate of "disregard of truth, neglect of duty, irreverent application of Scripture, and unbecoming levity." The Pomfret council was discreet; it passed the decision to a special committee of ministers and delegates. After several days of serious examination this body refused to ordain Mr. Dodge. Conceding that he had engaging manners and was undoubtedly very popular, the council wondered if he were quite jealous enough of the good repute of a minister. It thought that he was not. But he must accept this rebuke in the right spirit and so live that his natural gifts could be best used.

Oliver Dodge's friends were indignant and demanded that he be ordained just the same. The majority of the church members wanted him, and a full and complete church meeting was called. With suspicious good grace the conservatives granted the request. At first it looked as if Mr. Dodge's side had won, for an overwhelming majority was for him. But Dominie Putnam, dismissed too soon as old and feeble, invoked the Saybrook Platform which said that his one vote nullified all opposing votes. So Oliver Dodge was rejected, no matter how many people wanted him as their minister. The good old Saybrook rules and a few ecclesiastical sophists and politicians had kicked democracy out of the vestry door.

Pomfret was in no mood to take such treatment. Fifty years before, Canterbury liberals had defied the same authority and lost, but since then a war had been fought for liberty. People said openly that in a republic the clergy shouldn't have the power old Putnam had used. Soon all had heard of the Pomfret affair, and down in Windham arose Zephaniah Swift, lawyer, to defend Oliver Dodge and a liberal religion. It must be admitted that Mr. Swift had not loved the orthodox clergy since they opposed his election to Congress, but he did want a freer, more tolerant system, and he declared now that Oliver Dodge was the Second Luther come to Connecticut to battle against and destroy ecclesiastical despotism. Such allies strengthened the spirit of the Pomfret rebels, and they withdrew from the mother church and organized the Reformed Christian Church and Congregation of Pomfret. Of course, the Reverend Oliver Dodge was the pastor.

Apparently the old order had been defeated. Only eleven men and their families were left in the old church. The county association was helpless, and when Dodge refused flatly to appear before it, there was no way of making him obey. Half a century before the court had upheld the orthodox churches, and the poor Inner Light congregations had been easily subdued; now it looked as if, Saybrook Platform or no, the new Pomfret church was sure to survive.

From the first the Reverend Oliver Dodge preached and acted like a very unusual Puritan minister, and a delightfully different one. All hard points of theology were to be ignored, he said, and each man should interpret the Bible to suit himself. "The reign of long faces had passed," he continued. "Ministers were now to act and talk like other men and unite with them in mirth, festivity, and amusement. For God was best served by merry hearts and cheerful voices." The new Luther proceeded to carry out his own advice. He danced, he joked and laughed with all, and he said he met more people in a tavern who needed him than anywhere else.

Such doctrines and conduct would make any man famous, and the Reformed Church was crowded with people who came to hear him. Some of the listeners from other towns went home to spread the news that at least one town had an up-and-coming minister who called a spade a spade and dared crack a joke in the pulpit. And his words were real comforting too when he spoke of His mercy and love. Often the new man was asked to speak in other parishes. Once he gave a lecture in the Woodstock church, and the regular minister appeared and read a public remonstrance. The liberals of that town seem to have been a shrewd lot, for what did they do but serve a warrant on the protesting dominie for disturbing a religious assembly. The courts upheld the writ, and the poor man paid the highest fine the law permitted, and all for having remonstrated against the misuse of his own church.

Not all people were in favor of the Reverend Mr. Dodge; in fact, Pomfret itself was split into two warring camps. Children jeered and mocked those from the other side, and the town clerk lost his job because he opposed the new minister. His last entry was: "Here ends the services of a faithful servant of the public, who was neglected for no other reason than because he could not Dodge."

For six years the strife went on in Pomfret. The Reverend Oliver Dodge kept packing them into his church pews, and his ministerial calls were full of good cheer and laughter. Even his best friends, however, admitted that he did indulge in drink a bit too much, and maybe some of the things he said were a trifle loose, but on the other hand he was always ready to admit his faults and promise to be more discreet. And they guessed that most everybody except a few old grouches would rather have a human being in the pulpit, even if he did bend his elbow and crack a raw joke, than some sour-faced old fellow who harped all the time about hellfire. That was what Pomfret people, the ordinary citizens, said about Oliver Dodge. They were more than ready to forgive much and often if he would only keep on preaching glad words of salvation and come around and talk with them and let them know that religion could be pleasant and His servants much like anybody else.

The Reformed Church of Pomfret might have survived for years and its minister been remembered even today as one who helped break the old bonds if he had not gone on a monumental spree. It was a lusty experiment in a period when many a tavern haunter did his best to win fame as one described by those masters of understatement as "what ye might call a real thirsty man." For a week Pomfret heard of the ministerial progress from one tavern to another. In each he talked wildly, often telling lewd jokes. It was even whispered that once he offered blasphemous prayers in a blacksmith shop. The conservatives said, "I told you so!"; the liberals unhappily excused their pastor and said he would be all right come Sunday. That Sabbath the Reformed Church was filled; in fact, no Windham County place of worship had been so tightly packed since the days of the Great Awakening. At the proper moment the Reverend Oliver Dodge appeared. At first all seemed well; then, in the words of a shocked historian, "Rising to speak he fell upon the pulpit overcome with drunken sickness, falling forever from his high estate."

The Reformed congregation was very merciful to its beloved sinner. Although dismissing him for "intemperance and use of indecent if not profane language," it added that it did so " 'till by his reformation and amendment of life he shall be again restored to charity." Here is final proof that Oliver Dodge was a minister who gave his congregation more than laughter, a joke, and a slap on the back. For no Yankee town is going to be fooled for six years by such outward displays alone; they must be accompanied by indisputable evidence of deeper worth as a man and a Christian. And here Pomfret was, sorrowful at its hero's fall and conscious that he must be punished, but still ready to take him back if he would but act a little more discreetly.

But the Reverend Oliver Dodge did not try to reform; instead, he went on drinking and consorting with low characters. Inevitably his church died and its members drifted back to the old meeting house, there to be greeted no doubt with triumphant sneers from the conservatives. Before long the fallen minister left Pomfret, and nothing more is known of him until 1805. Then there is a Hartford record of an affidavit sworn against a notorious offender called "Dodge the Babbler." The accusation states that in an harangue at Glastonbury he said:

"God knows, angels know, saints know, all honest men, the Devils know, and none but knaves and fools but what do know, there ought not to be any laws for the support of religion. We should not then see the poor man dragged to jail to pay a minister's tax, while his family was left starving. We should not then have to pay four or five hundred dollars a year for ministers' dinners at Hartford; we should not then see ministers have the privilege of turnpiking the road to Heaven and erecting gates and collecting tolls upon it." Then Dodge the Babbler said: "Ministers' salaries are a stink in God's nose and a stench in his nostrils."

That is the last we know definitely of the Reverend Oliver Dodge, but he is supposed to have died a year after his harangue at Glastonbury.

A strange young man, this Dodge the Babbler. He laughed and danced and drank and made ribald and profane speeches; he told Puritans of an easier faith and freer salvation; he was not the Puritan Luther his friend Zephaniah Swift said he was; yet he was no Elmer Gantry. A hard-headed people loved him for years and begged him to reform and stay with them. But he went on drinking, and now and then he spoke blasphemously about ministers who owned the toll roads to Heaven. Perhaps he was just another kind of Puritan. After all, we are a strange people.

The established church won the battle with the reformed congregation in Pomfret, but only because its pastor had an unquenchable thirst and no discretion. It kept the Rogerenes and the Wilkinsonites from too many excesses, but it was helped by the instinctive distrust most Puritans had of fanatics. The old order of religion was victorious in many cases during the first decades after the Revolutionary War; or at least that was the case in Connecticut and Massachusetts, for over in Rhode Island there was little concern about religious experiments and what the Saybrook Platform thought about them. But in spite of these open victories over a more liberal spirit, it was obvious to all who would see the truth that the day was gone when the Congregational Church, through its ministers, deacons, and orthodox members could rule a town's spiritual life and also take a part in its secular affairs. From now on the church and its officers would be respected and listened to, but its power would rest on its ability to serve the people. Yankees were free men and women now and needed no stern dominie to rule them.

If you would understand the folkways of colonial Puritans you must know why the church had to be strong; if you would know the later Puritans you must understand why they rejected the rulers their grandfathers wisely obeyed. When a social group is building its life, there must be obedience; when that existence is stable, the individual can think and act as he pleases.

MAKING A LIVING

A good many activities were included under the very Puritan phrase, "making a living." Some men stayed at home and dug in the soil; some began to make gadgets; others sold those articles; and more adventurous spirits pursued gain into strange places and risked their necks to get hold of it. We are supposed to be a money-mad and very tight and cautious people up here in the northeast corner; other freer and more generous folk boast of how gracious and romantic their history is, or perhaps it was wild and woolly; at any rate, it had the glamorous, bold charm never to be found in our sordid chase after the shilling. But I say that some of our ancestors made the Cavaliers and

Prairie Men look like futile spinsters. It is true that those Yankees did manage to bring home quite a few dollars, but what a time they had getting them!

The Call of the Sea. Whaling, long the most hazardous and profitable adventure, began in a big way on May 20, 1784, when the Rising Sun sailed from New London. A year later that ship and the others which had followed her returned with more than three hundred barrels of oil. Then the New London *Gazette* forgot Puritan decorum and shouted, "Now, my horse jockeys, beat your horses and cattle into spears, lances, harpoons and whaling gear, and let us all strike out, many spouts ahead! Whale plenty, you have them for the catching!"

The Yankees were headed for the Seven Seas. From Groton sailed the Pioneer, with Captain Ebenezer Morgan, bought and outfitted for thirty-five thousand dollars. Fifteen months later it was back with a cargo of oil and bone that sold for $151,600. The Maclellan did even better, and broke the world's record with three hundred and sixty-two barrels of oil and forty thousand pounds of bone.

Some men found more than whales or profits. Captain Ambrose Burrows sailed for Lima, Peru, in January, 1823. After one hundred fifty-eight days of sailing he stopped at Callao and found that city having one of Bolivar's rebellions. After helping out in that little affair, Captain Burrows sailed on up the coast, only to be overtaken and boarded by pirates who forced him to navigate his own ship. The wily captain agreed but begged that his young son be allowed to go with him and not be cast off with the rest of the crew. The kind-hearted pirates agreed, and back came the boy, and with him his father's pistols. Soon the tables were turned and the pirates cast off in another longboat. Now the Burrows, father and son, sailed the ship back to Callao, which was busy with another revolt. This time the Yankees were rescued by the U.S. Navy. The adventure ended in good New England manner. Captain Burrows sold his ship at a nice profit, and he and his son rode home free on a U.S. frigate. Probably the abandoned crew also got along all right. It took a lot to kill Yankees.

Stonington was not to be outdone, and two of its men turned discoverers as well as whalers. Captain Edmund Fanning was only eighteen when he happened on the islands now bearing his name. Later he was a midshipman under John Paul Jones, and his brother maintopman on the Bonhomme Richard when it fought the Serapis. And in 1820, Nathaniel Palmer, aged twenty, sailed the sloop Hero for the southern ocean. A year later he discovered the Antarctic continent. Now there is a Palmer Land down there.

Now and then a Yankee just wandered without any idea of cashing in on his adventures. John Ledyard, born in 1751 in Groton, started to go to Dartmouth College, but studies bored him so much that he made a canoe out of a tree trunk and paddled it down to Hartford. Before long he was on a ship that took him to the West Indies, Gibraltar, and the Barbary Coast. In London he became a corporal of marines and was gone on four years of service that, miraculous though it sounds, apparently included trips to Hawaii, China, Siberia, and the Arctic. Back at last in America, John Ledyard took time off to publish a journal; then he began a cherished project—it was Jefferson's too—of exploring the Pacific Northwest by way of Siberia. Starting on foot from Stockholm, he traveled the fourteen hundred miles to St. Petersburg in seven weeks. On into Siberia he went, but at Irkutsk he was stopped and sent out of Russia, for what reason the meager accounts do not relate. Back again in London and far from discouraged, he modestly took Africa as the next continent to explore. Where he got his money, how he won patrons, both are mysteries, but he was in Cairo outfitting an expedition when he died at the age of thirty-seven. When Yankees branch out, some of them go far.

The Industries. While the coast towns built ships and sailed them all over the world, up in the hills men were also thinking up new ways to make an honest dollar. A good many started small industries. Sometimes the work might be given out to be done in homes, but soon tiny factories were built. In Town Meeting Country cotton mills were started at Vernon in 1804 and soon after that in Pomfret and Jewett City. Frequently, as in Pomfret, a mill was abandoned, but often it prospered until a small industrial city was built around it and the new buildings.

Even if a town did not have enough good water power for a

real mill, there were always little rivers, and when a man was really hard-pressed he could make a very small brook do a lot of work for him. All over this country you find the ruins of dams that backed up enough water to turn a wheel. In Hampton, Connecticut, there is a stream, called by courtesy a river, that is not more than fifteen feet wide. Yet in 1800 that river had eight dams and ten mills on it. Three of the dams were within half a mile of each other, and every dry spell there were hot arguments as to why the fellow farther up didn't let out a little water so other folks could keep from starving. That stream was a Missouri compared with two others that ran mills of some sort. One enterprising man put a dam across a foot-wide brook and started in business.

Puritans made their streams and mill ponds pay dividends in other ways. There were fish in them, and in winter you cut the ice and stored it. However, it was Sam Hunt who exploited his twenty by thirty lake to the fullest. It gave him ice, water for his cattle, and fish to eat, and every three years Sam let out most of the water, dug up the rich muck that had accumulated and spread it over the fields. While he was doing that he was careful to see that the fish had a deep hole to live in. Sam's grandfather had built the dam, and the grandson still had the record of the cost, one pound, fifteen shillings, and threepence, and he also knew how much that sum would be if left at compound interest.

"If I ain't pretty careful that pond'll turn out t' be a bad investment," said Sam.

The small New England town made its water power work. Hampton had grist, saw, fulling, clover, and cotton mills. One man made hats, another safety pins, and there was even a tombstone enterprise, not full time, however. All this water-driven industry was in addition to the regular shop work of a harness maker, cobbler, milliner, silversmith, cooper, several dressmakers, a cabinet maker, and three blacksmiths. Then there were the masons and carpenters who did their work as they found it. Three or four stores and as many licensed taverns brought in a few dollars. The professions were represented by a lawyer, a doctor, and two ministers.

Every now and then some town in the section started a new industry. Up in the northwest corner of Canterbury was the Backus foundry from which plowshares, fences, gates, and anything else of iron that could be cast were shipped all over the world. There was no iron ore within miles, but the Backus family became wealthy and lived in great estate on Backus Hill up above the foundry. Perhaps the strangest enterprise was started when, in 1775, a Dr. Nathaniel Aspinwall brought mulberry trees to Mansfield, Connecticut, and proposed that other people do the same and start a silk industry. The idea slowly spread, and in 1793 the state sent a half ounce of mulberry seed to every Connecticut town and also offered a bounty on trees and raw silk. Then David Hanks of Mansfield invented a double head for spinning silk, and soon after there was established in the same town the first mill to reel native cocoons by water power. By 1830 Connecticut was producing thirty-two hundred pounds of raw silk annually.

All over eastern Connecticut there were mulberry trees, and country women picked leaves and fed the worms. It was sort of fussy work, and you had to be careful, but there was a good profit in it. Then in 1845 a blight hit the trees, and another home industry was dead. Just a few mulberries survived, and even today you can find one or two near an old house or cellar hole.

The Peddler. If you make more of something than you can sell right in town it's only reasonable to look somewhere else for a customer. Of course, a busy man with a family couldn't go running around, but there was young Bill Snow; he was a shrewd, smooth-talking young fellow good at a swop, and besides he had been telling around that he'd like to get out of Woodstock and see a little of the world. So Bill Snow was given a few boxes of safety pins and told to see if he couldn't get rid of them. No, it didn't matter where he went as long as he sold 'em.

That was the way the Yankee peddler was born, those wanderers who carried a pack from Stonington to Savannah and became legendary figures. There had been peddlers before, but none like these Yankees. Even New England itself did not quite understand them. For the spirit of the road caught all sorts of young fellows and not just the ones you'd expect would like to go wandering around. The minister's son, the prosperous farmer's boy, and embryonic philosophers like Bronson Alcott, did as good trading as did the shifty blades and the village ne'er-do-well. Home folks talked in whispers about the sort of life these adventuring merchants led. They haunted low taverns and all sorts of musters and rough gatherings, and probably they drank too much. Yankees can forgive any young fellow who brings back a full pocketbook and an empty pack and says, "Fill it up with notions again; they're beggin' t' buy, an' while ye're about it ye might as well jack up th' prices a hull lot. Them planters down south ain't got no sense a-tall."

Naturally their customers were more than a trifle bewildered by these Yankee peddlers. Lean, wiry fellows who cracked a joke with a straight face, never told a direct lie and not too much of the truth, they were not gentlemen in the eyes of the southern aristocrats, or real he-workers to the western pioneers. At last their analysts gave up the job and decided that a new human species had been found, the Yankee Peddler. He brought gossip and news to the whole family: the latest fashion notes to the women, the best dirty joke to the men, and more than likely a night's adventure to the daughter. No wonder that he was welcomed everywhere and became such a national institution that Sam Slick, one of the first genuinely American characters of humor, was made in his image. And it should not be forgotten that *he sold his goods*. The Yankee might be a boon to the lonely farmer, but he was not on the road as a philanthropist; every joke and every gesture of this first great American actor was meant to hasten a noble end, namely the sale of what was in his pack.

The peddler was not always a man with a pack or saddlebags. Quite often he had a horse and a wagon laden down with heavier or bulkier articles; clocks of all kinds, chairs, books, and bolts of cloth. When the peddler had sold out, he was often as much loaded as when he started, for he had swopped one thing for another more often than he had taken cold cash. The peddler became the trader, the swopper, the dickerer, as much as he had been the salesman before. Now he was branching out and becoming a traveling merchant.

Inevitably, the Yankee peddler was accused of all kinds of sharp practices, selling basswood hams, wooden nutmegs, and clocks without works. Half of these indictments were made in fun, and even when he really did drive an off-color bargain, the victim was apt to swear ruefully and do nothing. For the drawling Yankee was a "character," and he was supposed to get the best of you; in fact, it wasn't quite the role of a gentleman or a sport to be shrewd enough to bargain with him on equal terms. And the Yankees knew how people felt and let such ideas bolster their reputation and sell more goods. The same thing is happening today. Just listen to city folks tell how they were outsmarted by the old farmer down the road; they are angry in a certain way, but in another they applaud his shrewdness and feel that he is acting the way a "Yankee character" should.

The peddler was created by the industrial growth of the small towns, and he left the road when the tiny shops he sold for became so big that they could afford to ship in big assignments over the railroads or canals. Then the drummer took up the role of the wandering driver of slick bargains. A good many of these flashy fellows came from New England, but they were a poor substitute for their foot-slogging brothers. True enough, they added a few classic fabliaux to American folk lore, but too often they were manufacturers' representatives, and not brisk young fellows branching out.

The Farmer. While the tiny factories and shops grew, and the peddlers tramped the roads, and whalers sailed all the seas, the Yankee farm was a multitude of industries in itself. There was not the same necessity now as in the old days to make everything on the home place, but just the same a husbandman had to be handy in lots of ways or he put out too much money and came out the little end of the horn. His wife was even more versatile if she won the accolade of—"She's quite a help to a man who's tryin' t' get ahead."

Those are the ways the Yankees in the Town Meeting Country made a living in the seventy or so years after the Revolution. Whaling, shipbuilding, sailing to every land, making all sorts of things and selling them in every state; starting mills and factories, inventing machines and processes for those mills; experts in a dozen trades, and always not far from the soil that first supported them. The people were busy and they were happy, too. They had done two things—built their towns and won their liberty; now they could branch out for themselves.

A Little More Schooling

When the people of this country began to branch out, they did more than change the old religious order and think up new ways of making money. In Colchester, Woodstock, Canterbury, Plainfield, and other towns little academies and private schools sprang up.

In the early days education had served the two righteous purposes of enabling a man to read his Bible and also keep his accounts straight, so if a Puritan wasn't going into a profession all he needed was reading, writing, and figuring. But as times changed there were new reasons why the average Yankee should get a little more learning than the district schools offered. Some kept on with their schooling because doing so satisfied their spirit. They would probably never be anything more than farmers or artisans, but just the same they wanted to know. Perhaps they had an idea that through knowledge they might become better citizens; perhaps the simple process of self-education satisfied them, for now and then we Yankees can forget the practical. At any rate, men and women asked for more learning, and the schools and academies were started. Some of them are still going strong, others closed after a few years, but they all helped the Yankees to branch out.

This Town Meeting Country welcomed all these schools except one, and that one experiment in education not only caused a scandal but also revealed the very worst side of Yankee character.

In 1833 the state of Connecticut passed a law stating that any school for Negroes would not be permitted except by the consent of the majority of civil authorities in the town where the school was to be located. It was a neat little piece of anti-abolition work and intended as a safeguard against ardent workers for the black brother. New England never did like enthusiasm.

A few months before this law was passed, Prudence Crandall, a Quakeress, started to teach Negro pupils in her school in Canterbury. Her little academy had been running peacefully for two years, and the town was proud of it, but now there was trouble. Before long Miss Crandall was arrested on the charge of violating the new law. No bond was set, so she went to jail. At the first trial the jury disagreed, but the Superior Court fined her.

However, the Judge remarked logically enough that whether or not the verdict represented justice, the legislature had certainly passed the law which Miss Crandall had violated, so if people did not like the outcome of the trial, they could choose better lawmakers.

Miss Crandall paid the fine and went on teaching her Negro girls. She and her friends tried to persuade the next legislature to repeal the offending law, but the representatives reaffirmed it; furthermore, the opposition pushed the case against the school and its teacher. Now it went to the Supreme Court of Errors, which finally stated that the law in question was designed to prevent setting up of schools exclusively for colored persons not inhabitants of the state. And Miss Crandall's had been established for white girls, and the Negro students were a later addition. Undoubtedly the justices thought that the law was a mistake and Canterbury a narrow, bigoted town, but instead of saying so they resorted to a legal quibble in their releasing of Miss Crandall. That's cautious Yankee logic for you. Never defy a vicious statute openly or criticize it; that sort of thing hurts the sound social order; it is far better to think up the right interpretation of the law. By that method the dignity of the accepted order is upheld while justice is being given.

But Canterbury folks were aroused. Every once in a while an otherwise sensible and law-abiding Puritan community gets its temper up and starts acting mean, and now the windows of the Crandall school were broken and a vigorous attempt made to burn the building. At last the young Quakeress gave up; Canterbury did not want a Negro school and was not going to have one.

In 1834 a Norwich mob entered the First Presbyterian Church and broke up an abolition address. The pastor who was speaking was then drummed out of town and threatened with a coat of tar and feathers if he ever came back to stir up more trouble. Norwich disliked queer notions even more than Canterbury.

Abolition was bad enough, but the reformers in Connecticut thought up a far worse idea in the first half of the nineteenth century. They started a temperance campaign. The official opening was the birth of the Connecticut Temperance Society in 1829, but the full enormity of the proposition struck home to Windham County when Samuel J. May, Unitarian minister in Brooklyn, emptied his cider barrels and gave his callers cold water as they read together from pithy tracts. Soon there were all sorts of organizations for the curing of a bad habit.

There were two logical reasons for the birth of this temperance movement. First, reform was in the air. Liberal clergymen read Christ's words instead of the Old Testament prophets and decided to help make their suffering brothers better and happier. The men and women of the laity had the same dreams of a purer New England. Puritans had been released from the necessity of conformity, and their new energy took new forms, one of which was a deep interest in making other people over.

There was another reason for the temperance tracts and sermons. Yankees were drinking more heavily than ever and with less decorum. Gone were the days when a stern dominie could punish the laborer who was overtaken with drink; the grandson of that thirsty fellow tanked up at the village inn and made more or less of a nuisance of himself. Public occasions seem to have been celebrated with great vigor. For instance, when the last public hanging took place in Windham County in 1835, there was an immense crowd which "caroused most scandalously." It was on this occasion that the doomed man got off one of the best of last-minute remarks. Looking out of his cell while he waited for the cart to take him to the gallows, he saw people hurrying by.

"Why are they running?" he asked. "Nothing can happen until I get there."

It was high time, said the ministers, that such license should be curbed, and they redoubled their efforts. No records can be found of how many bibblers were rescued from hobnailed livers, but there were always plenty of appeals for new workers, so I assume that staunch opposition was met. Very concrete evidence bears out this theory. Old inhabitants can tell you that their folks used to talk about Bill or Henry and how much each could drink; furthermore, plenty of legends tell of a carefree attitude toward the great sin of alcoholic indulgence. Two such tales come from Hampton, Connecticut.

Thomas Farnum and William Durkee, an ancestor of mine, were famed consumers. Farnum was a trifle the more regular churchgoer, so he was the one who heard the Reverend Mr. Weld preach a fiery denunciation of intemperance. As he left the meeting house, Thomas remarked to a friend, "Mighty searching discourse, mighty. I certainly pitied Bill Durkee."

Asa Kimball was meditating on the front steps of the village store. It was spring, and behind every house on the street the apple trees were in full blow. Down the road limped Asa's old friend, Jared Moseley. He, too, noticed the fragrant blossoms and stopped to admire an especially fecund russet. When he got to the store, a gleam of joyous anticipation was on his wrinkled face. He poked Asa with his cane and then pointed at the apple blossoms.

"Cider, Asey, cider!" he said reverently.

Apparently the steady drinkers of the county were quite undisturbed by all the commotion about temperance; in fact, they viewed the reformers most tolerantly. It was all right with them if old maids and ministers talked about the evils of hard liquor; such folks needed something to take up their minds. Of course, no sensible man was going to stop downing his daily quota, and by the same reasoning he wouldn't deprive the White Ribboners of their fun. But one neo-Puritan had more deviltry in him and went out of his way to torment the temperance addicts.

Until he was sixty-two, Ephraim Lyon was content to live quietly in Eastford, County of Windham, State of Connecticut. His farm gave him a fair living, and he was able to get hold of plenty of hard cider, applejack, rum, and now and then some whiskey. Local honors had come to him. He was frequently preached at by the minister and given tracts by the Temperance Society, and no one disputed his title of hardest man in town to drink under the table. One Sabbath morning in May of 1820, Ephraim's spirit was restless. By all rights he ought to be more than usually well satisfied with life. Here he was sitting on his front porch with a tumbler of good cider in his hand and a pitcher of the same amber fluid on the floor beside him. In his own orchard back of the house there was promise of a fine crop of russets, the best apples for a full-bodied cider and a potent applejack. From the barn came the jovial bellow of a young bull he was fattening for beef. The extra dollars he would get from the sale would buy rum and a bottle or two of whiskey for special occasions like a birthday or the anniversary of some battle. Yet deep inside the man on the porch some strange idea kept pecking at its subconscious shell.

Before long Jerusha Lyon stepped out of the front door. She gave her husband a disapproving look and started down the flagstone path.

"Have a good time at church, Rushy, an' listen an' see if th' dominie mentions my name," remarked Eph pleasantly.

"Huh!" said Mrs. Lyon.

Other families now appeared on the village street. All the women gave the porch-sitter mean glances, and a deacon spoke distinctly of the ungodly who wallowed openly in sin while others sought the light. Several men, however, waved a surreptitious greeting to the sinner, and he knew that there was a wistful gleam in their eyes and that tongues moistened dry lips. Yet Ephraim Lyon was not contented.

Ordinarily there was nothing he liked better than to tuck in the Sunday quota of hard cider while he watched folks go to church and heard and saw them disapprove of him. Ephraim Lyon gazed at the tumbler of cider in his hand and the pitcher on the floor; then he admired the apple blossoms once more. After that he looked northward to where folk were entering the Congregational Church. Wasn't there some sort of relation between cider and apple blossoms and Congregationalists?

Ephraim Lyon filled his glass and thought hard. The next idea that came almost frightened him, it was so beautifully simple and logical. There were lots of other men in town who thought that cider and applejack were worth being thankful for, and that a man should count it a blessing if he had the stomach and head to enjoy such gifts. And in that case, why should there not be a church where such men could get together and give praise for the good things in life? Then a disquieting thought came. Lots of the boys would welcome the new church, but they wouldn't dare uphold it openly. They were good drinkers, all right, but the dominie and their wives had them buffaloed. Well, he knew what he'd do; he'd run the church himself, singlehanded, enroll members, appoint deacons, keep the brothers worshiping hard, and throw out the backsliders.

Ephraim Lyon went into the house with the empty pitcher. When he came back it was full, and in his other hand was a black ledger, a pen, and an ink bottle. He sat down, poured a full tumbler of cider and took a deep swallow; then he opened the ledger, dipped the pen, and held it poised. What should he call this new church? Who had been a friend and protector of good drinkers? A vagrant memory of something old Bill Williams, once of Yale and later of any taproom and cellar, had said came to the christener. At the top of the ledger's first page he wrote, "Records of the Church of Bacchus." Below it was, "Ephraim Lyon, High Priest."

Before the apple trees bloomed again, the Church of Bacchus was going strong. Its high priest did not invite members to join, nor did he ask their consent to have their names recorded. He heard of a citizen who, according to Temperance Society jargon, "indulged in intoxicating beverages to excess," and forthwith that man was a member in good standing of the Church of Bacchus. The high priest himself was pledged to keep up a steady consumption of anything he could get hold of and also to become thoroughly pixillated several times each year. Deacons were appointed from those members who best followed the priest's example, for none surpassed it. If any worshiper gave up steady drinking, his name was stricken from the church roll, but if he reformed and proved by conspicuous intoxication that he had done so, he was welcomed back to the fold. Those who died in full membership were promised Bacchanalian joys.

The Church of Bacchus began in Eastford, but it soon had communicants in half a dozen surrounding towns; in fact, by 1830 there were a thousand or more names in the black ledger. Some members had backslid; others had gone to their ghostly jugs and barrels, but many hundreds still drank heartily. Most were men, but it was rumored that several women were staunch, even zealous members. Church meetings were held at no regular time or place. Perhaps the high priest was invited to sample a fresh barrel of cider in Woodstock or Hampton or Pomfret. As many local members as could get away from their wives dropped in, and right then and there a good evening of worship began. The high priest also liked to honor every national holiday or date of local significance, and of course the birthday of every deacon and honored member was celebrated in fitting manner. Tradition states that at every meeting Gargantuan amounts of liquor were consumed, but the high priest always tried to keep the members of his church from being too playful. Drinking good licker was such a joyous privilege, he asserted, that a fellow ought to go at it in a serious way, just as if he was thankful for his blessings.

Windham County looked at the Church of Bacchus in several ways. Independent, carefree men welcomed it and laughed raucously at a good joke on the temperance gang. The clergy, most women, and many sober citizens denounced the church as blasphemy of the worst sort and a deliberate attempt to hide the horrid features of the Monster Rum. Many good drinkers paid no attention to what they called "Eph Lyon's queer notions." When they heard that their names were in the church records and had been read aloud at meetings, they remarked tolerantly, "If Eph gets any fun doin' that, let him do it; it don't hurt me none."

The high priest was not too much hurt by such indifference. Of course, he liked to have people worship with him in the body, but his church was also of the spirit; so if any man drank nobly and enjoyed doing so, he was a brother in Bacchanalian bonds, no matter how much he scoffed. Then there were the guzzlers who wanted the public to think that they were abstemious men; such hypocrites objected vehemently to having their secret habits proclaimed. But threats and pleadings never moved the high priest; he did not weaken even when some young fellow who was courting a real nice White Ribbon girl begged that his name be taken off the rolls, or at least until he was safely married.

"Can't be done," said Eph. "Ye drink enough t' be a member, so a member ye be, an' y'r name stays on th' church records."

Ephraim Lyon was high priest and guiding spirit of the Church of Bacchus for twenty years. Twice he was defeated in drink-to-drink combat, but both his conquerors died soon after, one of stomach ulcers, the other from nervous exhaustion after a trip through a snake-infested jungle. All others the high priest drank under the table or sent away in confusion, while he strolled to his house or drove home to Eastford. Jerusha was dead now, and his housekeeping was a trifle haphazard, but he was happy with the church he had founded. Drinking in Windham County had taken on a fuller meaning; besides, he was having a lot of fun.

One April day in 1840 the high priest, now eighty-two, strained too hard at a cider barrel he wanted to move. Three days later he whispered to a deacon of the Church of Bacchus, "I would've liked t've seen them russets in blow jest once more. They make the best cider I ever tasted."

The fingers of his right hand bent as if they grasped a glass, and he tried to raise the hand to dry lips. It fell back on the quilt, but, as the deacon told the last meeting of the brethren, "Jest before Eph slipped off, he sorta smacked his lips as if he was tastin' somethin' mighty good, an' whispered, 'Ahh-hh.' "

The Church of Bacchus died with its high priest. Windham County drinkers mourned him, but there was no one to take his place, and as the oldtimers died of cirrhosis of the liver or from falling down the cellar stairs, Ephraim Lyon began to be forgotten. Then the Civil War years came, and the West opened, and before long few men knew about an old drunkard and his queer ideas. But I am pretty certain that up in the hills on a run-out farm there lived for a long time some old cider-guzzler who wiped rheumy eyes as he remembered the days when he didn't have to drink in lonely squalor; then he could sing and be cheerful at a good lusty meeting of the Church of Bacchus.

THE HOLLOW STILL LIVES

All this time the Gulls were much the same as ever. Maybe they were living a little bit better as far as food and clothing were concerned, but in them there stirred no urge to branch out. Their idiots crawled on the floor or wandered all over town, their women were whores or "housekeepers," and always there were the whispered stories that "them Gulls was what ye might call unnatural in some of their ways." No attempt was made by the town to stamp out the race that had spread up from the Hollow; as ever the Gulls were keeping to themselves, and if some wild young fellow was fool enough to get mixed up with one of the girls, that was his lookout.

So the Hollow and the life it had spawned kept on. Evil is as hard to kill in New England as is good. The town meeting, the dignity of the church, the beauty of our houses and commons, honesty, thrift, and hard work are evidences of our strength that persist century after century. So, too, persist shiftlessness, fornication, adultery, and incest.

Not a Popular War

The War of 1812 did not please the people of Town Meeting Country, particularly those who were in business. Connecticut was especially infuriated by Jefferson's embargoes and went so far as to refuse the government the use of its militia. Then in 1814 delegates from Massachusetts, Rhode Island, and Connecticut held the famous Federalist Convention in Hartford. Here the war was condemned for injuring the commercial interests of the three states; the drafting of soldiers was denounced, and in general the entire administration policy was given a thorough blasting in the traditionally vigorous manner of indignant Yankees who had been prevented from making an honest dollar. Unfortunately the convention was more or less of a secret affair, and soon the rest of the country was saying that those Yankees wanted to secede. That accusation was an unfair one. The malcontents were undoubtedly selfish in protesting so loudly about the dangers to their affairs, but their protest was a logical one at that time, and did not include any desire to quit the union. All that they said was that the federal government ought to know better than to start a war just when people were beginning to branch out a little and get ahead. That Hartford convention was nothing more than a very large town meeting at which disgusted men spoke their minds.

These same three perturbed states were ready to fight the British when war came; in fact, our privateers and ships did fine work against the enemy, and it was a Connecticut town which scored the greatest victory of the war, or of any war before or since, if you can believe the descendants of the heroes involved.

For three days in August, 1814, Stonington was bombarded by a fleet of five British ships, commanded by Nelson's famous officer, Captain Thomas Hardy. The enemy had a total of one hundred forty guns; the Connecticut militia answered with one six-pounder and an eighteen-pounder. Yet the little shore town won. Only three Yankees were wounded, while the British casualties were ninety-four and one of the five ships was badly damaged. How the militia did it is as great a mystery as why the British aim was so bad. Plenty of cannon balls came ashore, but most of them fell in woods and fields, there to be picked up as souvenirs, which, incidentally, are still proudly displayed.

While the battle was raging, one Connecticut soldier made himself mildly immortal. Private Abner Reed was loading the six-pounder when he found that all the wadding had been used. There was more in town of course, but the gun crew wanted to keep on pounding the enemy. Abner rememberd how a woman had sacrificed her petticoat for the same purpose at the seige of Fort Ledyard. He was as much of a patriot as any woman, he swore; in fact, he would give even more for his country. And off came the Reed trousers to be torn up and rammed into the gun. "Mebbe we'll need y'r underdrawers next, Ab," remarked the gunpointer. Abner Reed looked at a buxom vivandière who was serving a cool drink to the boys; then he made an heroic decision. "They're ready an' waitin' for their country's call," he stated; but Puritan caution made him add, "Jest th' same I ain't givin' 'em up until you fellers have used up y'r own britches."

At last the British ships withdrew, having suffered the most complete defeat of any in a proud navy's history. Ever since that memorable day Stonington has dwelt with true Yankee emphasis on the essential fact that it cost King George ten thousand pounds to take a crack at the town, and all the money was wasted.

The War of 1812 was not a popular one with the eastern Yankees, but after all it turned out to be better than anyone expected. The prizes taken at sea amounted to quite a bit, and Stonington showed the Limeys what was what.

SORT OF DIFFERENT

Many of the Yankees of this period seem to have done their best not to be like everybody else. Some were no more than mildly eccentric, but others startled even towns which had seen a lot of queer specimens.

Not even queer, just a bit independent and different, were the Hazards over in Rhode Island. Perhaps this family belonged by rights to the more expansive Narragansett shore life, but several of its members influenced the mores of western Rhode Island.

"Shepherd Tom" Hazard seems to have been the most articulate member of the family. His *Jonnycake Papers* are part of the

Holy Writ of Rhode Island and are, in fact, mildly interesting. One passage is worth recalling. In nearly every well-ordered family in Narragansett, says Mr. Hazard, there were three articles of faith. "First, that ye love one another and your neighbor as yourself. Second, that ye hate the Puritans of Massachusetts with a perfect hatred. Third, that ye hold the Presbyterians of Connecticut in like contempt."

Shepherd Tom also made a great to-do about the sacred jonnycake. White corn meal should be used, and it should be ground just so, and baked before coals of a quick green hardwood fire on a red oak barrel-head supported by a flat iron. At least that is as much as I can make of Mr. Hazard's enthusiastic account. At any rate, he was the leader of the jonnycake cult, and it was he who did most to make the feud between the white and the yellow meal schools of thought such a bitter affair. The argument still rages, and the State of Discontent will not admit that a cake which is good when made with white meal, is superb if made with yellow.

The Hazards were enthusiastic haters as well as champions. Sylvester and his brother John had not spoken for years. After the first decade of silence had passed, the neighbors began to think that it was about time for grown men to stop acting so foolishly. So a friend of both Hazards persuaded Sylvester to greet his brother who was coming along the road.

"I'll do it to oblige you," said Sylvester, "but I know he won't answer."

When John was near, Sylvester called, "John!"

The other Hazard stopped.

"When are you going to bring home that iron bar you stole from me, you thief?" continued Sylvester.

On walked John Hazard without a word, and his brother turned to the would-be peacemaker.

"I told you he wouldn't speak to me," he said.

Another Hazard would keep nothing but bulls. At one time he had thirteen of them. He said he liked to hear them roar, and besides, they kept the boys from stealing his pears.

Then there was the famous Stout Jeffrey Hazard who carried a stone weighing 1620 pounds "some rods." His sister carried on the family tradition by marrying a Mr. Wilson who used to take a full barrel of cider by the chines and lift it up so he could drink from the bunghole. The Plantations were deeply impressed by Stout Jeffrey and his brother-in-law.

A trifle more eccentric than any Hazard was another Rhode Island citizen, Captain Bill Wilson, who lived alone in a one-room cabin. His cooking and table utensils consisted of a two-quart iron kettle, two pewter spoons, one pewter plate, and a half-gallon jug. His diet was exclusively hasty pudding and molasses, and he never cleaned out his kettle until the crust on the bottom and sides was so thick that only one meal of pudding could be cooked. Of course that kettle was never washed; to do so, said Captain Bill, would spoil its sweetness.

Down in Westerly there was David Wilbur. Afraid of all human beings, he fled from them and walked great distances, always studying the stars, clouds, and winds. Undoubtedly he had parents and relatives who took care of him when they could, but apparently most of his time was spent tramping through the fields and woods. Whenever he came to a cornfield, he scratched numbers, signs, and figures on the pumpkins. People never mocked David or tried to shut him up. He was different, that was all.

For many years Jonathan Brooks of New London went over to the old earthworks of Fort Ledyard on the anniversary of the massacre of Groton. There he gave in a loud voice a commemoratory address. Once when only a few people were present, he gazed sternly over their heads and cried, "Attention, Universe!"

Up and down and across the Connecticut towns of this country walked a man clad in what was once a fine tailcoat, waistcoat, and trousers, but now each a solid pattern of darns and mends and patches. He was the Old Darn Man, who had been seeking a lost woman for years and would not put on other clothes until he found her. For how could she recognize him if he were not dressed the way he was on what should have been their wedding day?

From Dudley on the north to New London on the Sound, as far west as Colchester, and east to Foster and West Greenwich in Rhode Island walked the Old Darn Man. He had certain favorite roads and houses on them where he was sure of food and a night's lodging. About dusk he would appear at a home, rap on the door, and greet very politely whoever appeared. If asked to come in and eat, he accepted; if no invitation was given, he left, never to call again. After supper he would probably work on his coat and waistcoat, perhaps asking for a scrap of cloth or a little thread. Cobbling his shoes was too skilled a job for him, but every so often he wore a new pair. They were supplied, people said, by relatives who kept watch over him. The Old Darn Man would answer any simple question such as "Did you walk far today?" Otherwise he never spoke except to make some simple request. In the morning he left after a courteous bow and word of thanks. Perhaps he was back again in three months, or six, and once he must have been ill, for he was not seen in Hampton for more than a year.

The story back of the Old Darn Man is this in barest outline: He was dressed for his wedding to a beautiful girl when word came to him that she had died. There are various versions of the manner of her death, but the details do not matter. The groom was stricken with what people then called "brain fever," and when his body was strong again, he could not understand what had happened. For a week or two he roamed New London streets looking for his bride; then he began his long search through the northern towns. How death released the Old Darn Man is told in half a dozen stories, but each one relates that at the end he had a vision of the girl of long ago. Perhaps it did happen that way, for he probably died in some farm house, and the people there would not have invented that meeting at last.

The Old Darn Man was one of the few figures from another world who have visited our matter-of-fact towns. Yankees understood him. They knew that he was not bound by their sober reason; that it was right that he should search for a lost bride and darn his wedding coat so she would know him when they met on some country road or in a farm house. So the people were kind to this wanderer and gave him food and lodging and little kindnesses and never laughed at him.

BRANCHING OUT IN DEAD EARNEST

Emigration from New England started as early as 1775 or thereabouts. Then the Wyoming and Susquehanna land companies flourished, and restless Yankees trekked west. In the early nineteenth century this flow of people grew larger; in fact, it threatened to hurt the little hill towns most grievously. Down on the shore men were doing things that excited and satisfied them; up back life was too dull for many a young fellow. Not all could be inventors or peddlers or start new industries; the others had to find some way of branching out. They simply left the home town.

Some of these men who left merely took up daily life in some Ohio or Indiana community, but others went to college and became teachers, lawyers, doctors, and scientists. Look in the *Dictionary of National Biography* and you'll find a dozen stories something like: "Tillinghast, Horatio . . . educator. Born Brooklyn, Conn. Sept. 3, 1798. A.B. Yale. 1818. Professor . . . first president . . ." then the name of some Middle Western college. Most such men were from the farms of the Town Meeting Country. Dr. Albert Mead of Brown University had the right idea. He would lift the foot of a man and pretend to find something. "Just as I thought," he said. "Manure under the heel."

The little hill towns bred strong men, but it could not hold all of them. That is the inevitable result of any slow, careful building up of people by a way of life; the ones who have been created leave in order to perform the same act of creation in other states. The New England community did its work too well; it could not keep its sons.

That was the way the Yankees branched out: academies, shops, tiny factories, silkworms, whaling expeditions, voyages to every port, clashes with the old religious order, peddlers all over the land, more boys going to college, Unitarianism, Abolition, Temperance. A man hasn't time to fool with them when he's busy making things that sell like hot cakes at a muster. We don't want another war, but if th' British think they can take Stun'n'ton they're mistaken. New sects. Oliver Dodge preaches a happier religion for the common people. He becomes a drunkard, but to the last he rails against church domination. Men have built a sound social order; now they can let their own selves develop. Most become just set in their ways, or cussed, or queer; others become an Alcott, or Lorenzo Dow, or start the Beecher line. Yankees were branching out.

These were the years when the town was strongest. Not as self-sufficient perhaps as it had once been; it was more firmly established, and had a democratic quality that had not been expedient to cultivate when a stern rule by a few was necessary. Now the town and church were officially separate, and the last remnants of theocracy were being torn away. And all the time the small cities and the western lands are draining the towns of their men. Abandoned farms begin to appear; fifty years before there had not been enough land. Old maids live and die half-satisfied; the young men they could have married have gone. The town stands alone; it is as strong and as perfect a form of representative government as has ever been built.

CHAPTER 7

Our Grandfathers

ONE MORE WAR

AN INDIGNANT South believed once, and probably still does, that all pre-Civil War New Englanders were abolitionists and were so stirred by the slaves' plight that they were willing to fight to remedy these wrongs. The truth is that the abolition movement was never popular with the rank and file of Yankees. Probably most would have agreed that no man ought to hold his fellows in bondage. Their ancestors had done so, or at least permitted others to do so, but even the most realistic neo-Puritan realized that 1840 or 1850 had brought new ideas about human values. That is what the average intelligent Yankee thought of slavery; the more ignorant never bothered their heads about the whole matter. So it was left for a very small minority of abolitionists to launch a vigorous campaign.

This ardent reform spirit troubled the people of Town Meeting Country. They were willing to help an escaped slave get to Canada, but they also viewed with deep suspicion all these emotional appeals. For we are, and ever have been, instinctively suspicious of fancy theories which have not been tested and found to be workable. We have also desired peace and order and wondered if too much meddling feverishly with other folks' business would not lead to trouble. So our grandfathers listened to abolitionists and read *Uncle Tom's Cabin* and were not unduly excited, although they were slowly coming to agree with certain fiery orators that the South was an irrational and unpredictable place and one given to foolish gestures about honor, women, and other subjects.

In the meantime the South was creating for itself one of those misconceptions which send nations into disastrous wars. To the planters and their humbler brothers, the Yankee was a money-mad fellow with no spirit of fire in him. For the sake of a few dollars he walked dirty roads with a pack on his back; he worked with his hands; he built things or sold them rather than ruled broad acres; in short, he was plebeian and utterly devoid of martial qualities. Probably he would not dare face a Cavalier army, and if he did have the nerve, he would immediately run in panic from the charge of the Black Horse Troop, that brave and gay band of fighting aristocrats. Yes, any war that came would be a matter of knight versus peddler, clerk, farmer, merchant; and anyone knew the inevitable outcome of such a conflict.

Basing their defiance upon the assumption that it would not be punished, the South proceeded to do the one thing sure to arouse the North. It tried to break up the Union. Now the average Yankee had a very feeble concept of a theoretical union, but he did know that the federal government was something more or less like the setup that managed his town. And, knowing this, he realized how disastrous a real split could be. Say, for instance, the people up in the North District got mad because their roads weren't kept up right; they refused to pay taxes and vote, and finally went so far as to set themselves up as a town without asking permission from the old community or getting a charter from the state. That sort of defiance was dangerous and couldn't be allowed. Their ancestors had built a strong unit of living, and no bunch of soreheads was going to break it up. When the townsmen arrived at this simple idea, they were ready to fight.

The men the North sent to the battles were not much like the Cavaliers' notion of them. From Town Meeting Country went tough sailors and skippers to blockade southern ports and damn the torpedoes with Farragut. The South had forgotten that strip of water from Westerly to the Connecticut River. It's all right to know how to ride a horse, but the cavalry can't defend the Mississippi or keep a harbor open. Then there were the tough farmer boys and the mechanics from the small cities. They might be sober and thrifty men who had few graces, but they could march and shoot.

This country did its part in the Civil War. There was not a town that did not send a score or more of men, and in every cemetery you'll find at least one headstone in memory of a soldier who was buried far away from home. This land was not invaded by an enemy which burned and plundered; it was green and lovely every spring, and its old and young people carried on the business of life, but the shadow of death was on it for years.

There was not much talk about the war. Yankees are not ones to slop over and, besides, what could be said? A plantation home destroyed, the family silver stolen, a gentle lady insulted; those are the horrors of war out of which come legends and sad tales, but when a son or husband or lover was killed, women and fathers mourned silently and went on with their work. When I was young, I knew a dozen veterans, but I never heard them say much about their experiences.

"Sure, Bub, I was at th' Wilderness. Ye-up, got winged onct. If ye ain't got nuthin' better t' do 'n' t' hang round askin' fool questions, ye can run over t' th' store an' get me a plug a terbaccer. Tell ol' man Sessions t' charge it."

That was the way Yankees dealt with a small boy who wanted to hear heroic tales.

Perhaps the most matter-of-fact acceptance of the fortunes of war was shown by a widow. When Captain S. L. Gray sailed on a whaling expedition from New London, he followed the custom of many home-loving men and took his wife along. Off the island of Guam the Captain met the Confederate raider Shenandoah. There was nothing to do but sail away as fast as possible, but before the Yankees could get out of range a Rebel cannon ball killed Captain Gray. Almost all men who died at sea were buried there, but the Widow Gray declared that Seth was going to rest in the Liberty Hill cemetery in the town of Columbia. All his folks were there, and when she died, she wanted to be laid beside him. So the captain's body was put in a cask of strong spirits, and when the other barrels were full of whale oil, back went the ship to New London. There the widow hired a wagon and had the mortuary cask carried to Columbia where it was buried in the Gray family plot with a fitting and seemly funeral service.

The most casual and silent of the returned soldiers from my town were Bill and Hen Gull. The Hollow had sent three volunteers, and two came back. The moment they were home they took up their old ways, and before long Hen became so outstandingly irregular in his sex life that he shocked a town grown accustomed to Gull behavior and was given a jail sentence. He never pleaded his status as a wounded veteran, and the court did not give mercy on that account. Hen and Bill could never be persuaded to attend any of the infrequent gatherings of old soldiers. They had helped the town do a job, and now they were free to live as they pleased. The rest of the people had much the same idea about Gull heroes. There wasn't any sense making a to-do over them; they'd been good soldiers, none better, but the war was over, and a Gull was a Gull.

That was what my grandfather thought of the Civil War when he came home from it. It was over.

DOWN ON THE SOUND

Groton, Mystic, Stonington, Westerly, Noank, and New London were booming in the middle years of the last century. They built ships, and they sailed them everywhere. From Mystic yards came the Andrew Jackson, that beat even the Flying Cloud as it went from New York to San Francisco in eighty-nine days and four hours. And in one year New London had seventy-one ships in its whaling fleet.

By 1850, those miles of shore from Westerly to the Connecticut were as famous as any in the world, and as busy. Here were naval designers and architects who worked by rule of thumb and sent down the ways the most perfect sailing ships ever made. There were business men and entrepreneurs who gambled, not with dice and cards for those were agents of the Devil, but with cargoes and long whaling trips, and getting to China or San Francisco four hours before a rival, and with treacherous foreigners who tried to cheat an honest Yankee.

Down here on the Sound the Puritan was having his last great adventure. He was to be in three great wars, and one little one, in the years after 1850, but they were jobs that had to be done. Now he built and sailed and traded because he wanted to. Clipper ship captains kept an eye out for a neat profit on each voyage, but they were not business men alone; they were satisfying an urge in themselves. When other regions tell of dull, plodding Yankees, they forget those crews from the Sound who rode polar bears from Spitzbergen to Iceland, climbed the North Pole, cleaned out every saloon and brothel from Cardiff to Port Said to Shanghai, died at sea or in some strange land, or came back to Mystic to live to be ninety, left Yankee half-breeds all over the world, read the Bible to the mates every morning, and in general acted like true Yankees. The West can have its mountain men and wild cowboys; the whaling and clipper bravos saw and did more in a year than those staid fellows did in a lifetime. And a dozen of any crew, properly encouraged by rum and led by a Captain Ahab, could have torn a trappers' rendezvous or Dodge City up by its roots. And never forget that those voyages paid good dividends. They buried the cowboy on the lone prairie, and the mountain man's grave is unmarked; the New London skipper lies in dignified state in the old cemetery. A marble monument rises in his memory, and his grandchildren are still spending the interest on the money he earned. Under humbler, but neat and respectable, stones are the mates and the able seamen who sailed under that skipper. They owned their homes and gave a tidy bank account to their children.

That's New England adventure for you! The sky's the limit, but grab a handful of cash as you leave.

MILL CITY

During the middle years of the last century the inland mill cities of the region grew in population and wealth, but they showed certain signs that they were never to become more than oversized towns built around a few mills. The people of each little city liked to think of themselves as urban, and there was an Opera House, and a trolley line down the Main Street, and a Boston Store, and two hotels, one of which was respectable. Perhaps sin was also a bit more flamboyant here than out in the country. Saturday night on Union Street or the Stone Row was almost wicked, and there were sounds of revelry in many a saloon. Earlier in the day the city had been full of shoppers from the little towns, and now the weary clerks took a quick drink and laughed patronizingly about the "hicks" and their queer ways. But when you looked a little deeper at one of these tiny cities you saw in it the same virtues and defects you found in the small town.

In Willimantic and Rickville, as in Hampton and Woodstock, there was freedom, tolerance, pragmatic forgiveness, stodginess, thrift, shiftless people, a few degenerates, fornication, drinking, the code of honest work given in return for honest pay; in short, all the complex folkways of Yankees and Celts. In both the town and the city there were unmistakable signs of weakness taking the place of a dynamic power that had built the social order and sustained it until now.

Away back in the eighteenth century these little cities had begun to make use of their water power. For half a century the shops and mills had dawdled along peacefully; then in the 1820's when an agricultural section was converting to industry, they began to expand. By the Civil War decade each city was firmly established, some as cotton or woolen, others as silk or thread, centers. Willimantic thread and Talcottville woolens became world famous, but none of the mills grew very large. If one company branched out, it dominated the whole city, taking all the available labor supply and discouraging any new industries.

As early as 1880 each little mill unit had made its mold. The Company was an awesome power; the New York Office spoke like Jehovah, and the resident General Manager was greater than such nebulous beings as a president, a senator, or even the governor. The workers got fair wages and good enough treatment. They could rent nice, clean, white-painted houses, and if they were injured at the jobs the company was decent about paying damages. Once in a while there was a strike, but such rebellion wasn't considered very good form.

The foreigners started coming to the mill towns in the middle of the last century, and by 1880 or 1890 they were almost as numerous as the old-time Yankees. At first they had been mill hands and laborers, but some of the second generation were ambitious. The Irish turned to saloonkeeping and politics; the French and Italians to keeping small stores, and twenty years later you might think that the city had been captured lock, stock, and barrel by the Donahues, Lafrances, and Polettis. But you would be wrong. Alphonse Dufresne and Jerry McCarthy might divide the political honors; there was an Irish police and fire chief; the Catholic churches were big and rich, and still the old-time Yankees on the hill had the money. It was a typical New England setup of the 1890's. The newcomers up front running the machinery of the city; the descendants of Puritans sitting tight on their inherited wealth and adding a few dollars to it.

There was another quality in these little mill cities. Each one had created its pattern of life, and because its people knew and respected that way of life, life in Willimantic, or Putnam, or Southbridge was quiet and soothing. In too many New Englanders there is a deep-seated desire to "know where you're at"; to be free from disturbing experiments and innovations; instead, to meet the familiar scenes every day, follow the old customs, and be guided by fine, time-honored ideas. Even more than in the country towns, these fundamental requisites for sane, peaceful existence were found in the small industrial centers.

Especially restful were the details of ordinary life. When a man "ate downtown," he went to the same hotel he had always patronized, or he took the table d'hôte at a restaurant that had been going since before the Civil War. Men went to the barber they had known for half a century; they bought their tools and neckties and tobacco from old friends; the occasional drink was taken in a saloon with a tradition. The bums who shuffled up and down Main and Jackson were institutions slowly wasting away but never dying. Buildings grew older and dustier but stood firm. The N.Y., N.H., and H. depot smelled the same in 1910 as it had in 1880, and prodigals home from foreign states whiffed its aroma and knew that they were back where life was settled and free from disturbing changes.

Yes, those little cities were good places to live in if you were a sensible man who realized that a rolling stone never gathered any moss, and had already decided that the old home town was good enough for you.

HILL TOWNS

During the years from just after the Civil War to, say, 1900 the little up-country towns of this section were even more weakened than the small mill cities. Both of them, town and city, seemed strong; both were pleasant, very pleasant indeed to live in, but in both there were apparently the first signs of degeneracy. The old folkways were too smug and serene; life was too ordered, men and women had ceased branching out, and decay was inevitable. Or was it? Were the quiet mores more firmly rooted in human conduct than the critics knew? Was the New England town merely resting peacefully after the long generations of struggle?

There are those who believe that this hill town has been dead these many long years. They assert this idea sorrowfully, but as a fact not to be denied. For instance, Dr. Hamilton Holt, president of Rollins College, and a descendant of an old Woodstock family, is sure that the coming of the railroads was the first step in the disintegration of the town as a separate unit of life. He bases his contention on the famous Five-Mile Law. In the old years a Woodstock farmer could in one day reach a point five miles away from his home and return to that home. In other words, he could get five miles and back between morning and evening chores. Never forget those chores, for they were the chains that bound the family to the farm. A Cow Has To Be Milked Twice A Day is a law all-powerful in creating the folkways of country people. So the Woodstock farmer could get started as soon as the chores were over, and he could drive just as far as he could go and return in time for another bout with the chores.

Of course, that five-mile limit was only an average one. If a man had a good road horse he could cover a lot of ground in a day and pull off quite a few deals. There was Riley Witter over in Brooklyn who sent his black horses over half of the county between dawn and dusk. Some men hauled heavy loads of wood or other produce as far away as Norwich and were gone for days. My grandfather was courageous enough to take a loaded wagon all the way to Providence, thirty-five or more miles to the east. But he had been to sea in his youth and distances did not scare him as much as they did other Hampton men. And then, too, he had someone to do those inevitable chores.

Even within its own boundaries, the people of the town were influenced by the limitations of travel. No man wanted to hitch up horses that had worked all week and drive very far to church, and certainly he was not running off to the village store every day. If his son wanted to gad about and court a girl over in Pomfret or Chaplin he had to earn enough money to buy his own rig, or limit his trips to those days when the farm horses could be used. Of course, a good many prosperous farmers had a driving horse, but even a sleek bay pacer must draw the cultivator or rake.

Now and then a stiff-necked rebel would travel as much as seven or eight miles because he did not agree with the preacher in the church near him, but such devotion to principle was not approved of by sensible men.

"I see Dave Griggs is comin' over here t' church these days."

"What's wrong with th' Chaplin church?"

"Waal, 's far 's I can make out from what Dave says the preacher over there don't hand out th' right doctrine."

"Dave allus did have queer ideas 'bout religion. I never see a feller who could get more wrought up over it."

"I've heard from other sources that th' Chaplin minister ain't quite up t' snuff in some ways, but jest th' same Dave's a fool t' come way over t' church. Must be all of six or seven miles each way. A man ought t' give his horses a little rest one day a week instead of makin' 'em drag a load that distance."

Yes, a good many ministers were tolerated because a good one was outside the Five-Mile Limit. It is even said that a few weak-willed Congregationalists went so far as to enter a Baptist church because it was handy.

That restriction of the townspeople to their own territory gave them unity and strength even while it narrowed their interests. Dr. Holt is right in some of his emphasis upon the significance of a horse-drawn social and economic life. But I am not sure that the changes brought by the railroad and the auto route were the ones that ruined the towns, and perhaps after all they are not ruined. Most certainly there were other forces that have made the town of the 1940's a far different one from that of 1850 or 1900. That Five-Mile Law is neat and clear, but beware of such explanations of Yankees. We are a contradictory, cussed, and complex people who could not be put into an equation by Einstein himself.

One very obvious change in the hill town was in its population. A community which had 1,120 persons in 1800, was reduced to 800 in 1865, and by 1900 there were about 550 men, women, and children; and as Sam Hunt once remarked, "Some of them ain't what my father'd 've called living people; they jest ain't dead." This loss of population had its inevitable effects on the towns. More and more fine old farm houses fell into ruins or were occupied by shiftless day laborers. Fields grew up to brush, and the sheep pastures were thickets of alders and birches. The small industries were practically extinct. Now the pins and hats and plowshares were made in the factories along the bigger rivers. Men no longer started up new shops in Hampton or Woodstock or Dudley; they went to the cities with their inventions and ideas. There were still those in the towns who worked at blacksmithing and carpentering and ran a grist or saw mill, but the city was nearer than ever and, besides, there were fewer people to provide for. Slowly the towns, impoverished by the loss of people, began to drift into a very conservative agricultural life.

SOME GO AND SOME STAY

"The Yankees who had guts got out; the others stayed behind." In politer words this popular theory of why Yankees emigrated from the small town is supported by many historians. Yet the truth about why our great-uncles and cousins left the old place is too complex to be expressed in one epigram.

The only son of a prosperous family was not likely to leave home unless he got into trouble or was an exceptional youth who wanted to go into some profession. Quite a few Yankee boys did enter college and become teachers, lawyers, doctors, and ministers, but even so they were in the minority. Most of the other only sons were content to take over the family acres or store or learn a trade from the old man.

Out of a big family, only one son could take over the work. The others could have bought played-out land enough and developed it if they had been willing to work as hard as the early pioneers had, and the fact that they would not is proof of some degree of weakness, but after all too much cannot be expected of mortal flesh. So the three or four younger boys had to leave town.

Elijah Tillinghast's folks helped settle the town he lives in. He is one of the richest farmers; three times a legislator in Hartford; selectman often, and other years an assessor or justice of the peace; for quarter of a century a deacon in the Congregational church. Elijah is a fine example of the rural statesman, and his wife, who was Lucy Holt, came from just the same sort of family. They have three sons and a daughter. She is the oldest child and is engaged to the middle Rawson boy. He can't hope to inherit his father's farm, so he is working in a Willimantic bank. That means that young Lucy Tillinghast won't stay in Hampton and help in the Grange and Ladies Aid the way her mother does. Henry Tillinghast, the oldest boy, is already married and lives in a small house near his father's. He is a good farmer and could take over the farm when Elijah wants to slow down a bit. But Henry isn't any too strong these days; he ruptured himself two years ago, and once or twice he has hinted to his wife that maybe he had better think about getting a job in some bigger place where he wouldn't have to lift so much.

The second boy, John, is planning to go into Browne and Sharpe in Providence and learn the machinist's trade. Alfred, the youngest, hasn't made up his mind what he wants to do, but his father has been talking with a merchant in Willimantic about an opening in his hardware store. Even if young Henry Tillinghast does have an operation and feel well enough to take over the farm, he will be doing no more than filling his father's place in the town. A community does not grow strong, or even hold its own, when the number of its good men remains the same. There must be a reserve to draw from when the inevitable acts of God rob the town of a fine citizen.

Other families in town simply packed up and left. They were mostly small farmers whose places had heavy mortgages on them, or hired men, or struggling artisans, day laborers, the near-shiftless or, more charitably, the hardly solvent. Such people moved away from town or sent their children away because they were restless, or wanted an easier job, or, in the rare instances, had some vague notion of bettering themselves. Men like Elijah Tillinghast were scornful of such people.

"They'd make a living here if they'd only work an' save. Th' trouble with them is they haven't much sense an' gumption."

The Gulls never left town. If one of the girls did go over to a mill, she was sure to be back home soon, hanging around the house or living with a cousin or some low fellow. They did nothing for the town except give it idiots and disease, but they seemed to love it and cling to it. Even the very exceptional Gull, who was a partial reversion to the long-ago time when his people were respectable, seemed to hesitate before he escaped. Young Fred Gull was bright in grade school; then he went to high school, and after that the Boltons, who had lost a boy just Fred's age, took pity on him and offered to pay his expenses if he wanted to go somewhere and learn a good trade. Fred seemed to want to do it at first, but later on he told John Bolton that he guessed that after all he'd better stay on the old place. So he did and married a first cousin. Three of the seven children are not quite all there, but Fred seems unconcerned.

The worst people never left the town, and enough of the best and prosperous stayed so that the big farms were kept running,

Most of the families who left were of the middle group; the ones who should have worked hard. The future of the town was really in their hands. For the rich farmers were few in number, and conservative, and the shiftless ones would never amount to anything. If the community was to keep up with the times and retain its old power, the very ones who were leaving should carry on. But there was a strain of weakness showing in these Yankees, and too many ran away instead of doing what their forefathers called "buckling down to hard work."

Now the town became more set in its ways than ever, for most of its affairs were in the hands of a few people who inevitably supported the good old ways; the resilient power that had made safe, neat communities out of a rocky, Indian-ridden wilderness had become stubborn and clung to traditional folkways. No longer did the townspeople want to change and grow and branch out; instead, they were glad to conform to accepted standards. The gusto and dynamic force of this age of capitalistic development left them cold and distrustful; so, too, did the new ideas in social reform. The town had been built strong and sensible; now let it be kept in its sacred form. There came a lethargy of spirit over the life of the hill communities, and instead of the old strength there was an emasculated desire to be comfortable while a few stored up their dollars and the majority were content to trudge along the old paths.

These were the years when the little churches that had grown up in defiance of Congregationalism died like flies in November. Some of them had managed to keep alive ever since the Separatist and Inner Light movement more than a century before. But now there were not enough people to furnish a congregation; besides, a new spirit had robbed the faithful of the old determination to stick by their own church. It was a pathetic struggle as each church went down. A few old worshipers gave more money than they could afford to hire some superannuated minister who himself was sacrificing much to keep alive the faith. Then at last even he could not be paid, and a minister came over from another struggling church and held an afternoon service for ten or a dozen people. The next step was to close the church in the winter and open it for a few weeks in the summer. In that way the remaining parishioners felt that they still had a church of their own. But at last the one prosperous deacon died, and the rest of the congregation gave up the battle. Their church stood forlorn for a few years; then it was torn down.

Of course, the dying ecclesiastical societies seldom considered merging with one another. Yankees can be sensible pragmatists, but at times they are as stupidly obstinate as a shell-shocked mule. Take a town that had four meeting houses on or around its green. Baptist, Unitarian, Episcopal, and Congregational. Once they had all been well filled and strong, but as early as 1890 only enough worshipers to fill two churches were left in town. Yet the several ecclesiastical societies would not pool their resources or forget their theological differences. A man's family had been Baptist ever since the Great Awakening, and he wasn't going to change at this late date. Union with alien sects was unthinkable for the Congregationalists. Their church had always ruled the town, and it was going to keep right on doing so. The Unitarians listened to polite lectures, and the Episcopalians, in distasteful compromise, worshiped once a month rather than every week.

The rural churches that were still comparatively strong when I was a boy were almost always Congregational. They were supported by the more solid and prosperous families, and I believe that there was some kind of unofficial state organization which helped them if they were very poor. But even if they were more or less solvent they did little to influence the community. The typical minister was over fifty and content to accept eight or nine hundred dollars a year, an unfurnished parsonage, and perhaps a few cords of wood. Now and then he was a very young fellow who wanted a few years of experience before he was called to a bigger church. Such a man might revive the Christian Endeavor Society and make a few vague gestures toward satisfying the desire of the church that "something be done for the young folks," but nothing much ever came of his efforts. He knew that he was waiting impatiently to leave us, and we knew he was waiting; therefore his spiritual contacts with the town were decidedly tentative. Following such an experiment, the town was sure to hire a minister well over sixty. After all, it was more seemly and satisfying to throw him out than it was to be rejected by some young squirt.

All these old men who came to us were sincere, devout, and often well educated but, like the Society which hired them, they saw no reason why the old ways should be changed. Not once did they attempt to stir the town and the church out of the state of conformity into which they had fallen. The theology they preached was indefinite and weak; their contacts with local politics and society frightened and ineffectual. It is true that the church did not want a minister to meddle with secular affairs, but he in turn was only too glad to oblige. And it was a good thing that he was not asked to do anything; most certainly he would have been a miserable failure as a modern replica of the Puritan Roundsman of the Lord who hailed fornicators, drunks, and mockers before him. In all my early years I never remember hearing of a rural minister really interfering in a local problem. They avoided the Gulls and other low-lived families, preached one sermon on temperance, and did nothing when there was talk about this or that girl going wrong or a boy falling into bad habits. Their job was to preach on Sunday, call on church-going people, and keep the parsonage in good order.

Only once in a blue moon did a minister preach a sermon that really said something. When, after years of boring exposition of Old Testament prophets, one man gave a simple little talk on the folly of worrying, the town remembered it for years. Just last summer an old lady was reminiscing about bygone ministers.

"Mr. Smith wasn't what you'd call an up-and-coming worker in the church," she said, "but I'll never forget that sermon he preached on why it wasn't any use to worry."

The town's attitude toward these ineffectual men of holiness was hard to describe. It respected them, in fact, gave them high place. Women and men alike thought of the minister as one somehow set apart. Yet this same shepherd was paid but little, dismissed often, and seldom if ever permitted to take any part in the town's political life. The minister had at last been relegated to his church, and the last vestiges of theocracy had vanished.

Taxes, Legislators, and So On

There were few radical reforms in the small towns during the half century after the Civil War. The poor were given better treatment, schools became more modern, and idiots and insane people were sent to state institutions, but these changes were made very slowly and usually because of pressure from the large cities.

In general the towns spent as little money as possible. High taxes were well-nigh criminal, and selectmen spent more time avoiding such treason than in fixing roads. The Republicans were in power, not because they were any better than Democrats, but because they had sounder ideas on money, tariff, and taxes. This simple truth, valid even now, is seldom understood by outraged Democrats who think that their personal character has been maligned when they are rejected by a New England town. They are simply not careful enough with money.

The political relation of the small towns to the state was simple and, also, effective if not too many results were demanded. In the Connecticut and Massachusetts towns of Town Meeting Country a Republican and, therefore, conservative representative, was sent to Hartford or Boston, but in the Rhode Island lands once called Vacant, and now not too well-filled, there were complications. Over here each town not only sent a representative but also a state senator. According to the bosses this was a fine arrangement, since a rural senator's vote matched that of a city slicker's, and it was cheaper. Massachusetts and Connecticut scorned such medieval representation, but they had never aspired to keep up with the State of Resentment when it came to queer politics. No wonder the Plantationites could do such stunts, agreed the envious neighbors; they had been in training for years, and had once gone so far as to stage the best opera-bouffe performance ever given by Yankees.

That affair was Dorr's Rebellion, or War, as it is called by friend or foe. An advocate of more liberal suffrage, Thomas W. Dorr asserted that he was the rightful head of the Rhode Island government. His claims were rejected, and he at once withdrew with many supporters to Acote Hill in Chepachet where hurried fortifications were thrown up, and preparations made to meet the loyal state troops in bloody civil combat. However, at the last moment Dorr's followers were found to be too few, and he and a few of the nearest to him withdrew to Connecticut. All this happened back in 1842, but even today the War is evergreen in Rhode Island memories. The historians of the state will tell you that it was a very significant affair, and even those citizens whose grandfathers marched against the treasonable Mr. Dorr do not like to have it spoken of jeeringly.

Over in Massachusetts and Connecticut the people took their

state politics a good deal more sensibly. For instance, "going to the legislature" was no more than an honor which should be handed around. Let us say that both Henry Malbone and Fred Copeland have let it be discreetly whispered that they might be persuaded to "go." Fred is a prosperous farmer of forty-two who reads quite a lot and has sound ideas on politics. Henry is sixty-five, and his best friends admit that he "will never set the river on fire," or, in less polite words, he is stupid. His own poor farm brings him in half a living, and he works at odd jobs or does a little woodchopping in the winter. His seven children and peevish wife are never exactly destitute or hungry, but kind people often send in clothes. Henry's education stopped when he was twelve, and he often says that "All this talk about more schoolin' f' th' kids ain't good common sense."

Which man, Fred or Henry, gets the nomination for representative in the Republican caucus? The election is a mere detail; the Democrats always lose. Henry is the town's choice, for it is his "turn to go." If a white citizen reaches the age of sixty-five and has not shown positive signs of being degenerate, criminal, feeble-minded, or a Democrat, the town considers that it is duty-bound to send him to Boston, or Hartford, for a brief term of glory.

Very seldom did the town's official representative ever speak in the legislature, or introduce a bill, or buck the Republican Machine. Once or twice a session he felt called upon to rise and defend a proposal that was strictly local, such as an appropriation; he also hesitantly put in a bill to do something for the town he was from. Maybe it called for nothing more than getting some Civil War veteran his pension, or a law raising the bounty on foxes; at any rate, the legislator was very proud of it and talked for years after of how he did so and so. As for defying the state boss; well, that gentleman was as sacred as the Dalai Lama is to other worshipers. The Boss might admittedly be a crook in private life, and the representative did not approve him as plain J. Henry Bolingbroke, but he had been chosen; he stood for the Party, for the Established Order, for Them, and from many candidates he had been picked out to carry the banner. Confronted with the absolute proof that J. Henry Bolingbroke was a lecherous, hard-drinking, profane, and cutthroat individual who was waxing rich at the people's expense, the town's legislator and defender squirmed uneasily.

"Mebbe Hen Bolingbroke ain't all he should be in his private doin's, but . . ." he stopped to grope for words, "but he's head of the Party."

The town representative never seemed to feel much obligation to report to his electors what he had done. In fact, if someone asked how he voted on a certain bill, he was pretty likely to be insulted and answer that that was his business and nobody else's. Neither did the town demand an official accounting from its legislator. Of course, disgruntled enemies and Democrats might state loudly that Henry Malbone never done nothing at Hartford but smoke big cigars, but even they did not go so far as to suggest that Henry get out a full report of his activities. Apparently he had been a relatively sober legislator and had not disgraced his town by "shooting off his mouth" too much; and, since he had so comported himself, why ask more? To those who insisted that it might have been better to have sent somebody who wasn't quite so, well, mebbe ye might say, a little bit quicker t' think an' talk than Henry is, the majority of right-minded Republican citizens answered conclusively, "It was his turn t' go."

In religion, in politics, and in social philosophy, the small towns were, in these post-Civil War and late nineteenth-century years, so tradition-bound that there seemed to be little hope that they could again fight hard for any way of life, or, perhaps, even for the chance to survive. Of course, there were some virtues still apparent in these towns. Equal rights were given to all in the way of fair assessments and taxes and roads fixed and schools maintained. Justice was meted out fairly; the town meeting was open to all, and one man's vote was as good as another's. Furthermore, the individual was free to do very much as he pleased as long as he observed certain rules of communal honesty and cooperation. But in spite of these evidences that strength still existed in the small towns, there was no doubt but that they had become weak since the days when privateers harried the British, and the volunteers went off to save the Union.

KIND OF A PLEASANT LIFE

In *The Late George Apley* a character says, "When the individuals of one group find a complete peace and happiness and fulfillment in the association with one another, why should they look farther? . . . It is something to be an integrated part of such a distinct group. It is somehow reassuring."

Boston and the small town of Connecticut, Rhode Island, and Massachusetts had both builded so well and so firmly that the resulting order and decorum were overwhelmingly satisfying. If one were a Brahmin or a prosperous farmer, he had no reason to doubt the past that had created him or the present he supported. He was not arrogant or swollen with pride; he was merely very self-satisfied and content. Such men had little in common with the early Puritans and their crude and ruthless logic and religion, justice, retribution, virtues, and lusts. Those pioneers had weathered the storms; their descendants were living in the mellow haze of the New England Indian Summer.

It was a good life some people led in Boston or Hampton or Woodstock or Dudley or Ledyard or Foster. Like the Bostonians of the Golden Age of Gentility, many small-town Yankees managed to invest their folkways and daily life with far more satisfying charm than critics would ever imagine could come out of such a dour land and people. This gracious living was enjoyed most by those prosperous farmers, artisans, and merchants who had established themselves as the aristocrats of each town. They were the men who held mortgages, had money in the banks, and were deacons and Worthy Masters in the Grange. Their wives ran the Missionary Society and the Ladies Aid and did their share in the Grange. But other townspeople, such as the poorer farmers, the hired men, the shiftless odd-job workers, were satisfied with part at least of their life. For them it had the charm of established strength and security; it brought the reassuring certainty that they were in the best of all possible worlds. Even the Gulls, living in their Ishmaelitish squalor, seemed to have achieved some measure of the pleasant conformity that pleased their betters.

Yes, life in the small towns from, say, 1880 to 1910, was "real nice and comfortable." Since the markets had opened in the nearby city and the 7 A. M. train took the milk to Boston and brought back a good monthly check, the economic stress had eased up a lot. Forgotten were the political dissensions of years before; Republicanism was supreme. Gone too were the religious questionings, and to sensible people who yearned not after strange ideas the Congregational church preached an easy theology, and its ministers were content with a small salary and did not interfere with secular affairs. A nation, a state, and a town had all three shaken down and become comfortably settled; now people could take time to enjoy themselves.

It's hard for one who wasn't a Yankee small-towner in those years to understand what made life so satisfying then, for a lot of our little ways contributed to the sum total of pleasant existence. Some of them must strike modern critics as rather queer aids to joy, but just the same those quiet habits did their share. Take, for instance, the order cart. That was a noble institution that brought a lot of comforting entertainment as well as boughten goods to rural homes.

Every town had four or five general stores, but as a rule only two, and sometimes but one, was prosperous enough to solicit trade and deliver goods. The other proprietors couldn't afford a clerk to send around with the order cart; or, like Jirah Munro, they felt that such modern practices were weak-spirited. They weren't going to coax and beg folks to buy from them. "If anybody comes here t' my store, all well an' good," declared Jirah, "but I ain't runnin' after 'em. No, sir, not by a damn sight! I ain't lost all my self-respect."

Generally the stores at the center or "Street" of the town was the one which sent around the order cart. Every Monday there drew up at the farmhouse back door a snappy rig: a fast, strong horse and a good express wagon, which perhaps had a canvas stretched on wooden arches over its body. A man jumped down, snapped a rope with a weight on the other end to the horse's bit, and started briskly for the house, pulling an order book from his pocket as he went. He might be the proprietor himself, and in that case he was likely to be a trifle slow and ponderous, but more often he was a lively young fellow who was learning the business. Or he might be a gay blade-about-town who liked the excitement and contacts of driving the order cart. For this job was regarded highly and did not carry with it the mark of dull commercialism that branded some kinds of work even in the minds of Yankees all too ready to conform and earn.

Whoever the order man was, he rapped on the kitchen door, waited until it was opened, and then tossed a pleasant word to everybody present. Then followed five or ten minutes of quoting prices, and of suggestions, for a good clerk could stimulate the imagination of any woman. He was generally in a great hurry, but not too much of one to keep him from giving the appearance of devoting all his time and energy to this one family. He also did a bit of brisk retailing of any gossip he had picked up.

"I see Bill Holt's startin' t' shingle th' roof of his ell. They tell me th' oldest Moseley girl's started takin' music lessons over in Willimantic. Ye-up, does seem sort of a waste of time at her age. Bank's taken a mortgage on Sam Pomeroy's place, I hear. No, Sam ain't much of a farmer."

A good order clerk was a diplomat, a Winchell, a Marshall Field, and more of a practicing psychologist-salesman than nine-tenths of those now behind counters. Not everybody could qualify. I know, because I failed miserably. I had a satisfactory memory, the horse didn't run away with me, and I was punctual and honest; but when I went into Seth Waters' kitchen, I grunted instead of tossing a cheery word to Mrs. Waters. I also thought that purveying gossip was beneath me. Sorrowfully, since I was working for non-union wages, old Al Weeks dismissed me.

"Y're all right in some ways," he said, "but y'll never make a good order clerk."

If a farm was about halfway between two good stores, another order man arrived on Tuesday from the town to the north. In that case, a good housewife never bought all she needed from one man; she divided her trade and had two calls, rather than just one.

On a Wednesday or Thursday the goods which had been ordered were delivered. Many people paid cash; often part of the bill was met in eggs or butter, and there might be a little money coming to the woman. Some families ran an account at the store, but such a practice was frowned upon by solid citizens. They wanted to be square with the world, not only every month but every day.

"I don't feel right if there's as much as a dollar debt out against me."

"And ye feel wuss if there's a dollar comin' t' ye that ye ain't collected."

"Y're damned right I do. This idear of credit is goin' t' be th' ruin of this country yet."

Well, there you have the rural New England cart. It wasn't a colorful or dramatic institution, but it sort of fitted in and helped keep daily life from becoming too drab even while it retained its nice, comfortable ways.

Another quiet but satisfying custom that broke the monotony and did not overstimulate or breed dangerous rebellion was going on the train. Each town had its favorite shopping place, and ours was Willimantic. Danielson was only nine miles away, but no railroad connected us with it, so if you wanted to go over you had to use up a whole day; besides, it was only a borough with stores quite a bit less resplendent than those in Willimantic. That city was easy to get to. You could dash down on the 8:30 and right back on the 10:15, but doing that meant hurrying too much, and even the hardest workers tacitly admitted that when you went to the city you were going for more than the mere articles you bought, you were embarking on a mild adventure.

So it was better to take the 11:05 over and come home on the 3:30. In that way the shoppers had to get dinner in Willimantic, but even the tightest Yankees rather enjoyed eating out once a month. If a man and his wife both "went over," he generally stabled his horse in Irving Hammond's barn or, if the weather was fine, under one of Dwight Phillip's sheds. If "she" was going alone, someone probably drove her to the station and came for her. However, some women were quite capable of harnessing and hitching up a horse.

A trip like that, an all-day one, was prepared for well in advance. As soon as a woman got back from one shopping expedition she began to "make a list" for the next one, but the real planning began three or four days before the big day. Farm work had to be taken into consideration, for the most considerate husband sometimes refused to take a horse from farm work or waste half an hour of his own time. Then the weather had to be guessed at, the men folks' dinner provided for, and neighbors called up to see if they wanted any errands done. Husbands jeered a good deal at all this fuss, but they recognized that taking a day off to shop was part of a woman's heritage.

About every so often the man of the house went along, protesting, of course, that he ought to be home working, but in reality looking forward to shopping around and seeing old friends. On a Saturday a man couldn't go half a block on Willimantic's Main Street without seeing someone he wanted to say a few words to, and Jordan's hardware store and the Windham National Bank were full of farmers. Your true Yankee never exactly loafs; in fact, he is in theory always very busy, so the visitor shook hands with the other shopper and asked how things were. Then he hastened to remark, "Shouldn't 've come here today. Work's pilin' up at home, but she was bound 'n' determined t' come, an' besides I wanted t' see Will Grant about some fertilizer."

The friend nodded understandingly. He, too, ought to be at home working, he said, but his woman had insisted on coming, and he himself really did need to see a "party" about a mortgage.

Having thus observed the amenities and established themselves as busy men dragged from their work, the two settled down to a few minutes of pleasant talk. After about five minutes, one shopper looked at his watch and remarked, "Waal, this ain't th' way t' get any business done. Guess I'll be moseyin' along."

The friend hastened to declare that he, too, was driven by many details, and the two busy men shook hands and parted. A block farther up or down Main Street each met another brisk and hurried old friend, and the same scene was enacted again. That was the way conscientious Yankees kept their self-respect and reputation for being men who never wasted a moment.

As three o'clock drew near, shoppers began to converge on Railroad Street and the N.Y., N.H., and H. station. Down at that odoriferous place there was a sedately holiday atmosphere, for Willimantic was a junction where many lines met and from which at least half a dozen trains left around three in the afternoon. Exuberant Westerners would have said that these package-laden men and women were tired, dour, and miserable as they talked together in low voices or merely sat and looked around them. Tired they undoubtedly were of uncomfortable clothes and hard city pavements and too much noise and bustle, but otherwise they were enjoying themselves, not in the flighty manner of people who slop over out loud, but like sensible Yankees who find in a quiet shopping trip a fine, restrained joy and the needed assurance that life is serenely stable.

The best place to see neo-Puritans really at play was at the county fairs held every fall. The fair-going addict had plenty of attractions to choose from. I've forgotten which one opened the season in early September, but the Stafford Springs event in the middle of October was the last. Sturbridge, Oxford, Willimantic, Norwich, Putnam, Rockville, Palmer, Woodstock, and other towns had at one time or another a fair of its own. But the oldest and most typical of all was the one at Brooklyn, Connecticut.

There was the place where you best caught the real Yankee land as it completely relaxed for one day in the year. Over in Massachusetts there was the famous Brockton Fair where prizes were magnificent and the exhibits awe-inspiring. At Hartford in Charter Oak Park famous harness racing could be enjoyed, the Willimantic track was a sporty half-mile, and Sturbridge had its noted drivers. Brooklyn could not match such attractions; nevertheless, people seemed to feel that it had something the other fairs lacked. For one thing, it was a nice home affair that respected the old ways and exhibited a mode of life that was sound even while it pleased. You met everybody at Brooklyn Fair. You heard a woman say, "Why, I ain't seen her since last Fair day." And a man remark, "When I run into him at th' Fair he told me. . . ." Plenty of people went to the other fairs, but they never seemed to meet old friends the way they did at Brooklyn. As far as I can figure out, that Fair was a sort of catalytic which helped bring to a fine, satisfying blend all the sedate pleasures of a quiet, sensible people, who, nevertheless, could take a day off in the fall and spend a dollar or two and perhaps win a few blue ribbons and the accompanying cash prize.

There were three days to the Fair, Opening, Cattle, and Horse. The first was more or less given over to arranging exhibits in the buildings, although the Midway had started, and there were harness races in the afternoon. The second day was the big one, for then the cattle were on exhibit and were judged. On the third, the horses were shown, and there were some good races. Schools were let out for the Big Day, and only the sternest fathers dared keep their families home. Even Sam Hunt, famous among thrifty men for his more-than-thrift, bestowed one-half of a dollar on each of his seven children, sorrowfully accepting the fact that, as he said, "There goes a lot of damned good money I've worked hard for, but th' little cusses sorta look forward t' Brooklyn Fair."

By ten o'clock in the morning everyone was there, even Lester Gull, who walked the eight miles barefoot and put on his shoes at the gates. Up against the rails of the half-mile track were hitched the teams. Fancy rubber-tired buggies and black pacers, smart spans of horses and the canopy-topped surrey, farm horses hitched to lumber wagons with boards for seats. Ever since dawn the farmers had been driving their cattle toward Brooklyn, and now the long sheds were filled with calves, bulls, milch cows, hogs, and sheep. A man could spend quite a while, happily wandering from one stall or pen to another, commenting freely on each exhibit and telling a friend that he had a boar or yearling heifer better than any he'd seen yet. Over in the Main Exhibition or the Food and Fancy Work buildings the women folks were happy. Over the hum of voices rose the cry of the sideshow barker, the crack of the buggy whip wielded by the sporty vendor, and the occasional roar of the Wild Man from Borneo down in his pit.

In the afternoon the grandstand was full, and the crowd stood three deep against the rails. Next to the judges' stand was the platform where a band played when acrobats were not performing. The races were gallantly listed as 2/05 pace and trot, 2/13 trot, but if any horse made 2/20 he was very suspect indeed. This was the time when the young bloods had their big moment of the year, and the fellow who entered a horse and even drove it himself was a real hero.

When the last heat was trotted, tired celebrators piled into their carriages and express wagons and started home. Brooklyn Fair was over for the year, and there were chores to do. Most families in my town went to at least one or other fair during the fall, and a few reckless men took in four or five, but on the whole it was considered very bad form to waste too much time in this way. For in pleasure-seeking, as in other habits, the Yankees I knew were men of "measured merriment" and could not enjoy themselves if they broke the bonds of decorum. To them life was not an adventure; rather, it was a nice comfortable affair in which one day a year at Brooklyn Fair fitted neatly, a pleasant, almost gay eight hours, with just a touch of the sportive, even the exotic, but never unrestrained. For in the Indian Summer of a civilization, it is not coltish and wild; its joys are quiet ones.

Hired Men

If the Nineties in a New England town were years of weakness in many ways, and foretold the apparent decay of a strong civilization, it was in those very years that a fine institution flourished. Back in those last decades of the nineteenth century, and until almost 1920, there lived in the small Yankee town an unique kind of person, the Hired Man. No civilization or group of folkways save our own could have produced him, and ours could not have existed without his help. Van Wyck Brooks does not know him, O'Neill disdains him, and Frost is only condescending. Nevertheless, this half-forgotten man is as important as any other constructive member of the community. He was not genteel; he was not cultured or social-minded, but he was of the town and the ways of life that built and sustained it. Now, alas, he is out of the picture, gone with the Saybrook Platform, witches, the heath hen, and stern dominies.

There will always be plenty of mercenary yokels who work out on farms, but they are not the hired men I knew thirty years ago. Some were neat, dapper sports who drove a fast horse; others were dirty and always broke. They might be married or single, moral and staid and even church members, or mighty swearers and drinkers with whom no hired girl was safe. About half of them were unimaginative fellows who plodded through a life of hard work; the others labored just as hard and became legendary figures who added zest and color to sedate rural life. Most of them dreamed of how they would farm it for themselves if they had a chance, and a few did get their own places in time; the others died in an ell chamber or a rented room. But no matter what they were like, they were more than just laborers who took wages; they *helped* on a farm, not just worked out.

Those hired men I knew were the best exponents of the social-contract theory the world has ever produced. They knew that of their own free will and accord they had signed an agreement with the men who paid them, an agreement which, through long years of hiring and being hired, had so developed that now it took into consideration the demands of farms, farmers, and helpers, and was more binding than any piece of paper with seals and signatures.

A good hired man might tell his boss to go to hell, but he

would not quit in such farm crises as haying or threshing. Changing jobs was no disgrace; in fact, an independent fellow liked to show what he was made of by so doing, but he would not quit because an employer set too fast a pace of work. Mind you, I said, "Set too fast a pace." In other words, the boss was doing as much as he demanded. A hired man could lie all he wanted to about some matters, but he must tell the truth about what happened on the place in the way of crops, cattle, and buildings. He must never steal from the farm, and an employer's family was sacrosanct unless a Mrs. Potiphar was too insistent and Potiphar himself none too moral. All these things a good hand did or did not do, not because he was paid so much money, but because he was helping that family and that farm.

The employer lived up to his share of the contract or he lost a good worker. For instance, a hired man was accepted as part of the family, he usually ate with the folks, called them by their first names, and was listened to when he gave advice. There must be food enough to keep a worker in body and spirit, and he was capable of saying a few words about too much salt pork or dried codfish. As I have said already, a good boss got out and set the pace at working if he were physically capable of doing so. If slight and almost frail, he had to earn the praise of "tryin' his damndest t' keep up." A farmer could pay as low wages as the market allowed, and he expected a hired man to work overtime in case of emergency, but on the other hand he helped out that hired man if the latter were sick or needed money. Thirty years ago New England farmers had to be gentlemen before they could get along with their help and be given those words of accolade: "A goddam good man to work for."

After the contract of service between the hired man and his boss was drawn, the hired man had to think of his relations to the town. Very seldom, in fact almost never, was he a candidate for any office, but he paid his taxes, went to caucus and town meeting, and voted with more or less thoughtful deliberation. He was not a town father or elder statesman like the man he worked for, and he knew he probably never would be but, just the same, he felt that he was a real part of the town and was helping to make it a better place to live in.

Men like these have almost disappeared. A few of the toughest, bibulous, profane old rascals are still doing chores for their keep on little hill farms, but in another decade the last of them will have been buried by the town, and from our land will have gone another proof that a man can fill a humble role in life and still retain the comforting feeling that he is just as good as the other fellow.

Perhaps one quarter of our hired men were strangers to us when they came, but none were like the migratory laborers who follow the grain or fruit harvests. Although these Yankee wanderers might change jobs every few months, most of them seemed to feel that they were part of the life of each farm they worked on. There were many reasons why they never stayed in one place long. Several were so touchy that the slightest reproof sent them away, and others had peculiar standards. One old fellow would not work where there were young children to bother him, another wanted fried salt pork and boiled potatoes three times a day, and an equally determined man was always seeking the right kind of hired girl. The remarkable thing about the latter was the fact that when he was over sixty he found the woman he wanted, married her, paid five hundred dollars down on a farm, and began to raise a family and "be somebody."

Probably the most exacting man was the one who worked like a being possessed but who insisted that we stop every hour or two for a few minutes of supplication for the Lord's blessing on our work and His help in leading righteous lives. Unlike him was the fellow whose average stay on a place was about a week because he would swear luridly on all occasions. He did not wish to shock anyone; in fact, he was a mild and kindly man in all other ways. He simply could not stop cussing. The day he left, he shook hands with Father and Mother and said, "I wisht' Jesus Christ I could stop this hellish swearin' o' mine, but I guess the goddam habit's got too good a holt on me."

Some of these drifters worked well until it was time for a spree, then disappeared. I never understood why they did not come back, for they were almost always such good hands that any farmer was willing to overlook a week's absence, but we never saw them again. Perhaps they were ashamed of having left an employer in the lurch; more probably they wanted a change of scenery. Almost every year, a different hulking moron would come to town and get a job. Such fellows always seemed to hope that they could settle down on a place for good, but peo-

ple did not like to have them around, and they would plod off
to another town never to return. There were hundreds of farms
to be tried, and before the big stupid fellow could make the
rounds of them and come back, he would be an old man and in
some poorhouse.

Now and then, we had a man of mystery. Father hired a John
Smith one summer to help with the haying. He was a good
worker and pleasant to have around, clean, polite, and an easy
talker about impersonal matters. After supper he sat with us in
the living room and read the five books he carried with him.
None of us had the curiosity to see what those books were and,
when haying was over, he left, still just John Smith. Then there
was the man of fifty or so who forgot now and then to say,
"I done it." No one ever questioned such men about their pasts.
The contract with them called for their delivering an honest
day's work, and decent speech and behavior; it did not include
revelations that they did not care to make.

But even if these transients fitted more or less into our lives,
they were always strangers to us and quite unlike those hired
men who had always lived in town. These true natives were an
integral part of a closely knit life, giving to it as well as taking
from it, and never doubting for a moment that they served a
good purpose.

There was almost a hired-man class in each town. Such really
low people as the Gulls might help at haying or chopping, but
they preferred to be free to do as they pleased. However, there
were a dozen or so families which just missed solid citizenship,
and they supplied the farm help. We never expected the Field-
ings and Malbones and Henrys to be much more than hired men,
and they felt the same way.

Most of our farm hands were married by the time they were
forty. Now and then an astute fellow picked a good worker who
helped him save money and get ahead, but more often he chose
one from his own group, and she turned into a fat, prolific sloven.
Farmers liked a married hired man, for he was not so likely to
pick up and leave, but it was more or less of an unwritten law
that he keep his wife and children at home. Very rarely an especially devoted husband and father insisted that his family was
"as good as anybody else," but on the whole a hired man who
would quit if he could not eat with his employer's family was

willing to admit that "she" and "the kids" were to be kept in their place. He was a man among men by virtue of his working ability; they had no such claim to equality. Besides, some hired men felt the same as Mart Fielding did. When Father asked him how his wife was, Mart growled, "Don't remind me of th' ol' hag! When I'm up here, I try t' fergit I wuz fool enough t' git married."

Some of the married men lived in tenant houses and had just a garden and a cow and pig and a few hens, but others rented a little rundown farm and worked on it Sundays and whenever they could be spared. At least they did that when they first rented the place. After a year they would become discouraged, and when they came home tired, they went fishing or took a drink of cider and rested. Then the fields grew more up to brush than ever, and the hired man had a hard time paying the rent. But it was part of his code to be making the gesture of more or less having a place of his own and working out as a sideline. Now and then some hired man did manage to save enough to make a down payment on a farm. Two or three years later he was a hired man again, and people were saying, "He's all right working for other folks, but he ain't the kind to make a go of farming for himself."

The bachelor hired men were either young fellows who had not yet settled down, or they were extreme individualists. You might think that a sporty hired man who was getting good wages would like to keep his freedom, but only the strongest escaped the local Maud Mullers. If they were bachelors at fifty, they had minds and ways of their own and no doubt about it. Such men were Frank Glover, who wore red-flannel underwear in summer to keep the heat out; Bill Hussey, a "hard drinker" among some fair to middle guzzlers; and Seth Forbes, who heard the voice of God. None of them could be tied down to a wife who was bound to be bossy. Annie Gull did go to live with Seth one winter when he was in the woods getting out ties, but she left after a week. It scared her, she said, to have a man act as queer as Seth did. He said that God reproved him for living in sin, but he also added that Annie was a dirty slut and couldn't cook.

Mart Fielding and Joe O'Brien were the hired men I knew

best. Mart was with us for years, and Joe worked for Henry Moulton who lived a quarter of a mile south of us.

Six feet tall, wiry, aquiline nose, good forehead and mouth, hard gray eyes, Mart Fielding looked like a lean pioneer in overalls. In him were blended vices and virtues, and the result was his own form of integrity. According to his way of thinking, Mart was a pretty decent fellow. Profane except before good women, drunk on Sundays, adulterous according to opportunity, an awful liar about some things, a noted blasphemer and mocker of the clergy, and a very negligent father, Mart saw no reason why his virtues should not win him the respect of all right-thinking people, and especially the man he worked for.

Just as ready to work hard as Father was, Mart could also manage the farm and drive shrewd bargains, because he had good judgment except in his own affairs. He did more than just work for us; in his own way he was part of the family. Politely impersonal with Mother, he argued loudly with Father, and saw nothing amiss in slapping me down if I felt my oats too much. About once every two years he flared up over some trivial matter and left, swearing bitterly that we would never again see him on the place. Within two months at the most he was back with us, ready to defend the honor of the farm and give a good day's work in return for value received.

Mart began to work out when he was fourteen and was a hired man until he died at seventy-five. His last job was puttering around young Lyman Holt's farm, cleaning out stables, cutting brush and firewood, and driving the one old horse Lyman still kept. Mart's wife had died, but he refused to live with any of his children. He preferred to stay around a farm and keep busy. Then one day he didn't move quite fast enough to get out of the way of a truck as it drove into the yard. Some people thought that Mart suffered an ironic defeat at the hands of the machine age, but as old Lyman Holt said, "At least th' ol' buzzard died out in the barnyard where'd he spent a lot of his workin' days."

For years Joe O'Brien was our sportiest hired man and the acknowledged leader of all the young bloods for miles around. He dressed well, had a rubber-tired buggy and fast horse, and was as smooth and knowing as any city slicker. No dance or shivaree was complete without him, and he was the one who promoted every local minstrel show. Every fall he followed the horse races at the county fairs and quite often entered a horse himself or took a prize for his rig in the Gentleman's Driving Horse class. All these things, and the way he held his liquor, helped his repu- tation, which was really built on his escapades with women.

There were plenty of other hired men who did their share of wenching, but Joe had been famous ever since he got Mrs. Abel Wiston all wrought up when he was only eighteen years old. Abel discharged him and cussed his wife into repentance, but he did not try to revenge himself on the young Casanova; in fact, he said admiringly, "Th' little bastard suttinly has got a way with women." Abel was supposed to speak with authority, hav- ing himself been the hero of several affairs of love.

After that episode, Joe was a marked man, but he could always get a good job at high wages. For one thing, he was more than a strong, "soople" little man; he was an expert at all kinds of work, butchering, odd jobs of carpentering and blacksmithing, taking care of sick animals, training steers, and handling a team. Then, too, he was a moral man in his way. Mrs. Henry Moulton was a fine-looking, buxom woman and the two Moulton girls liked to joke and flirt, but Joe was always respectful to them, and Henry trusted him, even though he had to be careful to select an unassailably virtuous hired girl.

If he had wanted to save up and buy a place, Joe would have done well on it, and Norah Kelly was ready to marry him, but he was too busy being a sport to settle down. He was thinking of slowing up a little the winter he was forty and had a bad acci- dent in the woods. When he got out of the hospital, he was so crippled that he could no longer work as he had done. Lester Johnson wanted him as a clerk in the village store, but Joe pre- ferred to stay on a farm, and even if he couldn't do heavy work, he was still clever with his hands. But all the farms wanted able- bodied men, and all Joe could get in the way of work were enough odd jobs to keep him in tobacco and a few clothes and pay his board at Black Pat Kelly's. Gone were the sporty days and the rubber-tired buggy and the fast horse. Joe was begin- ning to settle down whether he wanted to or not.

The thing for him to have done would have been to marry Norah, who wanted him just as much as ever, and get a job in the city, but he wouldn't do that either. He wasn't going to let

any woman take care of him, and he wanted to be on a farm.
So he kept on doing odd jobs, and when he wasn't busy he hung
around Henry Moulton's place. One day there was a mean bull
to be taken from the barn to the pasture. Joe said he'd do it. A
year before, he would have been safe, but now his arms were
weak and his game leg gave way under him. Henry Moulton
paid for the funeral expenses, and his family and ours went to
the Catholic church for the mass. The Kellys and the other Irish
families resented Henry's usurpation of Joe after his death, but
Henry was unmoved.

"Maybe he was of your race and religion," he told Black Pat,
"but he was my hired man."

Rural New England created the genuine, old-style hired man,
and he in turn helped build the towns. Men like Mart and Joe
piled the stone walls and kept the fields productive; they fell at
Gettysburg, voted for sound men, and helped allot money for
schools and libraries and hospitals. Not many critics and historians of New England have noticed the hired man, but after
all, they could not understand what was meant when Sam Hunt
talked the way he did about Frank Glover after Frank was buried
by the town.

"Frank was a filthy ol' buzzard," said Sam, "an' mean-tempered
an' queer'n hell an' a bad man with a bottle or a woman when
he was young. Died on th' town, an' never saved a cent, but
when he was able, he was right on hand if there was work to
be done. I never heard he let a man down if he took wages from
that man. They tell me he tried t' get up an' go out an' help
with th' milkin' th' night before he died. Yes, sir, Frank Glover
was a good hired man, an' th' town didn't suffer none from his
bein' in it."

CELTS AND OTHER STRANGERS

Ever since the very first days, there had been some foreigners
in the shore towns, Jews, Germans, French, Welsh, Scandina-
vians, and the more exotic nationalities. Remember the crew
that sailed with Captain Ahab! And up in the hill communities
there were a few wanderers. Perhaps a Hessian group came as it
did up in Wales, and there were Irish from the beginning, and
over in Rhode Island the community called Frenchtown sent
some of its people westward. But almost all the names of Hamp-

ton or Woodstock or Columbia or Dudley or West Greenwich
people in the years before the middle of the last century told of
English or Lowland Scotch blood. Moseley, Fuller, Kimball,
Holt, Church, Button, Cornell, Burnham, Utley, Griffin, Baker,
Kenyon, Wade, Hammond, Converse, Lincoln, Sweet, Stone,
Hunt are examples, and the rest of the names were Norman-
French of the Conquest days or perhaps an occasional High-
lander.

Then the coming of the railroad brought the Irish laborers
to the little isolated towns. Some of the older folks could speak
only the Erse, and all had strange accents and even more peculiar customs, but the Yankees gave them justice and even a
little tempered kindliness, and when the tracks were laid, many
of the Celts decided to remain in town. True enough, their
welcome had been a trifle frigid, but they were ready to trust
these dour, calculating people they had come among.

The Yankees knew that these foreigners need never be feared
as dangerous competitors in business or farming. Too volatile
and given to irrational moods, they would not work well for
themselves, although they were good enough hired help; that
is, when they were sober, or not celebrating some saint's day or
mourning at a wake or letting something else interfere with the
serious business of work and getting ahead.

Neither was the strange religion of the newcomers feared by
the Yankees. It is only in weaker, less confident lands that the
Scarlet Whore is a seducer and Popish armies are ready to pillage.
Puritans are always sure of their ability to take care of themselves; besides, they had already subdued such very energetic foes
as Pequots, Baptists, and Quakers. So the new faith was not persecuted; in fact, it was often given a site for a church and money
to help build it. In the eyes of the selectmen, the assessors, and
the town meeting, a Papist was always as good as that most
excellent of all men, the Congregationalist!

From the very first, the town granted each and every foreigner
an even-handed justice. He paid accurately estimated taxes, the
road to his place was kept open and repaired, his children were
educated and, if some crafty Yankee stepped outside the law in
dealing with him, the authorities defended his rights. All those
things the town did for the Celt without stopping to consider
whether or not he was like other people. It was enough that he

and his family were legal inhabitants in a town which had certain obligations to fulfill toward all its people. For the citizens of a New England community are more than so many men and women with very human prejudices; they constitute a legal entity which has signed a contract with all who live within its boundaries.

That was the way the town treated the Celts. It gave them their rights and dues, then reserved the privilege to think as it pleased about them. On the whole, the verdict was a lenient one. However, there were a few Irish habits that caused a good deal of talk. For example, quite a few of their men would get drunk in a noisy and otherwise spectacular manner. Mark that I qualified "get drunk," for the act *per se* was not objected to as much as was the method of performing the act. As we have seen, several neo-Puritans put down large quantities of assorted drinks, but they were seldom, if ever, conspicuous.

Should a White Ribbon matron meet Ike Billings on the 3:30 from Willimantic where he had been celebrating his birthday or the anniversary of the Battle of Gettysburg, he tipped his hat and passed the time of day in a husky but respectful voice. And when he got off at the depot, he comported himself like a gentleman and offered to help the temperance woman with her bundles. She knew that he was soused to the gills, and Ike knew she knew, but he felt duty-bound to preserve the amenities, and she, disapproving heartily of drinking men, ignored Ike's deplorable condition as long as it was not conspicuous.

But the Irish were different. When Black Pat Kelly had three drinks in him he sang; two more and he wanted to free old Ireland. Given a few extra snifters to put him away, he started home crying piteously or perhaps singing or maybe just making a loud noise. With good luck, he arrived at his house with strength enough to start a lusty argument with his wife over why supper wasn't ready. As he shouted, he gave his kids a few slaps. A casual family affair of this sort could be heard quite a way, and as the Griffins on one side and the Fullers on the other listened, they shook their heads and remarked that these Irish weren't what you'd call real nice sensible-acting folks. Sometimes Black Pat or a fellow Celt did not manage to get home. In that case, he did not act as Ike Billings would have done. Ike would have gone to sleep peaceably under a tree off to one side of the road.

Oh, no, Black Pat collapsed right in the middle of the road and groaned like a dying man or called loudly for help. Then some disgusted Yankee had to rescue him, drag him home and reassure a few frightened women who were sure that at least a robbery with violence had been committed.

Some other Irish traits came in for milder criticism. Certainly they were not thrifty. Neither were some Yankees, but they did not spend their money quite as irrationally as did the Kellys and Cronins and Donovans. And you never knew what mood these unreliable people would be in. Black Pat might hoe all day in a spell of blackest melancholy, and the next day he'd keep you laughing at his gay talk. It disturbed Yankees to have such changeable people around them. They were more used to a man like Fred Ennis who got mad at his brother one day and never spoke to him again for ten years.

It was when death came to an Irish family that the Anglo-Saxons were most bewildered by strange ways and knew for certain that their neighbors were not of the same blood. Excessive display of emotion embarrassed men and women who did not like to "let go," no matter how grief-stricken they might be. They sympathized with the mourners, but they wanted to show it by doing things like bringing food and seeing to a lot of details. On the day of the funeral, teams were offered to help take people to the cemetery, and when the family got back home, there was a meal waiting for them. Not much was ever said in the way of condolence. If an aged person had died, the words might be, "Well, he lived to a good old age. You can expect it any time when folks get that old." If a younger man or woman had been "taken away," sympathy was even more sparingly expressed, "There isn't much a person can say at such times. Things like this *will* happen!" Not often were religious sentiments offered as comfort. The minister would do that sort of thing in an official way, but there were few amateur expositors of why the Lord tried the spirit of His children. Giving practical help, going to the funeral and grave, and saying enough to let anyone know you "felt for them," were the gestures of respect and sympathy that suited the Yankee character.

But the Irish mourned without restraint and asked that all their friends join them. Although some Yankees were never quite sure that such exhibitions were not "put on," most spectators conceded that it was an expression of genuine sorrow; nevertheless, that concession did not keep them from being acutely embarrassed by the Celtic emotion.

An Irish family and an old Yankee family each loses the oldest boy. Mrs. Henry Moulton may have cried when no one but Henry saw her, but the rest of the time she plunged tight-lipped into the work of preparing for the funeral. Yankee women have been known to clean all the woodwork in a ten-room house in the forty-eight hours between the death and burial of a loved one. The day of the funeral, Mrs. Moulton cooked until it was time to dress. Norah Kelly came in that morning and wanted to cry with the other mother, but the Yankee woman cut her short. "If you want to do something to help," she said, "you can wash up those dishes in the sink."

That was how it was between the Celts and the Yankees. They were two different races with separate ways of acting and expressing themselves, and it was inevitable that they should never rightly understand each other. Consequently, there were few intermarriages and little close friendship between the old and the new people. This inability to meet each other on the same emotional level did not mean that the two people could not live and work together as citizens.

From the very first, the folkways of the towns began their work of influencing the foreigners. No one person told them what they should or should not do; no set of rules or regulations was handed them. Of course, they were given definite help if they needed it. If, for example, a new property owner did not know about deeds and such matters as assessment blanks and school district taxes, someone set him right. But most of the Celt's education was conducted by more or less violent contacts with proper local behavior, the unfortunate Celt almost always learning how a good townsman acted by being told that he was not doing so. For instance, he found out that he must repair his half of the fence between his pasture and Ed Griffin's corn field; otherwise Mr. Griffin would shoot his cattle. It took him a long time to realize that the irate Yankee had no intention of shooting any cow or young critter, but he did learn that "good fences make good neighbors." In the same thoroughly roundabout Yankee fashion, he was taught to do such things as help out a neighbor in distress even if he hated that neighbor, refrain from bodily violence at all times, pay his taxes promptly, restrain his eloquence in town meeting, and, in short, behave as a decent citizen.

The Celts learned rapidly. They never lost their emotional fervor or their instinctive distrust of a dour, restrained people, but they were pretty fair townspeople before the last old man who spoke Erse had been buried in alien soil. The town might seem to be slipping, yet it was strong enough to put its imprint on the virile newcomers and mold them into its pattern as far as it needed to do so. Of course, it did not bother to change the Celts' private lives if these did not interfere with the town's efficiency, but it gently and firmly turned them into reasonable facsimiles of sensible dwellers in a tight little Yankee community.

The town showed its strength in another way; for better or worse it refused to allow the newcomers to create from Celt and Yankee a new race. Perhaps the thin blood of many a family would have been richer after a transfusion from healthy, fresh, peasant stock; and perhaps a Yankee boy was a fool for not choosing a gay, laughing colleen instead of a drab, colorless Anglo-Saxon girl. But then again he may have been obeying a law of his race. Perhaps he and others like him felt, for they could not have reasoned it out for themselves, that they must fulfill their destiny, whatever it was to be, with the strength or weakness that was in them. For generations Yankees had not called for outside aid; it was too late now to begin.

Those were the years when the towns and little cities stopped branching out, with the years the mold of tradition hardened and folkways became tyrants even as they allowed a conformist to lead a comfortable life. The real test was to come when the town limits expanded because people could go far on new roads, and more foreigners and city folks came, and the state and federal governments began to take over old town rights. Then the town found out whether it was as weak and conformable as it seemed to be, or whether there was still in its people some of the strength that had built a sound way of life.

CHAPTER 8

Today

WHEN the twentieth century dawned, Town Meeting Country was in a bad way indeed, yet today it is still strong. Its folkways have been tested and have proved worthy to survive. For instance, because my people built a custom called "having town meetings" and clung to it and only changed it slowly as the situation demanded, that custom is now helping the little towns and cities to retain their ancient heritage. True, of course, there have been some defeats and many more compromises, but the small cities and the hill towns are once more showing the world what a sound unit of living can be.

Sumner of Yale once wrote of all folkways, "They are the function of society and are developed unconsciously." A people makes its unit of life work in a certain manner because of social habits and traits specifically its own. It builds up these folkways without saying deliberately: "We will act thus"; "We will not do this or that"; "We must behave in this way." Instead, all peoples are plastic material acted upon and molded by the variety of influences and necessities in their daily existence.

Those truths are once more evident in the victory of this region over adverse influences. Today it boasts new strength because, deep beneath the apparent lethargy and the weak conformity, beneath the worship of the comfortable, there were folkways which could serve as guides to strong and sensible living. These ways of thought and action were not created consciously by theorists, philosophers, self-styled idealists, or politicians. They grew out of Indian fighting, religious quarrels, bothersome Quakers, bundling, original sin, stones in the fields, bad climate, many little rivers, tall wiry men, strong-breeding women, looms, spinning wheels, grist and saw mills, notions in a peddler's pack, district schools, dominies with a college education, Yankee cussedness, town bounds, rum, slaves, whale oil, clipper ships, privateering, hard bargains, and a dollar picked up here and there not to be spent except to keep young Jeremiah in college.

Out of these elements of the Yankee scene and dozens more like them stem our folkways. Once they seemed futile and too subservient to tradition. Now, in the fifth decade of the twentieth century, we know that they were valid and functional; that they had helped people to live and could help them again.

Railroad Street

Studies of towns must be something more than tables and graphs. Towns must be described in general terms too, and sometimes with symbol and allegory. Our New England towns or cities are the result of slow changes and developments starting so long ago that ample records and statistics were never kept. That is why I prefer to start talking of Town Meeting Country today by telling you about Railroad Street.

As late as only a quarter of a century ago, life in any small city of Town Meeting Country was as serenely beautiful as the last hours of an October day in the New England hills, one of those Indian summer afternoons when a golden haze softens grim neo-Puritan profiles, and the toughest-fibered man goes across the street for a pint. Those were the days when a few prophets wailed that the old juice had gone out of the Yankees. But no one listened.

Small wonder that men felt secure and contented! A sound Republican Party and its economy still reigned, N.Y., N.H., and H. common stock was gold-plated, and if a man earned an honest dollar, it wasn't taken away from him by taxes. Above all else, there were those nice, comfortable, soothing, ritualistic gestures of daily life which made a citizen realize that God was in His chosen corner of the Six Sacred States, and all was well. Such little factors helped to make small city life the satisfying thing it seemed, and there was none more potent than the gracious charm of Railroad Street.

Thirty years ago each little New England metropolis had such a fine block, contributing in its way to the joy of living. A young fellow of good family, a solid business man, or anyone who liked a nip and a bit of sporty life would have been hard-pressed without it. For such mild adventurers, the low saloons and hangouts across the tracks were forbidden. And the Old Guard of plutocratic Yankees at the Hooker House Bar did not like to be disturbed. But Railroad Street was democratic; it was lively without being tough; it filled all decent and reasonable needs. In that short block you could get a spot of whisky, or a cool glass of beer, a game of pool, a bit of something to eat, a glance at a newspaper and *The Police Gazette,* and, best of all, some good satisfying talk about the way the semi-pro nine was rounding up or the dire results of the low tariff.

Railroad Street was the boy's first safe step into the brave life of manhood; it was the rural visitor's first and last taste of city pleasures; it was the average citizen's cafe, club, and Times Square.

The Railroad Street I knew was in Willimantic, Connecticut. No city could have afforded a more perfect setting. Just the proper size, around twelve thousand, it was a prosperous little place where people could spare a few coins for mild dissipation. And there was the right proportion of sober Yankees to the more volatile Irish and French of the community. Willimantic was the place where travelers changed trains, and the shopping center for people within a radius of twenty miles. It was, in fact, the sort of city that needed and could support a good Railroad Street.

That short block ran due south down a little slope from Main Street to the N.Y., N.H., and H. tracks. The east side of the street was dead. There was nothing over there but a plumbing shop, the office and store rooms of a trucking firm, and a small, semi-basement establishment that changed hands every few months. Once a Greek started a restaurant there, but it died for lack of customers. It would never have occurred to Willimantic people to walk down that side of Railroad Street unless they wanted to see the plumber or Jim Murphy the trucker.

But the west side was perfect for business and pleasure. For one thing, the sidewalk met the depot platform, while over east it stopped abruptly at the tracks. That fact meant a lot to the west-side proprietors. Men who came and went on the trains dropped in for a paper, a sandwich, or a quick drink. More leisurely customers could keep their feet on the rail until the 3:30 pulled in and not have to waste any time at the smelly depot.

Then, too, it was part of the business of the day for a lot of citizens to look over the railroad transportation situation and, of course, they stopped somewhere on Railroad Street for a rest and a bracer before they climbed the steepest part of the slope. On this west side, the climatic conditions were better than over east, too. There the winds blew and the sun beat down and the rains came, but here it was cool of a summer afternoon and warm of a winter morning, and hardly any gusts of rain disturbed an habitué as he took his breath of fresh air.

No. 1 Railroad Street was the Elite Cafe, Jerry Maloney proprietor. You had to go down five steps to get into the Elite, but it was no basement boozing den. A trifle dark perhaps, but cool in summer, snug in winter, it was the spiritual home of some of Willimantic's best thinkers. Even the Hooker House could not boast of sounder conversation. In the morning the Elite was almost deserted except for one or two sedate barflies who disdained more casual saloons. Jerry served them with flawless courtesy and listened to their recipe for a morning pick-me-up. By ten or eleven o'clock, a few more leisurely citizens had arrived for a drink and a quiet word about the state of the nation. Jerry made no profit on such customers; in fact, some never paid a cent, but he took a deep pride in knowing that they looked upon his cafe as a refuge from a buffeting world.

From midday until the late-afternoon trains pulled out, Jerry had quite a few conservative rural clients. Such men were awed by the Hooker House, and the Natchaug Bar was too obviously a saloon, but when they slipped into No. 1 they were not "drinking men"; they were warding off a chill or doing something for that tired feeling. To such men, the Elite was a friendly hospice, and Jerry Maloney the soothing and wise family doctor.

By the time the mills let out, Jerry's helper, Jack Mulcahy, was on the job, helping to serve a lot of veteran mechanics and foremen who wanted a drink and a bit of good talk before they went home.

But the evenings were the Elite's pride. By seven or half past, the bar was lined with the city's Elder Irish Statesmen. Some were prosperous, others shabby and bent with work. But here all were equal; a hodcarrier's words on Wolfe Tone were listened to respectfully by P. C. McGuire, owner of the best livery stable in town and once-time mayor, and, in turn, P. C.'s remarks on the dire consequences of marrying out of the Church won a nod from his friend the hodcarrier. The Elite was a place where the brother of a bishop could find good company and the right sentiments.

Occasionally a few heretics in race, religion, and politics dropped into No. 1 in the course of an evening. They might be strangers attracted by its cheery glow, or perhaps they were citizens who liked Jerry's beer, a special brew he proudly imported from Hartford. Such men were never treated exactly as intruders. Room was made at the bar and their views on the weather accepted, but the Celts never let it be forgotten that the Elite evenings belonged to them. Afternoons it might be more cosmopolitan, but after seven P. M. it was a bit of the old country and a haven from strange notions.

No. 2 Railroad Street was Sam Henry's Pool and Billiard Parlor. From ten in the morning until after midnight, thin, pale men with coats off, vests unbuttoned, and sleeves rolled half to the elbow practiced trick shots or ran off endless games in this smoke-filled Temple of Sport. A cigarette dangling from the lower lip, eyes those of an ascetic, such men never seemed to sleep or work. The ivory ball and the cue were jealous gods and demanded all a man's energy. Sam Henry himself was the high priest of the cult, most austere and exacting of all. Yet he was a kindly man who let beginners use the rear table, and he often told a veteran to give a likely lad a few lessons. Many a Willimantic boy hit his first spheroid at No. 2 and could rejoice in later years that he had received a sound basis of instruction.

The Bright Spot Saloon was next door. Joe Smith ran it as the sort of place where the sporting crowd could get together and talk over the Windham High teams, the semi-pro nine, who had a 2/15 pacer, or how the local Young Corbett's left jab was shaping up. The Pool and Billiard Parlor was dedicated to one sport, and its guests worked hard to perfect themselves, but at the Bright Spot you merely talked knowingly or listened to the specialists. One such specialist was Joe himself. As a brawny young fellow, he had put up bare knuckles, London prize-ring rules, against the immortal John L. Sullivan. The battle had lasted one minute and fifteen seconds, but ever after Joe spoke with authority on all matters of training, form, and ring generalship. His assistant, Clem Monroe, had played first base with the

Willimantic Ramblers in the fine old days when that nine could beat Norwich or even Hartford, and now he was the acknowledged leader of the fans. Helping these two were such regular customers as Austin Cummings, expert on horses and harness racing, Gene Paulette, who knew his hunting and fishing, and Harry Walters, ex-high school basketball star. These men kept their fingers on the pulse of the city's sporting life and made the Bright Spot a place where you could hear the latest rumors and ask the soundest opinions. Joe never stood for any "rough stuff," and a solid merchant could drop in for a drink—or to see Austin Cummings about where to pick up a good carriage horse—without risking a bad reputation.

No. 4 was The Railroad Street Restaurant, Art Shores proprietor. It was no doggy place with tables. It had only a row of bulging-arm chairs along each wall and a counter at one end, but Art dished up the best short orders and sandwiches and coffee in the city. There was always someone in the restaurant stowing away a meal or a Western sandwich and hashing over the latest gossip. It was the only place on Railroad Street where women were permitted. That tended to give it a bad name, but Art never let any really loose girls hang around, and most people felt that his little friends added just the right touch to an otherwise strictly masculine setup.

The big place on the street, the one where Celt and Yankee, boy and oldster, sport and philosopher, bum and alderman met, was Danny Dwyer's News Room—"Cold Drinks and Tobacco also sold." Danny was mayor of the city whenever he felt like assuming the honor, or was not already busy being state senator or even treasurer, and no one disputed his title of boss of the eastern Connecticut Democratic machine. For all that, he was a tolerant man, and plenty of Republicans came to the News Room. Danny's two clerks, Mike Bannon and Patsy O'Hara, really managed the business and let His Honor spend his time talking. A fat little fellow with a red face, Danny was devoted to his city, pouring time and thought into the job of making it a nice place to live in.

Plenty of men thought a week incomplete if they did not drop into the News Room two or three times for a few cigars and some gossip. Others made it a habit to pick up their newspapers there every day. Efficient wives might complain about wasted time . . . why not have the paper delivered? . . . but their husbands liked that five minutes of contact with the real inner life of the city. The News Room was also the hangout for the high-school sports who were too young to go to the Bright Spot. A brisk young fellow who was on one of the teams was always sure of a little pleasing attention and a chance to talk about the prospects of trimming Norwich Free Academy next Saturday. Several citizens who enjoyed complete relaxation from work kept abreast of the times by a glance at Danny's newspapers. That kindly man never kicked them out; in fact, he often passed them an occasional dime so that they could buy a drink at the Elite and enjoy once more the company of their peers. They, in turn, called him "Your Honor" too and behaved like the broken-down gentlemen they were. Even Terence McGovern remembered not to kick up a row in the News Room after that last nightly drink.

No. 6, and the last place on Railroad Street, was Ernie Grigg's Natchaug Bar. Of the three saloons in the block, this was the most cosmopolitan. For one thing, the proprietor was not a professional Celt like Jerry Maloney of the Elite, or a devotee of sport like the Bright Spot's Joe Smith. These two men were polite to each and to every customer, but they preferred those who talked their subjects. Ernie had no favorites, no hobbies, and apparently not even many emotions save his pride in mixing a good drink and running a clean, quiet saloon. A slim, tall man with cold blue eyes, he dispensed drinks and a noncommittal word to clients and then left them alone. His example set the pace for the entire bar. You might not feel stimulated there, but sometimes it was soothing to get away from the specialized conversation of the Elite or Bright Spot and take a glass in objective serenity at the Natchaug Bar.

Ernie's clientele was far more varied than that of the other Railroad Street saloons. Travelers changing trains came to the Natchaug for a quick one. The railroad gang stopped in after work, and those mysterious men of every city who are not vagrants, not bums, but equally homeless, made this their rendezvous.

Such was the Railroad Street I knew, a short block with a pool and billiard parlor, a restaurant, a news room, and three saloons. The Hooker House might be more dignified, there were lively fights down on Brick Row, the drinks were more often on the house at Halligan's Corner, and you could meet a blonde at the York Hotel, but Railroad Street habitués were satisfied with their haunts. It was all right, they conceded, for a man to have his fling, and they kicked up their heels at times, too, but they didn't do it where they shouldn't. So the street remained quiet and decent as befitted the spiritual home of a lot of brisk up-standing lads and solid citizens.

Those fifty yards of good fellowship and decent joy have fallen on evil days. Only the Elite has kept any vestige of its old glory, and it has become the Taverne Quebec, serving a fifty-cent dinner and only beer and ale. Don't listen, Jerry Maloney, in your six feet of consecrated soil, but women are served at the tables now and a juke box drowns out the ghostly echoes of the Elder Statesmen who once uttered their deep thoughts here.

No. 2 is empty. In the last five years a dozen little enterprises have leased it, and then folded up after a month or two. Where the Bright Spot wise boys once talked knowingly, a bus line now has its office and waiting room. Tired women and squalling children buy cokes and chocolate bars and never know that a city's sporting life once throbbed on this very spot. Art Shores' restaurant is now a fruit store and, worse of all, Danny Dwyer's News Room stands forlorn and neglected. No. 6 is a magazine, tobacco, and soft-drink place. That is all that is left of the old street, and that little is dreary and sad. Once in a blue moon a Taverne Quebec customer lifts his voice in beery song; then the block sinks back into its apathy.

At first glance the end of Railroad Street is easy to explain. Prohibition and the sad mortality of men helped ruin the little street. All three saloons died when the cold breath of the wowser touched them. Then, in the winter of 1920, Danny Dwyer passed away, and his retainers, Mike and Patsy, hadn't the heart to keep on running the News Room after His Honor had gone. That same spring Art Shores died, and in the fall the medicos told Sam Henry that he must get into the fresh air and sunshine. And so when the Noble Experiment was repealed, Railroad Street was in no shape to stage a comeback. Two of its great men were dead. Another was far away in Arizona. The three who remained were too old or disillusioned to try again.

But there was another reason why Railroad Street had to die.

Willimantic had changed. The automobile had cut down to a mere trickle the steady stream of people who once passed through the block on their way to and from the depot. There had also been a spiritual metamorphosis in the citizens who once talked and drank in the Elite and Danny Dwyer's, for that same difference between the people of 1910 and those of 1940 can be seen all over the Six States.

The change might be summed up as follows: Back in a happy past, Yankees and alien brothers relaxed, not because they were inherently lazy, but because no more was demanded of them. Contrary to all accounts, we New Englanders do not work hard for the sheer joy of doing so. We do so to make money, to get better jobs, or for a dozen other good, utilitarian reasons. When we have got ahead and collected a few dollars, we know enough to take life easy. Of course, we continue to be sensible men and women who get full value for every dollar spent, and more indolent people mistake our carefree moments for ones of intense vigor and application, but the fact remains that we can and do let up a good deal when there is no need for answering the stern voice of duty. That fact is one part of the explanation of why Yankees took life so easy back in the Indian Summer days, and why all their cities had a Railroad Street that was soothingly comfortable. There was no reason why there should *not* be that kind of pleasant existence. That is how simple the explanation is.

The same sort of empirical reasoning tells us why the change came. Yankees woke up and started working because they had to. They were faced with one of those perennial crises that descends on the northeast corner of the nation. Wilderness dangers and hardships, Indians, British, British again, Rebellion, all had been dealt with at one time or another. Now there was a Depression and, therefore, no more loafing around on Railroad Street. Yes, Prohibition helped kill that happy block; so did the automobile. But it would have lived on in some form or other had not the necessity of giving up many comfortable gestures struck the death blow.

When 1929 came, and then the New Deal, Willimantic fared better than some little cities, but just the same it had no time for many leisurely moments in a news room or over a pool table. Loafers and bums were undisturbed, but the respectable middle class was buckling down. Those were the men and young fellows who had made Railroad Street something bigger and better than merely a block with saloons, a pool room, a restaurant, and news room on it. It was the presence of solid citizens and their sons that constituted the difference. When they were too busy to carry on the good old ways, those habits were doomed.

That is the essential point to be remembered about the 1940 small city of Town Meeting Country: the serenely beautiful, languorous Indian Summer days have gone. They will return, of course, for life in New England, as elsewhere, moves in cycles, but a lusty vigorous spring has followed the winter of our discontent, and city folks are too busy right now to make themselves another Railroad Street.

Small Town

This cannot be the story of the 1944 small town, for these war years are interludes that bring tragedy and pathos without greatly changing the deep-rooted folkways. Jim Holt and Andy Posloski and Fred McGuire go off to war in Italy or the Pacific, and at least one family in every three is sorrow-stricken before the war is over. But taxes are assessed fairly, town meetings held, and justice decreed even if these boys and others are away and, if Jim or Andy is killed, other soldiers will come back to go on being good citizens. They may be a little more given to drinking and to moody fits of temper than they were before, but they will make pretty good town officers and help support their churches. So I shall try to forget that my town is strange and troubled these years. I shall write of her as she was before this war and as she will be again after it is over.

In some ways, the town is very much as it was a hundred or even two hundred years ago. The two ranges of hills with the half-mile-wide strip of river lowlands between, the swamps and meadows, the outcroppings of ledges, the little brooks have not changed. The sacred town boundaries are just as they were.

Some of the stone walls have been taken away to the crusher to make foundations for the black-top roads that took the place of the old dirt ones, but plenty of other walls stand as firm as when they were laid with sweat and profanity and rum by the old Puritans.

The burying grounds are as austerely neat and beautiful as

ever, and the village street still runs along the crest of the west line of hills at the place where the valley is deepest and narrowest. Maybe half the houses on the street and out on the roads are the same as ever, only a little more rundown in some cases and better painted in others. A few more cellar holes have begun to be hidden by those final conquerors, the lilacs. But, take it all in all, the physical aspect of my town has not changed much. Abiel Durkee, who died in 1810, would still recognize it if he came back. Of course, he'd be worried about why the road to the village goes right through Elisha Fuller's barnyard, but he could find his way around.

Different People

Although the houses and the fields are the same as in the old days, the people are not. There are two hundred-odd dwellings in town. Perhaps one-fourth of them belong to city folks; of the remaining hundred and fifty, at least one-third are owned by people who were born in another country or whose parents came here as immigrants. In between these obvious aliens and the old New Englanders are the Irish. Though they are obviously not of the original stock of the town, some are two and three generations removed from Ireland, and they never think of themselves as foreigners any more.

All these people, Poles, Italians, Finns, French-Canadians, Bohemians, and half a dozen other races, are legally part of the town, and most of them quite readily learn to take part in its politics, organizations, in fact, in every activity that is not directly connected with the Protestant church.

People who come to our town for the summer cannot understand this adoption of the alien by the town, and his capacity for learning to be the same kind of citizen as Hen Moseley and Sam Hunt. They know that Anton Wosmensky has bought the old Harrington place, and they tell Hen Moseley that it's too bad such things happen and isn't it awful how the old-timers are being crowded out of their own town. Hen agrees that he does sort of wish Fred Harrington's boys had wanted to carry on the old farm after Fred died, and it *is* kind of a shame the way the old families are petering out, but even so, probably this new Polack'll turn out all right. Take his brother, the one who bought the Upton place five, six years ago; he ain't a bad citizen in many ways. Got on the school board for the Democrats this fall, and probably he'll be the third selectman next election.

"But you'd rather have a Yankee in those offices, wouldn't you, Mr. Moseley?" insists the city dweller.

Thus driven to the wall, Hen admits that probably, take it by and large and making reservations for the cussed no-count fellows that crop up in every nationality—"and mind you that other Wosmensky man is a damned good farmer"—it might be better if somebody "we was what you might call used to" was in those places. Then he hastens to qualify such direct and unguarded statements.

"Don't get it into your head," he cautions, "that fellows like that Wosmensky ain't fair-to-middlin' citizens. Of course, I don't go to his house the way I do to Seth Osgood's an' my wife don't see anything of his wife. An' furthermore I don't approve of some of their ways, such as workin' most of Sunday and havin' their women folks help with the hoein' and milkin'. But the way I look at such things don't keep me from giving them Polacks their just and rightful due and sayin' they don't make half-bad citizens."

The funny part of this reaction to the "foreigner" is that the critical city man will, within a year, be calling on the Mr. Wosmenskys for aid, asking them to sell him all sorts of things as well as to plow the spring garden, haul rocks and manure, and in general be father confessor and rural cicerone. But Hen Moseley will be going along as before, granting that Anton Wosmensky seems to be a pretty fair citizen, nevertheless one with some rather peculiar habits.

That is rural New England for you in its most puzzling dual aspects, aspects that baffle non-Yankees and almost all city dwellers. Out in the little towns we can approve of an alien as a citizen and grant him complete rights in that capacity. We can also ignore him socially, and for generations refuse to marry his people or let him come closer to us than he does as a legally constitued fellow citizen.

As I have intimated, many people cannot understand our way of accepting and yet rejecting the alien in blood, religon, and politics. They think that when we accept a man as our equal in town meeting we should take him into our parlor and let our sons marry his daughters. A New England town is not run that way, for a town is a complex group of people with many divergent social ways, held together by mores that define communal behavior. And just as the individual has prejudices, so the townsman has principles. That is the way the foreigners have come to town and been accepted.

Of course, all has not been harmony. We have had unbelievably crude and dirty peasants, some of them almost as bad as the neo-Puritan Gulls and certainly more given to loud and raucous drinking. And some have repaid New England justice and tolerance by showing us a few tricks of chicanery. But on the whole the aliens have been willing pupils as the town has taught them how to live in it. The methods of teaching were just the same as the ones employed to teach the Irish; no direct admonition, just plain example and, if that didn't work, a little discipline.

The way the aliens once poured into town it looked as if they would soon overrun the old Yankee stock. But the balance of the population is about the same as it was ten years ago, and looks as if it will remain so for a long time. For although the foreigners have more children than the Anglo-Saxons, the former are pretty likely to go to the nearby mills to work instead of taking up land and developing it for themselves. We old-timers are bolstered by the fact that when a farm goes up for sale, it is more than likely to be bought in by a city man who, although he is prone to get sentimental over aliens, does, in the last analysis, side with us against the newcomers. And if he is on a place, why then a Pole or Italian can't buy it. (In the eyes of some, that fact is the best explanation of why summer folks should not be exterminated.) So, even though we dwindle in numbers, we manage to keep ahead of the aliens, and I believe the time will never come when our folkways are rejected in favor of foreign mores. It may be that, in the year 2050, the defenders of the small town behavior-patterns will be called Wosmensky, Pellitti, Lafleur, O'Hara, or Coupla, but they will still be defending an Anglo-Saxon community. For the old men and women built well; they created folkways that were more than narrowly racial: they were basic and fundamental. The new citizens will be running the town according to the rules slowly and carefully formulated by Elisha Fuller, Ebenezer Griffin, Phillip Pearl, Henry Kenyon,

William Lincoln, Abiel Holt, Christopher Hevey, William Hammond, Jerome Woodward, Henry Button, and hundreds of other men like them.

CITY FOLKS

Town Meeting Country is the best place in New England to observe those strange newcomers, city folks, as they fit into the life of the town. Note that I make a sharp distinction between them and the people who live in the tightly packed rows of cottages from Westport to Point Judity, in a quaint cottage on Cape Cod, in the Maine woods, or at the New Hampshire resort hotels. Such visitors care nothing about the villages and the people around them; or, if they care, find only what they came to find, the "salty humor" of the "staunch, strong, stalwart natives."

It is rumored that up in Vermont the natives still manage to keep the city folks in their place, but after all it's a long way up to that state, and people can't skip out from the city for a weekend quite as easily as they do down here. Besides, there is more room up there, and a disgusted farmer can always find a little relief in soothing solitude. But Town Meeting Country is thickly populated, more or less diminutive in size and, furthermore, close to Hartford, Worcester, and Providence, and not too far from New York. So we suffer more than Vermont ever can do. More people come to us, and there is no room for us to escape them. We have to fit them into our life, go mad, or turn the whole section over to them.

They tell me that the Squire section down southeast is in the hands of the Hound and Horn gang, and, of course, New Hampshire's mountains and Cape Cod went under long ago, but we still manage to run our towns pretty much as we want to. The aliens couldn't capture them; in fact, we turned them into good New England citizens. That is more or less what we aim to do with the new folks on the Trowbridge place; at least we aim to if they are halfway amenable; if not, well, we can ignore and tax them.

City folks cannot be scientifically classified or described; the only way is to sketch their general habits and then wait and see what they will do next. There was the woman in New Hampshire who bought a dozen Guernsey cows. A month later she realized that her herd was biologically incomplete. So she bought a dozen bulls! When I told my next-door neighbor about the twelve happy cows, he was not greatly surprised.

"Person just outa th' city's liable t' have queer notions," he remarked tolerantly.

On the whole, the city folks we get are not too hard to understand, if you want merely a rough working estimate. They are just children playing in an extra large backyard, and they have all the cussedness, charm, and general unpredictability of brats. At least that is what most of the old-towners think of the city folks. There are a few citizens who moan loudly, and mean it, that the place has gone to the dogs, but most of us feel quite kindly toward our new neighbors. However, I am afraid that we would be less lenient if the city folks had not come among us very gradually.

Thirty years ago there were only three families who had summer homes in our town. Plenty of sedate couples and nice spinsters stayed at the Inn, but three houses were all that opened in June and closed after Labor Day; other places were lived in all the time or, if empty, fulfilled that state with authentic emptiness. Two of the transitory families were not actually newcomers, for "his" or "her" parents had come from the town, and the children were taking over their old home for the summer. They knew all about us; our folks had gone to school with theirs, and we did not resent their better clothes on weekdays or their city ways. The members of the third family had no roots in the town and were just plain summer folks.

The year-rounders never paid much attention to these three families. In June they noted casually that the Monroes or Carrs or Allinghams "had come"; in September they took a moment off to notice that the visitors "had closed up." In those days no one thought of city folks as a crop to be cultivated profitably. When a farmer sold them milk or vegetables, he was doing them a favor, not developing a source of revenue. "Come an' get th' stuff if ye want it; I ain't got th' time t' deliver as little an amount as that." Some stern men even went so far as to make customers pick their own peas and ears of corn, but other farmers thought such efficiency was too brutal; besides, the city folks probably trampled down more than they paid for if they were let loose in the garden. It was the same with odd jobs like carting a load of manure or plowing a garden. We gave the three helpless families a distinct gift of our superior skill and more valuable time when we "helped them out." It was a wise city man who first used that phrase "help out," instead of "Come over and do it."

Even the professionally employed carpenter, mason, or painter was not eager to accept summer trade. For one thing, it was liable to be ephemeral. In town a man was sure of a certain group of patrons. Bill Ennis had painted for the Trowbridges ever since Bill was a little shaver helping his father put yellow paint on old Hezekiah Trowbridge's buildings. If Sam Trowbridge had hired Frank Spalding, the other town painter, Bill Ennis would have been genuinely hurt and shocked. But the Monroes or Carrs were different; they hired one man this year and another the next; they even sent to Willimantic for workers, saying openly that the local men weren't good enough.

Then, too, the city folks were fussy and domineering, since they were accustomed to dealing with urban workers who had little spirit and less independence. Suppose Bill Ennis got word that Sam Trowbridge wanted a room papered. "Drop around when you're up this way and bring your books so the woman can pick out what she wants." A week or two later—to have come earlier would show a servile spirit, to wait longer would insult the Trowbridges—Bill Ennis goes up and lets Mrs. Trowbridge pick out the wallpaper. "When'd ye plan on startin'?" asks Sam Trowbridge tactfully. Note that he does not order or even suggest; he allows the worker to set his own time. Bill Ennis does a little mental reckoning. Mrs. Lucy Scott wants her front room done before next week when she has the Ladies Aid, and he's working right now painting a house over in Chaplin. Probably the quickest he can get to it is by the end of next week. In rare instances, the year-round man or woman remonstrates, but ordinarily he or she accepts Bill's verdict. They may suspect that he is sandwiching in a few days of work for someone else, but they assume, and rightly so, that it must be a special case like Mrs. Scott's.

When Bill arrives to paper the room, he is not met by a flustered woman who announces that on second thought that isn't the paper she wants and won't he please come back next Friday for by that time she'll have gone to Hartford and got the paper from Fox's. No, Mrs. Trowbridge has the room ready for him

and agrees that the paper "looks real good." Maybe it isn't quite
as nice a blue stripe as it looked in the book, but you get used
to a thing after you've lived with it a week. Nor does Mrs. Trowbridge try to boss Bill, tell him how to cut his paper, match his
edges, and "look out for that tricky corner around the fireplace."

In those days a good worker was certain that he was an honorable man who could be trusted to turn in a good day's work, and
he was not used to being bossed around by any city man, much
less by a woman. Aside from such temporary difficulties, the city
folks got along fairly well in town. They had a good time; we
ignored them when we weren't obliged to see them; otherwise
we exercised the tactful patience we used with children and
peaceable dimwits.

This period of quiet did not last long. People who had stayed
at the Inn and had come to like the town, decided to own their
own summer homes. Then their friends came and admired, and
the next year they, too, were looking for a place. Today more
than one quarter of the two hundred-odd houses in town are
owned by city folk. "Summer" is not quite the right word to use
in describing them, for a few stay in town all the year round,
and others from early May until after Thanksgiving. But at any
rate these fifty or sixty houses are distinctly not occupied by people who make their living in the town. Oh, yes, the visitors may
tell us that Hampton, Woodstock, Brooklyn, or Dudley is
"home" to them and that they are happy only there, and at the
moment they probably mean what they say, but the town rightly
considers them outsiders. That last statement needs qualifying.
You remember there were some summer families whose ancestors had been true townspeople. Such people may live most
of the time in Hartford or Providence; nevertheless, the year-
rounders think of them as a little more at home here than the
run-of-the-mine city visitor.

It is these raw newcomers who have to learn how to fit into
the sensible life of the community. As in the case of the foreigners, no one ever lectures them on behavior; we simply let
them find out what they ought to do. Take the question of property rights. Strange to say, let some law-abiding city folk get out
in the country and they seem to think that they can run hog-
wild. For instance, a jolly little group goes blueberrying. Everyone is carefree and so happy to be out in the open fields where

you can do as you please. Pretty soon they see some likely bushes in the corner of a field near the road, and with glad cries they climb over the wall and start filling their pails. Five minutes later a stern, but not too indignant, voice demands, "What ye doin' here?"

The spokesman of the pickers remarks casually that they are picking berries.

"Get permission?" asks the visitor.

"Why, no."

"Didn't think it was necessary, did ye?"

A young matron is not amused by the sarcasm.

"Certainly we didn't think it was necessary," she declares. "Here are all these berries, and nobody is using them."

The farmer draws a deep breath and tells himself that he is a gentleman talking to ladies and, possibly, to people who are not quite all there.

"Didn't ever hear of a big fam'ly needin' some t' eat an' more t' can, did ye?" he enquires. "An' it never struck ye a man could pick his own berries an' sell 'em?"

This indirect and therefore authentic Yankee explanation does not impress the city folks; in fact, one or two of them continue to pick berries. However, a man who prides himself on getting along with all sorts of people does condescend to admit to the farmer that possibly they were theoretically in the wrong and, if he insists, they will pay him for the berries they have picked. This is the last straw, and the trespassers are told to get off somebody else's property. How this command is worded depends upon the character and disposition of the embattled farmer, but in every case the city folks understand and depart.

That is how nine out of ten farmers handle such a case. The tenth may be a thoroughly bad-tempered fellow, or one who has suffered too much from city folks. He forthwith proceeds to do two things: he orders them off his land; he calls the state police and has them arrested for all the misdemeanors he can think of. Before the justice of the peace, the astonished city folks are given a reading from the law and made to pay a few dollars in fine and costs.

Whether the berrypickers are simply put off the land or are arrested, all the town soon hears of their disgrace. Paradoxically enough, year rounders are the more sympathetic. Their attitude is one of firm parenthood which punishes, but without sadistic joy, and really hopes that the punished will learn his lesson. Of course, a few reactionary farmers and artisans assert that the whole damned crew of city folks ought to be shut up, and look at how they act, and see how the town's going to the dogs since they came. But such reactions are seldom met, and on the whole the culprit family can expect tolerance and merciful silence from the real citizens of the town.

His own friends, the other city folks, are a different proposition. If he remarks bitterly that these damned farmers are definitely anti-social in their attitude, he is given the Bronx cheer, or the more polite reminder that after all he really had no business on that man's property, and certainly he ought to know that fruit is not common property, even if you meet it out in the open. The disgraced man probably moans that he expected better treatment from the townspeople. Some brutal friend expresses what was left unsaid: "You thought these 'natives,' as you call them, would look up to you and treat you as something special, didn't you?" he asks.

The offended man asserts vehemently that he had no such idea, but he protests too much, and everybody knows he is lying; that is, they know it if they have lived five years in a country town and have an I.Q. of over eighty. For they, too, had that same delusion when they came here. They thought they would be adored and allowed all privileges by a humble and forelock-pulling peasantry. They had to learn that living even for a month in a country town is a matter of obeying laws as scrupulously as you would in the city; furthermore, it entails a profound respect for a great many unwritten laws and ways of behavior. In short, they had to realize that people live in this community, and living in peace and security among other people means that you yourself are an integral part of the social structure and not a selfish rebel. All those ideas and some others the freshman summer family learns, and before September rolls around even little Junior hesitates momentarily before he raids that raspberry patch.

Although the newcomers do learn to leave all obviously private property alone, not a summer passes for many years without other lessons in how they should behave. Eventually they learn that cows walk through bars left down or gaps made in a fence;

that oats and grass are hard to cut after being trampled down; that cows do not give more milk after being chased by dogs and small boys; and that hens are nervous creatures. They learn slowly that a farm is a delicately adjusted mechanism of production and not the jolly playground they thought it was. About the only parts of the farm that can take care of themselves and actually go on the offensive are bulls and poison ivy. Poetic justice has been wrought on more than one supercilious city family by a sour-spirited Jersey sire and some beautiful green leaves. Of course, bulls and poison ivy also humble rural people, and skunks, too, are impartial, but these doughty representatives of country prowess have far greater opportunities when summer explorers are around.

Now and then a stout character buys a summer house and resolves to admit of no power greater than his own. In the city he is a sensible fellow who respects all potential dangers and would not think of setting himself up as stronger than they. But let him out of the urban limits, and he is infuriated by the mere hint that he is not master of all he surveys. He bought this place and paid good money for it, and, by God, he is boss of whatever comes along! Of course, he does not express his philosophy in that direct manner, but that is the spirit in which he meets rural life. "I'm a city man, and you're nothing but a country skunk, or bull, or patch of ivy, and you'd better remember your station in life." Such a challenger's experiences are inevitably written in bandages, salve, and disinfectants, but does he capitulate? Does he surrender to the ignoble enemy? Not by a damn sight! He fights on bravely. It is almost unbelievable the amount of punishment such a neo-Puritan can take and still go on at least tactily asserting that he is master of his soul. There are stories of men, and women too, for the latter are easily infuriated by the assumption of power by rural forces, who have spent a whole decade in defiance of the humiliating facts that every summer they swell up and itch, that they are scratched by thorns, that a skunk is under the barn and does not like their dog and cat, and that squirrels, rats, and mice invade the house. Such people almost always leave the country before they surrender. They evacuate with their own equivalent of colors flying, and assert valiantly that they are still in love with country life, but . . . and here follows a good excuse. So back to the city they go, their spirits bruised but still defiant.

Another important lesson city folks have to learn is how to get along with the natives. Men and women who act sensibly and with more or less kindly tact when they meet their social inferiors in the city are fairly liable to turn into Lords and Ladies of the Manor as soon as they buy a Cape Cod cottage in extreme disrepair and five brush-clad acres. There's something about owning one's own land that brings out the hidden desires in us, and one of them is the deep longing to act like a pompous fool in our relations with the yokels around us.

A few inherently kindly and amiable women trot about with jelly and old clothes to needy natives, lecture women on diet and sanitation, or start a Village Beautiful Society. But the more normal procedure is to avoid such altruistic efforts and merely to order all natives around in a firm and uncompromising tone. It is conceded that Lord and Lady Smith must avoid open discourtesy and tyranny in their contacts with the peasantry, but they insist that they be obeyed, and that right smartly. Any other little gestures of recognition of the manorial station are welcomed.

In some parts of New England, yes, even of Connecticut and Rhode Island, two proverbially cussed states, the natives play the game just the way Lord and Lady Smith desire. Of course, they can never catch the tone of admiring servility that some sections of a democratic country achieve, but they do manage to produce an attitude that does not openly tell the city folks that they are in town on sufferance.

But up in my country we are a stiff-backed people; we refuse to kowtow, touch the forelock, and say, "Yes, sir." Of course, it has been hard to preserve our integrity. We look at the Bronx and Broadway Squire region down around Greenwich and see the forehead-bumpers cash in on the triple prices they can charge for everything as long as they are faithful family retainers. After that we go into solemn conclave with our souls and the ghosts of a strong past, and we emerge determined to live as if we were as good as anybody else and probably a damn sight better.

When a potential Lord or Lady of the Manor comes to Town

Meeting Country, he at once runs into what is called "the cussedness of the natives." Generally, the first trouble arises over the way to get a farmer or artisan to do something. Let us say that some more stones are needed for the terrace at Far View, the manorial home of Mr. and Mrs. J. Humphrey Smith of Worcester. Far View was the old Carey place before it was rechristened, and the Smiths bought it three months ago. When Mr. Smith is told by the stone mason that the stones are needed that afternoon, Mr. Smith hies himself to the farm of Joe Tillinghast, the man who brought the first load. Mr. Smith had noticed then that Mr. Tillinghast seemed a bit crude and abrupt in his manner, but Mr. Smith never suspects that any native would dare be openly rebellious.

At the Tillinghast farm, Mr. Smith raps on the kitchen door. That was his first mistake. Intimate friends can use that door; others must make the gesture of formality and take the side one. It would have been even better for Mr. Smith to have been laughed at for trying the tightly closed front door. Mrs. Tillinghast answers the peremptory summons and gives Mr. Smith a cold, dour look.

"I want to see Joe," announces Mr. Smith, who imagines that all natives are delighted by being called by their first names by such as he.

"Mr. Till'n'st is out at the barn, or he *was* last I saw of him," answers Mrs. Tillinghast with the air of one who is not interested in locating her husband or having the stranger locate him. Then she goes back to work. Mr. Smith is almost indignant at this treatment, but he soon remembers the well-known fact that all country people are very diffident when in the presence of their urban superiors. Mr. Tillinghast is found under the barn, filling a manure spreader. Mr. Smith halts a discreet ten yards away and calls: "Oh, I say, Joe!" His words are an obvious request, even command, for the laborer to quit work and come out and talk in more pleasant surroundings, but Joe gives a casual glance and a "Hi, there!" Mr. Smith waits. Mr. Tillinghast shovels manure; Mr. Smith surrenders and comes to the shed.

"I want a load of flat stones this afternoon, by one or half-past, if you can."

That "if you can" is tactful and gracious according to Mr. Smith's way of thinking. Mr. Tillinghast disagrees violently, but he does not show his resentment at being ordered around; to do so would be to lose his advantage, so he pretends to think a moment.

"Can't do it t'day," he decides. "Busy haulin' out manure."

Mr. Smith preserves the outward dignity of one born to command.

"The stone mason will have used up all the stones by noon," he explains. "If a load isn't there soon after one, he will not be able to go on working."

"Can't see how I can oblige ye," asserts Mr. Tillinghast. That "oblige ye" is lost on Mr. Smith, who decides that it is time to stop all this nonsense.

"I must have those stones this afternoon," he states. That is the way to deal with these natives, he tells himself. Be firm. Let them know you won't stand for any monkey business.

"Need them stones this afternoon, do ye?" inquired Mr. Tillinghast with the pleased interest of one who hears of this bit of news for the first time. Mr. Smith decides that he has won.

"Yes, I must have them, and by . . ."

"If that's th' case, I guess ye'd better get somebuddy else," interrupts Mr. Tillinghast casually. His whole air has been, and continues to be, one of serene good nature in the face of a mildly irritating blow-fly. There are several other approved methods of dealing with this kind of situation, but he has found that this one works as well as any.

Squire Smith is surprised and hurt.

"But I must have those stones!" he states.

"Plenty of other trucks in town," says Mr. Tillinghast with supreme indifference.

"But you brought the other load, and I was relying on you," says Mr. Smith reproachfully. He has heard of the myth of the faithful native who took the city man's burden upon his shoulders so efficiently and so gratefully.

"Happened t' be free that time," explains Mr. Tillinghast. "Ordinarily I can't be bothered with such little jobs."

This description of the all-important task of working on Far View is an insult to Mr. Smith, but by now he is beginning to realize that he has been defeated, or at least will be if he continues to talk to this native in the approved squirish manner. For Mr. Smith, although he has acted more or less like a fool ever since he came to town, is really a sensible fellow and will make a good town dweller when he has been educated to our folkways.

So Mr. Smith surrenders. And he does so with that complete and abject totality that so often marks the city man's capitulation. "If you can't do it, who can I get?" he begs humbly.

Mr. Tillinghast smiles to himself, but his outward mien is as casual as ever. However, he does consent to stop work and meditate. Just the same, he does not intend to let this smart city man off so easily.

"Damned if I know who you could get for a job like that. Breaks up a man's whole day. Bill Griggs might do it with that broken-down ol' outfit of his, but he sprained his back last week. As I say, I can't think who you could get."

Mr. Smith, now completely beaten and humble, moans piteously that if he doesn't have stones the stone mason will have to be paid for doing nothing, for Smith can't let him go since he is the only man available for miles around. Mr. Tillinghast relaxes a little. He has made the city man realize that his work is a nuisance and not a blessing to be sought. Furthermore, he has displayed himself as a freeborn citizen who respects his own spirit. This being the case, the independent fellow can afford to make a few concessions. So he remembers that Hen Billings most likely might consent to bring a load of stones sometime tomorrow. Squire Smith makes one last stand: he must have those stones this afternoon, and why can't this Billings man . . . ? Mr. Tillinghast cuts in on the protest and assures Mr. Smith that even Hen Billings, who ain't quite as driven by work as some folks—even he ain't ready to drop everything and haul a load of stones.

"But you can call him up when you get home and see what he says," finishes the now very affable and helpful Mr. Tillinghast. Squire Smith plays with the idea of trying just once more to command this surprisingly strong-minded native, but he relegates it to the realm of other pleasant fancies.

"Thank you for helping out, Mr. Tillinghast," he says in a humble voice.

"Don't mention it," says Mr. Tillinghast cordially. "Glad to help out a neighbor any time I can. An' if Hen Billings can't haul them stones, and ye can wait till day after t'morrer, why mebbe I can bring ye a truckload of 'em. I ain't promisin', mind ye, an' do as ye see fit, but mebbe if things turn out right I could snatch an hour or two, seein' ye're in trouble."

Mr., no longer Squire, Smith's future relations with his neighbor Mr. Joseph Tillinghast now hang in the balance. If he refuses this kind offer of help and tries to persuade Hen Billings to bring the stones, there will never be another chance to secure Mr. Tillinghast as a helper, adviser, and general guide and expert in the tricky business of keeping up a country home. For Mr. Tillinghast will be mortally offended by that refusal and go around telling how that city man up the road wants people to drop everything and wait on him hand and foot. It does not matter that Mr. Tillinghast told Mr. Smith to get Hen Billings; Mr. Smith should have known that Mr. Tillinghast would help him out.

If Mr. Smith has a sudden burst of intuition, or if his guardian angel whispers to him, or if he is so worn out he can't think of battling with another rural Yankee, he may say gratefully, "That's real kind of you. I don't know what I'd 've done if it hadn't been for you."

Mr. Tillinghast will then make a few last remarks about being busy, and it's being a damned nuisance to haul rocks, and so on. They will part the best of friends. The stones may arrive that afternoon and, if Mr. Smith is still a wise and discreet man, he will say nothing about the change in plans; instead, he will again thank his neighbor for helping him out of a dire crisis, pay him promptly, give him a drink, and once more speak fervently about the great debt he owes him.

Under these circumstances, Mr. Tillinghast is more or less obliged from now on to do all sorts of odd jobs for Mr. Smith. He will be telling the truth when he swears that he really shouldn't take the time from his farm work, but he does see to it that this helpless but essentially decent city fellow is taken care of. And on his part, Mr. Smith is supposed to rely on Mr. Tillinghast, follow his advice, wait for him to do jobs when he sees fit to do them, and in general submit to a firm and fatherly guidance. Now and then it will occur to Mr. Smith that instead of his being the Squire, and Mr. Tillinghast the peasant or, at best, the yeoman, he is little more than a small boy visiting his country cousin. He then decides that a good neighbor is worth more

than the joy of feeling like a Lord of the Manor. He is con-
firmed in his decision by the fact that by now he has realized this
section of New England does not take kindly to the Squire, Pa-
troon, Ol' Massa, Big House, Manor idea; in fact, it insists that
city folks conform to a large and loosely stated number of folkways, or else spend their days in a conflict with the despised natives which will inevitably end in defeat for the proud family in
the Hall.

There is another variety of summer visitor that has to be
dealt with. He, or oftener she, is gracious and peaceful by nature,
but she raises more trouble in a quiet town than three Manorial
Lords. I refer, of course, to the reformer who starts some sort
of a campaign to do something for the town. There is no telling
what will be advocated: possibly lower taxes, another road, new
schoolhouses, new privies for the old schoolhouses, signs for the
roads, flower beds anywhere, electric lights on the Street, none
of those glaring lights on the quaint old common, better selectmen and representatives, an Old Home Day, a new fire engine,
or a communal center, a comfort station, or any one of a thousand things the fertile brain of woman can think of. Every year
there is liable to be one such person in each town. In fact, a community raps on wood and expects the worst if three, or even
two, years pass without a wave of reform. Then, sure enough, the
spinster schoolteacher or the librarian who bought the old Utley
place and fixed it up as a summer home, gets the idea that a little
urban enterprise and vision are needed in "this dear, quaint
village, and of course I love every inch of it and everybody, but
just the same there is no denying the fact that the natives are a
little bit conservative and behind the times, not very eager to
accept new ideas, and I really do believe that it is our bounden
duty to show them how they can make their splendid beautiful
town even more glorious to live in than it is now."

Another, but somewhat rarer variety of reformer, is the man
who has built a home in town, and now decides to run the
town's affairs. He is always a citizen of complete honesty and
great would-be helpfulness; he is also kindly, generous, and
sympathetic; but he is a born patronizer of rural folk and can
never get it through his head that these humble people and their
ancestors built and have sustained a strong, efficient way of life.
Instead, he openly tells us that we should call upon him to help

us in every possible way. For, as he points out, he is on the Worcester Chamber of Commerce Ways and Means Committee and is very well qualified to advise us about proper community management. A week or two after this offer there has been no response, and the helper decides to wait no longer. Probably these country people are bashful about coming to him. Very well, he'll start a movement of his own.

As soon as the spinster or the business executive starts to help the town, that long-suffering body takes up its favorite defense, a passive resistance that makes Gandhi seem positively violent. Selectmen cannot be found, or they are busy, or very obtuse; or, when driven to the last corner, they begin to talk with great fluency and at the end of five minutes have said that the idea proposed isn't a bad one in some ways, but on the other hand. . . . The non-official citizens are equally evasive. "Yes, the idea seems to be all right in a way, but you can't ever tell how things are going to turn out. You'd better go see what the selectmen have to say about it." All summer long this conflict goes on. The Forces of Progress and Reform talk, plead, scold, orate, and campaign, but by Labor Day they have usually withdrawn to their tents and are sulking in a You'll-be-sorry-you-didn't-let-me-help-you spirit. They are not quite ready to consign the town of their adoption to the dogs, but they feel the moment is not far off.

What happens next depends upon the intrinsic worth of the idea proposed by the reformer. A foolish scheme is soon forgotten; a worthwhile suggestion is adopted after a seemly wait of two or three years. If the latter action is taken, no credit is given to the original proposer unless he or she demands recognition. In this case, the first selectman does remark casually that, come to think of it, some such idea was talked about a few years back but it had slipped his mind who it was thought it up.

When you understand why the town had to refuse to act the first time and why the reforming spinster or business leader had to be defeated, you will know a lot about our protective folkways. The answer to the whole mystery lies in the fact that a town is run by vested authority and not by the vision and imagination of any one person. It is safer to be wrong with legally established selectmen than right with a prophet, and especially one from the city, for a town goes on a long time, and in the end the batting average of selectmen is higher than that of prophets.

These are some of the lessons city folks have to learn before they can live in our town: respect for private property and rights; how to treat us as equals; how not to meddle with town affairs but to cooperate tactfully. If the city man does those few things, the town is his as long as he pays his taxes and bills. That sweeping statement does not mean that he will not be talked about if he paints his house the wrong color, wears too little in public, or commits any or all of a hundred possible follies. However, if he obeys the basic rules of good citizenship, he will escape with the verdict of: "Queer-actin' but means real well, take it all in all."

From this it may seem as if we, the twentieth-century inhabitants of these little New England towns, were the ones who molded raw city folks into good citizens and neighbors. But such is not the case. We merely enforce the rules made by the folkways which have been slowly created and are very wise and strong. It is these that really govern all New England towns.

A Place Is Sold

Even if most of our city folks are turned into pretty fair townspeople by the pressure of our folkways, there is still one good reason why their coming is dreaded.

When they decide to settle down with us, city folks can choose between a farm, or a house and a few acres on the Street. If they take the latter, the economic structure of the town is not disturbed very much. Some old lady goes to live with her folks, or a couple moves away or builds a modern cottage. Part of the land that went with the house is turned into gardens, and the rest is kept mowed by a farmer who takes the hay for his labor. Whoever buys such a place generally fixes it up and keeps it looking well. Of course, it is assessed for more than it was before, and any new taxes always please the town. So, taking it all in all, nobody complains when a place on the Street is sold to city folks.

But when a farm slips out of the hands of the real Yankees, a good many people wonder what is going to become of the town. In a way, of course, they say it is better to have Anglo-Saxon folks around you, but on the other hand if a Pole or a Finn had bought that farm, the life of the town would not have been as much disturbed as it will be now. A town is more than so many human beings; it relies for its strength on people who live in certain ways, produce certain goods and values, and keep alive the old habits of life. The surest way to lose people who will do those things is to have them leave their farms.

Joe Ennis sold his place to some city folks not long ago. He hadn't been planning to do so, but a couple from New York stopped and asked if they couldn't see what the woman called "this dear old house." Joe said he didn't mind, and he and his wife showed the fireplaces and the Dutch oven, and the paneling in the north downstairs bedroom and the wide oak floors. Then the New Yorkers walked around outdoors. They weren't interested in the farm buildings or the crops. Instead, they praised the view to the east and said there were definite possibilities for a flower garden in the south mowing lot!

When the couple came back to the house, the man asked Joe how much he wanted for his place. Joe didn't know what to say. He and his wife had talked once or twice about how much they could get if they decided to sell, but this spring they had made up their minds to hang on to the old house. So now Joe laughed and said he couldn't say offhand how much he'd take. The New Yorker kept on wanting a definite figure, and at last Joe said, "Six thousand dollars." He knew that was a high price, but he wanted to scare these folks away. They said they would think it over and come back the next day. That evening Joe told his wife that they had seen the last of those people, but early the next morning the couple was back again, and the man handed Joe a check to bind the bargain. Another place has been sold to city folks.

Joe Ennis was born on the place he has just sold, and he worked on it until he was twenty-two years old. After he married Alice Holcomb, he was in the Willimantic mills for a few years. Then the old folks began to get feeble, and he and Alice and their two sons came back to the farm. It wasn't one of the biggest in town, about forty acres of tillable land free from stones, perhaps twice as much good pasture, and a big woodlot. Joe kept fifteen cows, and a truck called every morning and carried the milk to Providence. At first he had a good team of horses, but five years ago he bought a tractor and kept one nag for raking and cultivating and such jobs. Of course, he had a couple of pigs every year and thirty or forty hens. The milk he sold brought him in the steadiest revenue. However, he picked up quite a few dollars getting out stove wood or railroad ties, plowing gardens in the spring, selling potatoes and oats, and, when work was slack on the farm, helping to oil the roads or cut brush. But primarily he was a dairy farmer, and every year he added a little to the fertility of his fields and the grazing of the pastures so he could buy another cow and keep her without having to buy too much grain.

As it was, the Ennis farm came very near being a two-man job. Joe did as much of the work as he could, but old Bill Rindge helped with the chores every night, and at haying time Joe hired another man if he could get one. The boys were seven and nine and helped quite a bit already. In a few years they would do so much that Joe could branch out a little and buy more land, or at least rent some from a city man who was letting his fields run out. By the time the boys were grown up, the old Ennis place would be one of the best in town.

And now it was sold to summer people! The evening of the day when Joe Ennis gave the deed of his place, he and his wife talked over their plans. Their first thought was to buy another good-sized farm. Quite a few men would sell if they got a big price, but Joe wanted to put part of that six thousand dollars in the bank. There wasn't any low- or even medium-priced farm to be had. Of course, they could move to another town, but it didn't seem right to leave a place where there had been Ennises and Holcombs ever since before the Revolution. Or they could buy some abandoned farm land and put up new buildings and bring the fields back. Joe said he would have done just that ten years earlier; now he was afraid he hadn't the nerve. It would mean too much hard work.

"I guess we'd better buy a little place first," Joe said at last. "Then I'll look around."

"How would you make a living?" asked his wife.

"I can get plenty of odd jobs," Joe reassured her. "We'll keep a cow and chickens and a couple of pigs and have a big garden and get a lot of our living that way. I'll be back on a farm before a year is over."

"People say there's money in chickens," she suggested.

"That's what they say," agreed Joe.

The Ennises will buy a small house with a few acres around it, or perhaps they will build on some land that is not much good for farming. Joe will use up quite a bit of that six thousand dollars putting up a complete layout for raising broilers. He figures that he will get his money back in a few years and have enough over so that he can buy a good farm and return to the life he really loves. If Joe Ennis works hard and long, studies the bulletins the Agricultural College sends him, and learns all the new tricks about raising broilers, he may make money. But the chances are fifty-fifty that he will go at it half-heartedly and with the feeling that fussing with hens isn't a man's job.

If Joe Ennis does not make money at his poultry venture, he can do one of three things. First, he can borrow money and buy a good farm at a top price and get right down and dig to pay off the mortgage. Second, he can go back to the Willimantic mills. In that case he will keep his little new place and drive back and forth to work every day. It is just the sort of life the sociologists are praising so fervently. Every factory worker, they say, should also be a man working on the soil to help his family get the benefits of country air and freedom. Or third, Joe can begin to take odd jobs around town, work on the road, help a farmer at haying time, and even mow lawns and garden for the city folks.

If Joe Ennis has the nerve to try to be a farmer again he will save himself, and the town will be better off for having him. But if he goes over to the mills, he will cease to think of himself as part of the community his forebears helped create. Before long he will stop going to the Grange meetings; he may stay away from the Republican caucus or town meeting. Of course, he will not then be able to hold any office, for he won't be in town except after work and on Sundays. Within a year he will have to ask a neighbor for news of what is going on in town. A good citizen will then have become just a man who lives nearby.

As an odd-job, or hired, man Joe Ennis will still be spending all his time here in town, but his attitude toward local affairs will have changed. For one thing, he won't be vitally concerned in taxes, good roads, milk and grain prices, and a dozen other problems that a good farmer has to think about. Someone else will do his worrying for him; he will merely work out and collect his wages. Why should he go to the meeting the County Agent has called? He isn't a farmer any longer. Being a Yankee, Joe will keep a good deal of his self-respect, but there will always be a sense of failure in his spirit. He may have part of that six thousand dollars in the bank, but sometimes he will yearn to have his old place back.

The J. Irving Stouts bought because they liked the fine old house and the view and that nice sloping field to the south. Both of them are city-bred, but it is the correct thing nowadays to have a place in the country, and evidences of antiquity, a sweep of fields, and the rim of hills from your windows are the best proof that you have bought wisely. Of course, there must be a garden. Perennial borders, a cutting bed, and a jumble of rocks are sure signs that Mrs. Stout has the right instincts.

The Stouts will spend three or four thousand dollars driving a new well, putting in a furnace and modern plumbing, tearing out a few partitions and putting several in, making a garden, moving a stone wall, and doing the hundred and one things necessary before a country farm becomes a house. The family will come out week-ends from April to the middle of June; then Mrs. Stout and Sister and Junior will stay until after Labor Day. J. Irving plans to come up from New York on Friday nights and go back very early Monday mornings. In the fall, the week-end trips will be resumed and kept up until cold weather comes.

After a while the townspeople decide the city folks on the old Ennis place are pretty decent. They give for preaching and to local projects, they patronize the food sales and suppers, and in general fit nicely into the community life. The only spectacular stunt they've pulled off to disturb the town's equilibrium might have happened to anyone. It was a nice dry Sunday morning in May. For three weeks there had been no rain, and a brisk wind blew from the west. It was just the time a city man takes to burn off a little patch of grass. Mr. Stout had heard once about the law that stated that he must have a permit to light a fire of that sort, but he had dismissed it long ago as a bit of rural red tape which, of course, could not apply to a city man, and especially one from New York, even though out of Kalamazoo but recently. So J. Irving touches a match to the dry grass, smiles happily at the gay flames that start, and walks away to do something else. Five minutes later he has an uneasy suspicion that perhaps he should curb this raging line of fire; it is getting dangerously near his neighbor's field. So he takes a broom and makes a few admonitory slaps. Nothing happens, and J. Irving begins to realize that he may be meeting a crisis. He yells loudly for his family to come and help, but their aid is not enough, and things look bad for that section of town when a truckload of men with fire-fighting equipment drives up. J. Irving in his role of all-wise city man starts to give orders. The fire warden says five words, and J. Irving is left deflated. Half an hour later he is a humbler, better man for his trial by fire, profanity, a large bill, and a comprehensive lecture on local laws and customs. One thing is left a mystery in his mind.

"How did you people happen to be going by at the right time?" he asks the fire warden. That rural czar smiles pityingly and points to a skeleton shape just visible on a hill to the north.

"See that tower?"

"Yes."

"Well, that's a fire lookout, and the feller up there knows just where every city man lives and watches real careful for something to happen just as it did today. When it does he phones me, and I come and keep you city fools from burning up yourselves and the hull damned town."

But as I have hinted, the fire episode might have happened to any city family, and generally does; therefore, the Stouts are not to be blamed too much. On the whole, they are very acceptable citizens, and even the most skeptical year-rounder admits that they pay their taxes right on the dot and don't let any bills run round town.

However, all the virtues of the Stouts cannot make the town forget that there has been a big change in the old Ennis place since it was sold. As far as the Stouts were concerned, they bought a house, a view, and one lot; the rest of the buildings, the fields, pastures, and the woods were thrown in. The horse barn was turned into a garage and playroom. The first few years some pretense was made of keeping up the big barn and hen houses and tool shed, but then Mr. Stout swore he was tired of bothering with them. So a local man took them down and carted them away for the fine old beams and the wood. It was the same way with the mowing lots. For a while J. Irving had a man to plant corn and potatoes, and seed down the field, but before long he found that he was not getting enough in return to pay the taxes. So he began to lease them as pasture. Now they are growing up to brush, and the hay on them is thin and poor. The pastures are dense with brush and saplings, and the woodlot has been sold and cleared of every good bit of timber.

That is the way a place dies—a place that supported a family and let it put money in the bank and have a sense of independence and pride.

That same tragedy of death of the land is happening all over the town, and the sight of it makes the old-timers wonder how much good these city folks do bring. A man has a perfect right to do what he wants to with the buildings and fields he has bought, but at the same time it is a waste of all the work gone into building up a farm. When a Polish family buys a good farm, the neighbors shake their heads and talk about the good old days when such changes were unthinkable. But pretty soon someone is sure to say, "Well, anyhow, there's one place that won't go to rack and ruin. Say what ye will about 'em, most of them Polacks are pretty fair-t'-middlin' farmers."

The greatest danger that faces the small town of Town Meeting Country is that too many of its places will cease to produce. Then the end is near; for we are supported by an economy of production within the community itself, and I doubt if we could survive as a summer playground or the home of workers who commute to an industrial civilization. You have to work a place, and work for it, before you can make it live and be *worth* keeping alive for a few hundred years.

THREE CHURCHES

During the last century, in the decades when this region seemed content to lead a comfortable existence and let its strong folkways slip into reaction and indifference, the critics said, "This is the Indian Summer of a glorious civilization the like of which we shall never see again." At that time, there were three churches in our town.

Two of these churches were on the Hill, as the village itself was called. The first of these was the Congregational Church and the second was the Catholic mission, visited every other Sunday by a priest from some nearby city.

The third was three miles from the hill down in a narrow valley that had once been the center of a brisk mill community. There was nothing left of it now but a few farms and broken dams and sluices, but the church still stood beside the road that cut across the meadows. It had been the center of a fairly strong Baptist community thirty or forty years before, but now, in 1890, it was poor indeed. Services continued to be held there every Sunday unless it was so cold that the one stove would not heat the building. The preacher was a devout but not very learned man who was a farmer six days in the week. There were a few hundred dollars' "endowment" of the church, money left it by old people who had attended it when they were young and looked upon it even in death as "their church." Every Sunday a collection was taken up, and now and then some city man whose folks had worshiped there sent in a few dollars. Somehow the Ecclesiastical Committee got together the money which paid for the minister, the wood, and such repairs as were absolutely necessary.

Time and again sensible Congregationalists up on the hill told the Baptists down in the valley that they ought to close up the church and come up to the big one to worship. But the Baptists shook their heads. It was pretty clear, they admitted, that Reverend Holmes wasn't much of a preacher, and probably it would be better to disband the church, but after taking everything into consideration they guessed they'd try to keep things running a little while longer. That was all that was ever said, but they knew, and the Congregationalists knew, that their attitude was not merely one of obstinacy. They were reluctant to kill a force that had once been powerful for good and still had a little life left in it. Too often they had seen the rebirth of a custom or an idea that had been given up for dead. Perhaps the old church was on its last legs and there was no saving it, but it was better, they guessed, to let matters take their own course. That is New England for you. We believe too strongly in the resurrection of moribund folkways ever to take it on ourselves to deliver the death blow.

The Catholic Church was the same then as it had been when it was started. It grew a little this year, or lost a faithful family the next. One priest was kindly man who preached tolerance and good neighborliness; another might try to stir up enmity against the heretics. Not too much attention was ever paid to such remarks; the old Catholic families had been in town long enough to know that you can't have a strong happy community if you go around saying that so-and-so is going to hell and is a dirty black-hearted Protestant.

Those were the three churches the town supported fifty years ago. One was almost dead, a second adhered to an old faith and played little part in the town's life, and the third, the one most closely identified with the past, was little more than a spiritual reaffirmation of the code of conservative laissez-faire that governed the conduct of the people.

Today there are still three churches in the town.

The one down in the valley is more forlorn than ever, but it is kept repaired just enough so it does not fall to pieces, and two or three times every summer some preacher holds a service there. Then the folks in the valley come and worship in the pews their ancestors sat in. There is still that tiny "endowment," and when some big job of repair work must be done, such as the replacement of rotten beams or the laying of new shingles, a Baptist church in the city remembers its very old relative and helps out, or else a city man whose grandfather lived in the valley hears of the emergency and sends a check. Perhaps he is wealthy enough to give a million to a college, and he could reinstate that little church and give it a regular preacher, but he does no such thing. He knows that its usefulness is over, that if it is kept alive it is as a symbol. For the hope that was held fifty years ago that this church would again be a living force was apparently vain. Now it is nothing save a reminder that once there were more people in town than there are now, or at least more who went to church. Still it lives on, for who knows but what it may some day spring to life again.

The Catholic Church up on the hill has changed little since the '90's. Rome is not given to sudden and violent transformations, so an oil furnace and electricity are about the extent of the church's participation in the new life of the town. They tell me that the priests, who now come every Sunday instead of every other, are tolerant men who tell their parishioners to live in peace with the heretics around them. And the heretics in turn forgive the papists for a religion obviously too gaudy for sensible descendants of Puritans.

I remember my father telling us that a friend of his had become a Catholic to please his wife. This apostasy did not bother Father, because he hastened to assure us, "But her folks couldn't make him turn Democrat."

Yes, the chief cause of friction between Catholic and Protestant in our town is just this: one sect is almost inevitably Democrat; the other is as stoutly Republican. I heartily approve of this basis for disapproval. A man's religious beliefs are his private concern and seldom if ever affect the community; but his political beliefs lead him to vote in a certain way and may or may not help bring a sensible regime of control. In a small New England town the Lord is loved and Caesar obeyed.

But if the Catholic Church is the same as it was fifty years ago, another set of influences has changed the Congregationalists. As in 1890, their minister does not interfere with local politics or worry too much about what he vaguely terms "conditions" (a state of affairs that includes everything from a wave of petty thefts to adultery and incest). Neither does he give the people too ornate a service, sermons too long or too short, or too gaudy or too matter-of-fact lectures. He pays just the right number of calls at the proper time, he keeps the parsonage looking neat, and his garden is as spick and span as his wife's kitchen. All these things a good rural dominie does for fifteen hundred dollars a year, a parsonage, and its fuel.

Year after year, though he preaches the same safe, indecisive theology, changes have been overcoming him and his church. At first glance, you do not recognize that the man in the pulpit is anything more than a thirty-year-old replica of the shepherd of sixty-five who stood there fifty years ago. But after you have spent a summer in town you will note the difference. The present minister will turn up at a cocktail party given by some summer folks who are interested in the church. He comes dressed as smartly as any man there, and his wife is a little woman who lets you know that being a minister's wife does not keep her from liking pleasant company. Neither one of them takes a drink, and she does not smoke, but he uses up half a pack of cigarettes. Next Sunday afternoon the minister may drop in at the tennis-court rendezvous and do a good job of rooting for his favorite side. He very frankly says he does not dare play on the holy day for fear of being criticized by the older church members, but he sees nothing wrong in it. After you play a game of bridge with the new shepherd you are ready to accept him as a "human being," one more or less like the rector of the church you attend in Worcester or Hartford.

Then it occurs to you that probably the year-rounders are upset because this young squirt is playing around with the ungodly city folks. So the next time you go up there for butter you ask Bill Perry how the new minister is getting along. Bill spits meditatively and after much irrelevant detail gives you the following verdict: "Most folks like him. They say he preaches a real sensible sermon and calls regular and don't stay too goddam long right when a shower is comin' up and a load of hay still out. One or two old folks have sort of objected to his smokin' and playin' cards, but that didn't get 'em anywhere. The day's past when a minister is much different from anybody else, I guess."

"How do people like his running around with the city folks?" you ask.

"They give to the church, and give a hull lot too, don't they?" answers Bill.

And so the Congregational church of the average small town has become pretty adaptable and urbane these days. It has discarded the self-confident lethargy of half a century ago and is raising money and demanding that it get value received for those extra hundreds of dollars it pays out. More than ever before the church is a social center. The minister cannot be a village reformer or meddler, but he can and must function as an affable fellow who believes that a good church supper helps a congregation as much as a sermon, and that a Sunday School picnic is a vital part of religion.

The old days have, in a measure, returned, even though they are in new dress. Back in 1700 the Reverend Mr. Billings, in robes and profound dignity, the only college graduate in town, worked hand in glove with the selectmen to make Hampton a tight little town. Then there were long years when the town was getting along very nicely without the help of the Man of God, for, sad to relate, he was loath to keep up with the changing times. But now, when the communities are faced with a new and terrifying complexity of life, when they are menaced by all sorts of changes from within and influences from without, they need the church on the hill. To its glory let it be said that that church has responded. Throwing off its complacency, adapting to the times, and somehow getting hold of spiritual plasma as well, it has once more begun to be a power in the community.

MAKING A LIVING

The town is still basically agricultural as far as making a living is concerned. But slowly two changes can be seen. First, more and more heads of families are working only a few acres of land and relying on jobs in the nearby mills or on the road for their main source of income. Second, every year some two or three men quit their general farming and concentrate on some form of poultry raising. The result is that the old-time large farms aren't as numerous as they used to be. In fact, there are only a dozen or so big units of production that use two, or perhaps three, men on them. Those dozen farms are better than they ever were before. Their buildings are modern, the fields yield big crops, and the herds are tested and approved and are often made up of purebred stock. Electric milkers do their work, the milk is cooled in big refrigerators, and the workers are positively antiseptic as compared with the farmers of fifty or even twenty years ago. A tractor and a truck stand under the shed together with a lot of machinery the other generations never dreamed of. The farmers on these places will tell you that they lead a hard life and hardly make a dollar. But there is a good car in the garage and, if he wants to, the son can go to college.

The poultry men have their good and their bad years. That is the chief trouble with this specialized form of production. Let the price of grain go up and the value of milk go down, and a dairy farmer won't make any money, but he can fall back on his farm for food and still pull through thanks to the dozen devices known to a Yankee. But when the poultry man has a bad year he has no big farm behind him, nothing to fall back on, and he is more than likely to throw up the whole thing and take a city job that will give him security if not freedom. The new tendency to specialize has brought new dangers to the economic life of the town. It was no accident that, back in the best days, the elder statesmen of these towns were men who owned and worked big farms which were almost self-sustaining units. There is something in the power and responsibility that go with this form of

life likely to turn a man with good stuff in him into a sensible,
just town officer.

Quite a few men earn a fair living in town by doing what you
might call "maintenance work." It's hard to tell just what to
call a Yankee odd-job man, but there may be four or five who
can paint, hang paper, and do a neat job of carpentry. Then
there will be another fellow who is a good cabinet-maker, an
expert carpenter, and will if necessary paint your room, hang
your paper, and build your fireplace. Another will do all those
jobs and also your butchering, cutting up of meat, and smoking of hams. Still another is a rough plumber and the town's
best man with septic tanks and cesspools, in addition to being a
fair-to-middling carpenter. Only one worker can shoe a horse
and do expert blacksmithing, but he won't display his skill unless he is obliged to; he wants to be a specialist at all kinds of
carpentry and stone work. Almost all have some skill with garden tractors, power lawnmowers, and the other mechanical garden tools. And most can fix a broken-down car on a country
road quicker than the average city mechanic.

The only one-job man in town is the doctor. One mail car-
rier runs a farm on the side, and the other is just about our best
gardener. The station agent and the garage owner are at present
more or less limited to their immediate work, but either of them
can turn his hand to almost anything. And this is the way our
town gets its non-farming jobs done: you go out and get hold
of the man your folks asked to help them—I didn't say hired—
or his son or grandson, and then you tell him what you want
done. You do so very humbly. After that you wait patiently, and
sooner or later your work is all done by that one man. If your
project involves such mysteries as wiping a joint, he will remember some friend who was once a plumber's helper, or he
will tell you that you need an expert. This announcement is
made more or less shamefacedly, for a Yankee workman likes
to feel that he "can do anything around a place."

Commerce is represented in our town by a village store, controlled by a corporation, and a feed, grain, and fertilizer store,
also one of a chain. Both are very modern and efficient, and town
afficionados look in vain for the cracker barrel, the potbellied
stove, the loafers, and the checker game. Progress has arrived!

That is the way we make a living: farming, raising poultry,

doing maintenance work, running a post office, garage, store, mail route, and working on the state road or the one big estate that employs more than a solitary helper.

Although a big farmer has a more obvious stake in the community than the man who works out by the day on his farm and then goes back at night to a rented house and garden, both these men are equally good citizens in their basic concepts. The farmer will know more about how the town finances stand, for he is one of the assessors, and he works with the County Agent and Pomona and the State Grange. But the hired man sizes up things pretty well too, and in the long run his judgment is to be trusted just as much as the prosperous farmer's. Take, for instance, some case that needs careful handling, one of sex delinquency that involved more than the theoretically guilty parties. Both men will arrive at a wise and sound verdict; both will weigh the desire to punish against the disgrace that might come to innocent people and take into consideration family tradition, up-bringing, and a dozen other environmental factors that the State Police would never know about.

If a man stays in town and feels that it is his home, he keeps on being a good citizen within the limits of his capacities. His job does not make or ruin him. When I wrote about the hired men of another era, I said they never expected to be selectmen or representatives; but I also pointed out that they took an intelligent interest in local affairs and knew that they stood just as high at town meeing as the men who hired them.

The hard facts about the citizen in relation to his job give one good reason why the small New England town has managed to survive. The worker is a man and a citizen over and above his identity as stone mason, carpenter, sexton, farmer, mechanic, painter, or hired man. When he changes work or becomes richer or poorer, he does not allow himself to be transformed as a townsman. Our forefathers built a sound economic structure, but they also created a spirit and a consciousness of what right living in a community should be. That spirit is the force that has sustained us.

GETTING A LITTLE FUN OUT OF LIFE

Some "experts" will tell you blithely, "Oh yes, the small town is now a part of the city that is only ten miles away, and the rural amusements have been discarded in favor of the movies." That is another of those one-eighth truths printed by the man who spent three weeks visiting "those crackpot artists over Bear Hill way." He saw three families drive over to Willimantic to see Bette Davis; forthwith, he concluded that the Ladies Aid Society, Grange, Harmony Club, Catholic Women's Club, Young Folks Society, Home Economics Club, and Junior Grange had all died or at least were attended only when the bright city lights palled on this new breed of natives.

Year-round townspeople do go to the movies now and then, and about once a year they may neglect a local meeting so as to see a special film, but ordinarily the trip to the city is made only when there is nothing going on in town. Here is one of the paradoxes of modern life in a small community: the people can get away from it more than ever before, but there is more to amuse them at home, for, just as they can go to the city and other towns, so the city and towns can come to them. A whole day used to be needed for a Grange meeting with a sister group for a friendly visit and supper. Now the members go in their cars and are back by ten o'clock.

Farm agents cover the county; Home Economics experts go here and there; lecturers of all sorts come to town. If the Grange in Canterbury puts on *Charley's Aunt,* the chances are that the cast will go to half a dozen towns before the winter is over. The Chaplin Congregational Church holds a Fellowship meeting with Woodstock and Pomfret, and the young people of Brooklyn come over to Hampton to a Sunrise Service.

All this activity does not seem much like staying at home, but if Hampton Grange goes away visiting one month, it is host the next, and in this way the people get double the amount of social pleasure. The automobile and good roads have released the towns from geographic bondage and have increased their sense of separate identity. Hampton goes calling; then it receives callers. Its people drive the seven miles to Chaplin for a church supper. Do they lose their individuality as citizens of a special town? Of course not. They come home and put on a bean supper of their own and expect Chaplin to return their call the next month.

What the town does to amuse itself has already been described indirectly. Church, Grange, Home, Farm, those interests create the clubs and the meetings. And because there are more of these groups coming together, the interest in homes and farms is increased.

Just the same situation exists in the churches. In the old days the pioneers had to work together in one faith; now new problems demand an expanded social and religious consciousness.

Sins, Misdemeanors, and Just Plain Slips

The small New England town is fully as moral and sober as it ever was. Foreigners, summer visitors, good roads to the city, the death of original sin, and liberal churches are relaxing influences that, after a couple of centuries of stern rule by Puritan codes, still have not turned the little communities into hotbeds of crime. Neither have the new social consciousness and the contacts with broader sensibilities done away entirely with all evil. But there has been, in some ways, a slow, deliberate change for better. There is less hard drinking in town than there was back in the days when Ephraim Lyon could start a very strong Church of Bacchus. Plenty of rural inhabitants consume their daily quota of whiskey, but there is little hard cider made, and I have not heard of the making of applejack for years. Beer seems to be the favorite tipple now, and the foreign families go in for wine rather than hard liquor. Gone, apparently, are the staunch characters who became famous for their drinking capacity and for their drunken exploits. The last citizen I have seen who was soused to the gills has now passed on, and he was seventy-five when he limped across the village street dispensing kind words of advice on many subjects. Don't ask me why this change has come. It may be due to the fact that beer seems to have replaced cider. In the old days, the brew was hard to come by regularly and was more or less of a holiday treat when you went to town. Or it may be that when the prejudice against drink began to die, the obstinate defiers of respectability no longer found such pleasure in their defiance.

We are still far from being a Blue Ribbon town, but the spectacular drunks have gone, and you don't hear tales about how much other men consume. Probably the truth is that we are entering on a period of outward conformity when it is considered bad manners to display an unchecked taste for whiskey and song. Now that we are less alone as a town and more a part of a larger social unit, we do not feel as free as before to be stark, devastating individualists.

Back in 1890, Andrew Rindge got drunk when he felt like it and, being drunk, sang loudly or composed libelous poetry about his neighbors. There was no reason, as far as he could see, why he shouldn't do as he pleased so long as he refrained from physical violence, paid his taxes, and, sooner or later, his other debts. Today an equally thirsty townsman hesitates before he acts as independently as did Andrew, and the chances are that he decides against such open flaunting of respectability. He realizes dimly that he is living in a less individualistic age, and the complete self-expression of a cider- or rum-stimulated ego are not for him. As in the earliest pioneer days, he is disciplined by the community. The likeness between the first years and this modern period persists. Then and now the social unit forbade the individual to assert himself too wilfully—then because the unit was being created; now because that same unit is waging its bitterest war for continued existence. In between the early and the late years, and especially during the last century, individual conduct could be free, for the town had settled down and become self-confident. Such license may have been allowed too long and thus contributed to the years of apparent decay. Certainly it cannot be allowed today. So the thirsty citizen brings home a case of beer and consumes it slowly, thinking perhaps a trifle wistfully of those brave stories his Uncle Horatio used to tell of flagons of three-year-old cider and demijohns of rum.

A few minor thefts and assorted misdemeanors of little importance are the extent of our towns' crimes, except for acts of violence and sex. Every year or so an angry man strikes another a harder blow than he expected to strike, or some degenerate kills his wench, or a solitary farmer is beaten to death for the money he is supposed to be hiding. Such crimes of violence are not dealt with by the town; instead, a highly efficient State Police steps in and sees that justice is done. Because of this, and because any one town seldom has a murder more than once in half a century, we do not think of this crime as part of the real life of the community. Rather is it some strange phenomenon that visits us every so often. Naturally enough, a murderous assault for revenge, greed, or in deep anger reveals something about the assailant, but we fall back on the good old Puritan theory of original sin for the answer. "There is," we say, "the potentiality of being a criminal in all of us, and now and then it rises to the surface." We do not wait supinely for murder to crop up in our town; we do, however, say that murder is done for abnormal motives that may be latent in all men, and not alone in those who live in small New England towns.

We pay more attention to fornication, adultery, incest, and the very rare cases of what is broadly defined as "unnatural acts of sex." So far as I know, this town has never had an authentic case of rape. One young girl did state tearfully that she had been violated by the son of a prosperous farmer. His answer was the effective one of producing several witnesses who swore that they had had carnal knowledge of the would-be virgin. But we have had plenty of other proof that man and woman are carnal. Most of these cases never get to the police; the town itself decides what to do. Nine times out of ten, the verdict is, "Do nothing." Such failure to act is not a sign of weakness or of fear; it merely indicates that other people think there would be nothing gained by arresting the guilty couple, bringing them to trial, having a lot of publicity, and finally jailing the guilty pair. After all, both were willing to sin; furthermore, the town's basic structure has not been threatened.

Perhaps this conclusion needs explanation. People outside New England are puzzled by our definition of what constitutes a danger to our towns. "Aren't fornication and adultery crimes?" they demand. Yes, they are crimes, and town life would be better off without them. But, and here is the Puritan and neo-Puritan logic, these crimes are caused by innate desires and lusts of which no amount of legal castigation can rid our frail, carnal bodies. When Man is nearer the angels he will cease to lust after Woman; until then the law can do little for him. That is the first part of our reasoning. The second asserts that these sexual irregularities do not damage the roads, raise the taxes, hurt the crops, make the school system less efficient, or even render the churches impotent; in short, they are detrimental only to the individual, and not even entirely to him. The town agrees that a famous lecher might be an honest and efficient town official.

Now, mind you, the good people of the small New England

communities are not convinced that sin and degradation should ever be excused; they are merely capable of seeing the difference between a personal and a social crime; furthermore, they understand that a sinner-in-private may possibly be a public figure of rectitude, even of definite value to the town. Here in New England we know our sins and sinners and have them both in complete control, perhaps even doing a little useful reclamation work in virtuous moments.

RUNNING THEIR OWN AFFAIRS

Very often the observer of the New England town will tell you it is "dead." Sometimes he will assert that it died because the railroad and the automobile broke the Five-Mile Law, and, therefore, the town's separate and jealously guarded identity was spilled all over the landscape; or it died of old age; or the foreign invasion; or the New Deal; or almost anything else, except of course from the blight of city folks, for the observer himself is almost inevitably one of them.

A popular reason for the supposed death of the town states that practically all local affairs are now in the hands of the state and federal governments. To hear this story is to decide that not even the town dog warden dares touch a pooch unless Hartford, or maybe Providence or Boston, says he can; and Washington itself has to give the selectmen permission to buy a new pair of felt boots for old Jim Rindge who is on relief. Gone are the days, wails the distrait admirer of rural independence, when the "staunch, strong, stalwart, and quaint" town could and did tell the state and national meddlers where to get off; it was going to raise taxes just as it saw fit, and it was nobody's business how many paupers there were in the town and how they were being taken care of.

The truth about this supposedly glorious past and ignoble present is, as usual, quite complex. In the first place, the early towns never asserted that they were free from the power of the Court of General Assembly; in fact, they often turned to these bodies for aid and support, and their authority was always respected. Not to have done those things would have been poor policy for, just as a man was an individual who also acted as a citizen, so the town obeyed higher legal and legislative bodies while it kept its identity as a community with its own bounds, rights, and privileges. Second, the town of today has lost far fewer of its powers and rights than the alarmists are inclined to believe.

Take the job of First Selectman of any one of a score of towns in this country. In 1740 the harassed man had gaugers, fence viewers, pound-keepers, and other minor officials to help him run the town, but he was the one who helped the dominie punish drinking, fornication, and disrespect for the cloth; he was a bridge and road builder, militia trainer, Indian agent, distributor of lands, tax expert, and general financial wizard. He thought he was persecuted and unappreciated; and, sure enough, just as he was getting things in fair running order, the ungrateful town elected somebody else.

By 1840 the town had shaken down into comparative security, and the selectman's duties were not quite as spectacular as before, but he was still a very busy fellow who handled many different problems. For instance, not many new roads had to be built, but paupers were more numerous, and the school districts were a nuisance. Already the state was sending out more and more regulations each year, but that did not worry the selectman too much. He obeyed them in the letter at least, and let the spirit be guided by the needs of the town.

One hundred years later, in the 1940's, the First Selectman of Dudley, or Woodstock, or Ledyard, is a brisk man, respectively twenty and ten years younger than his 1740 and 1840 counterparts. He has an office, and enough paper work so his wife has to help out. An expert oiler of roads and general highway maintenance engineer, he is also a very practical engineer who can make a stab at solving half a dozen other problems before he calls in the state men. Instead of working with the dominie as his 1740 ancestor did, this town father cooperates with the health officer. For he still watches over the town, and his vigilance is as faithful when the public nuisances he abates are privies, as when it dealt with blasphemers against the Congregational Church.

The town officials of today have new duties because the towns they work for have new problems. Furthermore, some of the solutions are so intricate and involve so much money that the town must be helped by the state or national government. The school situation is an example. There is a school board of nine members, and it finds a lot to do, and every year there is a large appropriation of money by the town for tuition, transportation, salaries, and so on; but the town simply could not bear all the expenses of educating its children in grammar and high schools, and it could not spare the time to do all the necessary supervision. The school board might be willing to assume both burdens, but it has neither the dollars nor the hours, so it accepts financial aid and permits a supervisor to be the real master of the school system. Of course, it still retains much authority, and that is why one town may have better schools than another but, on the whole, the state has the control. Almost all communities accept the logic of this situation and do not rebel. Now and then, however, some town goes on the warpath of cussed independence and proceeds to throw a tomahawk into the best-laid plans and programs. Then the schools get so bad that there is a community rebellion. The individualists are told very sharply that the children of the town are suffering, and, therefore, that there must be more cooperation with the state.

It is the same way with the State Police. On the whole, they do a very good job, and the towns are gradually getting accustomed to the idea of being governed in a measure by the state. We could not afford to pay efficient, trained constables and provide them with patrol cars equipped with radios. So the "cops" make the arrests, and only the toughest old diehards bewail the day when we were free to arrest our own.

The old-age pension scheme helps a lot, too. Almost gone are the town farms and the boarding out of paupers. It is obvious that when the town lost its control of the indigent, those unhappy people achieved relative independence. There was old Ike Gull. About the most decent citizen his family ever produced, he refused to live with his relatives, so when he got too old to work in the woods or on a farm, the town had to take care of him. Ike was a cantankerous old fellow in many ways, and he found a lot of fault with the room and board he was given —not any wood stove he could sit by, and salt pork far too seldom. Then came the old-age pension and liberty and the pursuit of happiness for Ike. When the first check arrived, he hobbled up to the town offices, told the long-suffering First Selectman what and who he was and then announced that Isaac Gull was no longer a goddam pauper to be treated like a dog. From now on he was paying for his own board and room and finding it where he pleased. So Ike changed rooming places and for the first time in years was heard to sing in a feeble, cracked voice, a happy man who had once again become his own master. A kindly town never pointed out to the rejuvenated Ike that his pension was being paid for by someone else just as certainly as his pauper's bill had been.

UP A BACK ROAD

Drive along the village street of any one of a dozen towns in this region. On either side are neat, clean, painted houses with green lawns before and around them. Here live orderly and prosperous people. Out in the country, the smooth black road takes you through fields and woodland. There is not the tropical richness of the black soil belt in the South, or the well-regulated fecundity of Iowa or the Pennsylvania Dutch country, but neither is there equivalent poverty or disorder. These are old respectable mowing lots and pastures and groves of birch and oak. This is the land of steady habits, and the landscape must not be too lushly rich. Still, it would be a disgrace if it failed to produce an exemplary profit!

Then you turn on to a dirt road that twists up the side of a long-lying hill. Here the woods are more like thickets of under-brush with an occasional oak or maple, and the farms are poorer, with only a few stony fields around the old house and the dilapidated barn and sheds. But even here there is no squalor or degeneracy. The people on these places are just tired out. Their folks came here around 1700, and somehow, with living and working, the family has lost its old vigor. The children of the couple who live here now are scattered, and whichever dies first, he or she, the other will probably apply for old-age assistance and board out somewhere. Until then, the old folks are bound to keep up appearances. They drive to church in good weather, give a few dollars for preaching, keep on in the Grange, take *The New England Homestead* and *The Congregationalist*, and go to a Grange or church supper once in a while. That is the way old people of good Yankee stock go to their end. They have little money to spend on things, and it's hard driving themselves to show up on Grange nights, but they don't want the town to think they're dropping out of everything.

There are three such places on the dirt road before you come to a different sort of New England home. Perhaps this house isn't very much more rundown than the others, but there are other signs that the people who live here have given up caring or else they never wanted to be like other people. The yard is strewn with litter, and the chopping block is close to the front door instead of decently around to the back. But there is something else that sets this place apart. Under a maple tree near the house is a crude pen. There is a child in it but, although it is large enough to be ten or twelve years old, it does not seem to be able to walk. Sometimes it pulls itself up almost straight by holding on to the sides of the pen, but its big head is too heavy, and it falls back and lies in the dirt, making noises that sound as if it wanted to speak and could not. When it makes these noises, a woman comes to the door of the house and looks out. She is shapeless in a filthy gingham dress, but on her dark face is a sort of evil strength. Perhaps evil is not the right word, for it denotes active revolt against good, and this woman's nature is passive. She does not act; she merely lives, and yet she is a menace to this orderly, self-respecting New England country.

From the barn comes a man who slowly crosses the road and enters the house. As he goes by the pen the child in it tries to stand up again. The man lifts his hand in a casual wave, but he does not stop or notice that the child is making a noise to attract his attention. This man seems to fit into the fields and hills better than the woman does. A gaunt, lean frame, once tall, now bent, and a face that could be almost strong if the eyes were more alive and the mouth would close firmly, reveal that he is an old-stock Yankee.

He drops down in a rocker by the kitchen window.

"Ain't ye goin' down t' th' Halseys t'day?" asks the woman, who is fiddling with an old battery radio.

"Too damned hot t' work," he grunts. "An' besides my back's been achin' bad ever since I got up. Must've sprained it pitchin' off that last load of hay yest'day."

The woman shrugs.

"Do as ye please, but if I don't get some money pretty soon from ye, I'm goin' t' get it some other way."

"Why you . . ." declares the man, but his undeclared threat does not disturb her.

"Guess I'll go out an' lay down in th' hammock an' see if that won't help my back," he remarks, looking furtively at the woman to see whether she is in a better mood. She does not bother to speak or even glance at him. "The Life of Mary Marlin" is coming in over the radio.

As the man goes by the pen, the child squeals with some sort of emotion, and this time its father stops and looks at it.

"Hello," he says, and picks up a stick and pokes the child gently in the ribs. It gurgles as if it were pleased and tries to pull the stick away from the man. The play goes on for a moment or two, but the father tires of it and shuffles across the yard to an old woven hammock that hangs between two trees. Left alone, the idiot whines miserably for a minute; then it sleeps in the dirt.

Stretched out in the hammock, Frank Greenfield was doing a thing he seldom allowed himself to do. He was wondering exactly where he had got himself. That was the way he put his problem: "where he had got himself." He was still honest enough to want to take the blame for things if he ought to. Yes sir, the Greenfields never dodged a debt or responsibility of any kind. The thought of Bill Halsey and all that hay to be got in came to Frank Greenfield, and he squirmed with guilt. Maybe he was letting Bill down, but it was the truth, in a way at least, that his back ached. Tomorrow he'd go down and put in a good day's work. Maybe Bill would take him as regular hired man. If that happened, he would be making steady wages, and she might be more or less satisfied.

Frank Greenfield cursed softly to himself. He did that about once every year, swore to himself about himself, about what a fool he was now and always had been, at least since he left home when he was a boy. But after a minute he had a strange new idea. It was a disturbing one, more so than his own sense of shame. For now he began to wonder if maybe his family hadn't been partially responsible for the way he had turned out. He didn't want to think such an idea had any truth in it. It was bad enough that he, Frank Greenfield the individual, had gone downhill until he was married to a Gull woman and had an idiot boy out in the yard this minute. But it was still worse to think that Frank Greenfield was that sort of a man because his family had lost its strength, had run out, just as he had seen other old families run out.

His folks had been in this town since away back before the Revolutionary War. They had never been very prominent. A staff officer in the colonial army was all they could boast of, but they had always managed to make a good living off their own farms. One Greenfield boy was a minister, and another who went west taught in some college. The rest of them were farmers and artisans and storekeepers with, now and then, a factory worker. Thinking back in this new spirit of discernment, Frank Greenfield wondered if maybe his own father had not been the first to give in and stop fighting the tired feeling that comes to all old families. Josiah Greenfield, Frank's grandfather, hadn't been much of a farmer; "slack and listless," people called him, and he married a sickly girl. Their only son was Henry, and at first it looked as if he might amount to quite a lot. But when he was seventeen or eighteen he began to run around with the wrong young fellows. All of them drank too much, and every so often they went to Gull Hollow to visit one of the dark wenches there. Getting a reputation like that hurt Henry Greenfield's chances for marrying a real nice girl from one of the better families. The one he did pick out, the oldest Blake girl, wasn't exactly fast or low, but people talked about the way she acted with the men. But she and Henry Greenfield settled down all right after they were married; in fact, those two or three years of mild hell-raising were the extent of his sinfulness, and she too was content to settle down.

That was the sort of family Frank Greenfield had been born into, one that had been decent and self-respecting once and even now was just on the edge of shiftlessness and had not really gone downhill too much. Of course, Henry Greenfield had lost his farm and had to work as a hired man, and his wife was sickly a lot of the time, but still they tried to keep up appearances in certain ways. For instance, both of them were Grangers and made an effort to go to the meetings even in the dead of winter. Frank remembered once that his father had to go through a mowing lot, the road was so drifted. His mother had wanted to stay home that once, but his father had been stubborn. Now that he thought about that incident, Frank Greenfield realized that attending every meeting and being somebody in the Grange was the gesture his father made so he would not quite drop out of the life other people led. Well, that was about the only effort the old man made. . . .

He had paid scant attention to what Frank did as a boy. Once in a while he might say something, but ordinarily he shut his eyes and ears and pretended that he did not know his son drank too much and was running around in the nearest city when he could get there. Frank never stayed on the old place after he was through school at sixteen. There in the hammock thinking about the past, he got a feeble joy out of remembering that he had not done badly in school, certainly a whole lot better than the children from some families. No, the Greenfields hadn't lost their brains; it was the will to struggle his folks had lost and now it was lacking in him too.

Fancy ideas did not come to Frank Greenfield very often, but this morning he couldn't get rid of the thought that somehow or other the Hollow was responsible for his going downhill the way he had. In the first place, his father had gone down there when he was a young fellow. He wondered if a man inherited that sort of desire. He supposed not, but just the same it had always seemed to him that he took up with that black-haired wench in the house because some force was pushing him toward her. Well, there was no sense thinking such things; the truth probably was that the Greenfields had begun to peter out in his father's time, and had gone fast ever since.

He wondered if any of his children would ever bring the family back. Probably not. They hadn't heard from Albert for two or three years now, and the chances were mighty good that he was in some kind of trouble. He looked like a Gull, thickset, and a heavy, black beard if he didn't shave, and that sort of crushed-in, square face. Gertrude was working down in Norwich, but she would never tell him what she did. Gertrude looked like a Greenfield, tall, slender, and blonde, but she had the Gull disposition. That was all his family, and not much to be expected from it.

Oh yes, there was the third one in the pen. Every so often Frank Greenfield tried to remember if he and the woman ever did give it a name. They must have before they realized what it was going to be, but for years now they had only called the creature "It." Sometimes he proposed sending It to the County Home, but she was always dead set against such an idea. In a way she took pretty good care of It. Gulls weren't disturbed by such animals, he supposed. Certainly there were plenty of others here and there in the towns, and one or two were worse than his. And in a sense he himself had got used to It; he even liked to poke It with a stick and make It giggle.

Frank Greenfield began to be sleepy. He ought by rights to do a little handmowing for himself, especially if he was going to work steady for Bill Halsey. But he might as well catch a few minutes' sleep. Come afternoon he'd pitch right in to work. From the kitchen came the voice of that tortured but brave woman, Mary Marlin. Frank Greenfield laughed to himself. That woman of his certainly did slobber over such stories. She was hard in lots of other ways, but she'd cry when some radio person put on an act. He tried to stop thinking about his wife.

Up the back roads of the Town Meeting Country live the dying families of the old Yankee stock. Some pass away in the seemly dignity of respectable people; others in squalor and degeneracy. And around these families and sometimes with them is a stronger clan, one that is as strangely, terribly virile as it was three hundred years ago. Up the back roads of New England are the dying Greenfields and the living Gulls.

TOWN MEETING

There is final proof that our 1940 New England towns are still strong and are worthy of the people who built them: we still hold town meetings. Andrew Durkee, buried in the North Cemetery in 1743, and Jonathan Rindge, who fought at Bunker Hill, and Elisha Fuller, born in 1812, could go to any one of them without disappointment in the twentieth-century crop of townspeople.

Nowadays we hold two regular town meetings each year, one in the late fall, the other in February. The first is on the day of the election of town officers and in it is transacted most of the run-of-the-mill business of the year, except for approval of the annual budget and establishment of the tax rate. That last bit of high finance is talked over when the selectmen have a good idea of how much money they are going to need to run things. Aside from these usual meetings, there are the rare meetings convoked for some special purpose by the town fathers, or demanded by a petition signed by a certain number of voters, who, incidentally, are almost always in a very bad frame of mind.

Every voter in town can attend these meetings and cast a ballot, or say "Aye" or "No." It doesn't matter who or what he or she is; black, red, or white; rich or on the town; deacon or lecherous scoffer. Any person who has lived a year in town, who can read and write, and has not had the right of citizenship taken away, can become a voter and forthwith be eligible to attend town meeting and help make its decisions. This right of participation is not merely a legal fiction. Literally and without qualification, the town lives up to its promise. Become a voter in the community, and you can go to any meeting, talk in your turn, and vote as you wish. But though the basic framework of the New England town meeting looks very simple, these assemblies of the people are not as uncomplicated as they seem.

For example, more often than not a New England town meeting is a very dull and also perfunctory affair at which little of interest or value happens. After the October assembly has been called to order by the first selectman, the town clerk reads the warning, or official notice. Then a moderator is elected. If there is no battle in the offing, any honored citizen may be chosen. In every small town, there are several men who may be picked as moderator. Inevitably they are fair and just, and are also capable of handling a quarrel or ruling on a knotty point of order.

Fred Holcomb takes the chair and announces that the first business to be taken up is whether or not the town wishes to empower the selectmen to use for another purpose the $535.50 left over from the road appropriation. It is a matter of routine management, and a citizen in the front row says, "I make th' motion that th' town. . . ."

"Secnthmshn!" calls a voice.

"Mshnmadensecnd! Any discussion?" asks the moderator.

Out of long habit the inevitable critic of the administration gets up and states in a loud voice that he don't see why the selectmen need that $535.50. They handed in their budget last year and got the money they wanted for various things, so let 'em be satisfied. The moderator glances at the first selectman. He rises, far from disturbed, and asks casually, "Well, Joe, what would you say we ought to do with that money if we don't need it on the roads and can't use it anywhere else?"

Confronted with even a hint of the dire tragedy that the town should lose $535.50, the critic mumbles that he ain't been elected to take care of such matters. The selectman presses his advantage.

"If I don't get that money transferred from one appropriation to another, I'll have to turn it back to the state."

Driven to the wall but resilient of wit, the opposition immediately demands why this state of affairs arose; why wasn't the estimate of how much that stretch of road would cost made more carefully? If it had been, all this fuss and bother wouldn't have come up.

"You're th' one that's makin' any fuss there is," the selectman points out. He is a patient man but, as he tells his wife that night, Andrew Bugbee can rile him.

Instead of being squelched, Andrew is now on sure ground and speaks a few minutes on his inalienable right to talk, how little good his talk will do, how much good it should do, and, lastly, how there ought to be a change in town officers.

No one is greatly moved by this flow of oratory. All present know that Andrew is basically a loyal citizen who pays his taxes and, ironically enough, votes right and keeps his mouth shut when really important issues come up. Now he is talking to give himself pleasure for the moment and, furthermore, to provide satisfying proof of his assertion in later private conversations that he "said what he had t' say." Knowing all this, the assembled voters are tolerant of Andrew's remarks. Some, of course, mutter to neighbors about hot air and windbags, and one or two hot-tempered conservatives swear fervently to themselves, but not until almost five minutes have elapsed does anyone interrupt to call for a vote on the question before the house. This act of extreme discourtesy to a speaker who has a right to speak is frowned upon by the older members, but young blood is hot and, after all, Andrew is wasting time. So the moderator does no more than say that Mr. Bugbee has the floor. That indignant orator is now very near the boiling point but, an expert in gauging the temper of town meetings, he contents himself with a pungent concluding remark to the effect that the town is going to the dogs and he's going to keep on saying so until something is done to save her. Then he sits down—a man who has enjoyed his annual spiritual outing, his redeclaration of independence, and his demonstration that he is a free citizen.

The moderator calls for a vote, and the motion is unanimously carried. Even the articulate rebel does not shout "No." As he tells a friend later on, "I don't like t' kick up a rumpus in public." The four other items on the warning are dealt with quickly. Only once is there any opposition to a motion. This time an old farmer asks why the Cedar Swamp Road is being hardsurfaced while the one he lives on is in such bad shape. The selectman knows this question is made in good faith; therefore he answers at length, explaining how the farmer's road is going to be repaired this year and that it is next on the list for surfacing. A motion to adjourn is made, and another example of democratic rule by the people is over.

In February when the yearly budget is presented and approved, together with the tax rate, there is even less excitement than in October. Once again the rebel speaks, this time to the effect that this paying out of good money to teach music to kids is all tomfoolishness.

"Seems to me I remember your boy did pretty well playin' the piano at the exhibition they put on last spring," remarks the moderator.

The critic gulps with embarrassed pride and subsides. A good town-meeting moderator can give Anthony Eden lessons in tact and diplomacy.

There are, however, two occasions when the New England town meeting is as heated as Yankee assemblies ever get. One is the time the city folks present a petition and force the calling of a special meeting to vote on appropriating two hundred dollars for beautification of the village street. On questions of expenditure of town money not only legal voters have a voice, but also all adults who own more than three hundred dollars' worth of property in town. This peculiar state of affairs may cause occasional annoyance to the year-round inhabitants of the town, but they recognize that a taxpayer has a right to say how his money is spent.

A city-versus-town assembly is easily described. Of course, the city is for the appropriation; the town is against it. Just as naturally, the former do nine-tenths of the talking and provide all the eloquence, pleading, exhortation, appeals to town pride, and other forms of influencing the vote. The outcome is forty-eight for the appropriation; forty-two against. The victors go home jubilant and speak happily of the way they would run the town if they tried to. But in February, when most of the city folks are absent, the town rescinds the vote taken in July. There is no beautification.

The second variety of hot debate is the one in which the year-round inhabitants battle over some motion that has come as the result of a year or two of bitter undercover talk and campaigning. Let us say that the Curtis Valley voters want the money available for road improvements this year to be used for a bridge over the Muddy River, and the North District voters are just as determined to get a continuation of the road up Alworth Hill. Ordinarily this question would be dealt with in October, but the First Selectman, caught between two very lively fires, has at last declared that he is going to haul this quarrel out into the open; then perhaps he can get time to do some work. As it is now, all he does is listen to people "griping against each other." This complaint is well founded, for a New England town, although ordinarily serene, gets het-up about once a decade. The result would not impress a more hotblooded community as anything other than an interchange of preliminary courtesies, but, in the Land of Steady Habits, it is the equivalent of a Central American revolution.

The meeting is called for eight of a Saturday evening in June, and by seven-thirty the town hall is comfortably filled. A few city folks have come to defend their section of the town or to enjoy the fireworks, but the majority of the people is made up of genuine residents. Old friends spot each other for the first time in months, and news and gossip are pleasantly exchanged. This meeting is to be a struggle to the finish, but before forces are joined there is no reason why citizens should not enjoy themselves. At quarter of eight Jim Pierce arrives. His coming is heralded by the nostalgic wheeze of a Model-T Ford and the loud "Made it in five minutes flat, and it's a good four mile from my doorstep!" Everyone realizes that Jim has decided that a special town meeting, and on a Saturday night, calls for a little extra celebration. Now he stations himself by the main door and greets old friends.

"How fare ye, Seth? Lookin' kinda peaked these days, ain't ye? What you need is less of your wife and more of th' cider barrel. . . . An' if here ain't my ol' schoolmate, Deacon Osgood! How in hell be ye, Deacon? Sellin' much bob veal these days? . . . Now don't go skinnin' by without speakin' to me, Julie. That ain't th' way you treated me when we was both young 'n' gay."

Soon after this last remark, Mr. Pierce decides to find himself a seat before it is too late. In the doorway he pulls off his hat and waves it jovially to the assembled voters, then he weaves his way to a back corner on the men's side. Once comfortably established, he belches with loud and dramatic emphasis, says, "Begypden," and goes to sleep. He may be drunk but, as a veteran town-meeting-goer, he can be trusted to behave properly.

For the first time in years there is a vote taken over who shall be moderator. Fred Holcomb and another famous presider have decided to stay away from this meeting. Officially they are "under the weather"; actually they do not like to have anything to do with these bitter town quarrels, so a vote is necessary. The North District candidate wins. The Curtis Valley group is not too worried. "Asey Kimball more or less tries t' be fair 'n' square," it concedes. Such seemingly meager praise is in reality proof absolute that Mr. Kimball is a man of unquestioned honesty and integrity.

Now half a dozen men clamor to make their motions, for there is supposed to be great virtue in putting a positive statement of your wishes before the voters. The moderator looks at the ceiling, the floor, and out of the window; then he casts a furtive glance at the assembly. Finally he compromises by "recognizing" Newt Dudley, who lives on the village street and may be considered a partisan by principle, and not by personal interest, of the North District group. Newt rises and makes the desired motion; a seconder pops up, and the moderator mournfully asks if there is any discussion.

A valley champion states emphatically that the folks down his way are always left out when any money is being spent, and it's about time they got something to show for all the taxes they pay. "Why, they need a new bridge a whole lot more'n the North District people need a hard-surface road. That bridge that's there now is liable to cave in under the next truck that goes over it, but *any*body can get over that Alworth Hill road, in fact, it's better than most down his way."

Now, a North District champion is recognized. "Who says that Alworth Hill road is passable?" he demands. "Maybe it is three months of the year, the rest of the time . . ." and he gives a detailed account of the terrors of trekking that road. Another valley man argues fairly reasonably and is answered in the same spirit.

Then there is the inevitable blowoff. Up leaps an excitable valleyite. "It's about time," he declares, "that the selectmen stop playing favorites and hand out a little justice and fair dealing." Town Father James Munroe is on his feet before the hotheaded speaker is through. He'd like to know what all this talk about playing favorites means, states Mr. Munroe. "And who says the selectmen don't give fair dealings? Let him say this again. . . ."

With those two speeches, the flood gates open and anyone present who thinks that Yankees are a silent, inhibited people is in for a big surprise. Charges and countercharges, old injustices remembered, details about this or that bit of past town history, personal references, insulting answers, everything has its moment. No one sticks to the issue at hand. A chance remark that the town wastes money cutting brush beside the road leads here and there until the moderator has to stop a fervid argument between two men over whose ancestors were first in town.

When the vote is finally taken, the North District motion wins by two ballots.

"I protest!" shouts a valleyite. "I see one man put in two votes!"

"I demand another vote."

"I make a motion we have a standing vote."

"Second the motion."

The next vote is taken standing, and the tellers disagree among themselves. At last it is decided that the motion is carried by a majority of three votes. A stranger to New England folkways is sure to think this bitter fight will be resumed with fists or even clubs and knives after the meeting, but he is disappointed. One or two hotheaded citizens do pass a few remarks about soreheads or crooks, but the rest of the citizens go home quietly. The valley crowd is bitter enough, but it knows that it was outvoted in honest battle and it can look forward to doing better at the next town meeting.

These are real New England assemblies of the people, but they seldom satisfy the professional admirers of these noble institutions. For there has been so much talk about the last vestige of pure democracy, the lone remaining stronghold of popular government, the most authentic expression of the people's will, that the newcomer always expects too much of his first town meeting.

all over town. Snow plows for the roads. The selectmen's office looks like big business. School-board chairman talks like Teachers' College. Soil tested every year. Thoroughbred sires for a lot of herds. Subscribing to agricultural magazines and breeders' gazettes. Nobody misses the 11 P. M. price broadcast. Cars in the garage. Tractors and trucks in the sheds. Trips to the movies and for shopping. Townspeople are not hicks any more. Just tweneieth-century folks who live in the country.

This is a land of villages.

Some are on hills: Woodstock, Dudley, Thompson, Pomfret, Hampton. Others are in valleys or on level plains: Windham, Brooklyn, Eastford, Westchester, Salem, Canterbury. There are fertile stretches of farming land. That little valley just outside East Woodstock village. The big farm in Wauregan. The ones on Sterling Hill and in North Franklin and Lebanon.

This is poor and desolate country.

The Father Dunn region up around Warrenville where an up-and-coming Catholic priest helped the farmers to market their crops. And, if you wanted, you could go on back roads from Somers in the west to the factory section above and below North Grosvenordale and not see more than one house in a mile. Over beyond the mills, the country stretches in desolation through the East Douglas woods to the Blackstone valley. Then the poorly settled land falls away south from Douglas by Wallum Lake and through Glocester and Foster and West Greenwich and Beech Pond to within a few miles of the Sound. That T-square of land is about ten miles in width on the average, and when you pass through it, it is hard to remember that you are in the midst of three densely populated states.

This is a land of factories and mills.

Rockville, Willimantic, Putnam, Taftville, Wauregan, North Grosvenordale, Attawaugan, Occum, Hanover, Baltic, Talcottville, Killingly, Southbridge, Mechanicsville, Norwich, Greenville, Webster, Jewett City, Fiskdale, Brookfield, Three Rivers, Ware, Plainfield, Central Village, Moosup, South Coventry— those are a handful of the towns and cities that rely on their factories for support.

There is wealth in this country.

Shore estates. Pomfret Street. A bank in any one of a dozen little cities. The mills and factories in those same places. Lovely old houses on village streets. Watch Hill. Country homes all through the land. We do not flaunt our money, but we have it.

There is poverty in this country.

Shabby tenements in any mill city. Still poorer houses on the outskirts. A shack up a back road. Tumbledown houses half a mile from the chaste, lovely, quaint village street. People on relief, living on old-age assistance, or just plain on the town. Others no more than getting by but hanging on to their house as long as they can. Some people in this country are lazy and shiftless, others have had bad luck, and some are only tired. This is an old country and even pioneer blood runs thin at the last.

This is a beautiful land.

The meadows at Brookfield and Lake Quacumquaset. The view from almost any hill. The Thames River above New London. Many village streets and greens. Riding along half a hundred roads. Old houses. The stone walls near the Russian Bear in Thompson.

This is a sober, god-fearing land.

Grace is still said in country and city homes. Men and women work hard to keep their church going. Some give more for preaching than they can afford. They are kind neighbors and honest, godly people. They do not shout that they have found salvation or been washed in the blood of the lamb, but they live as decent folks. Their boys and girls are upstanding, well-behaved children. They go to dances and card parties; perhaps they smoke and take a bottle of beer. Times have changed in little ways, but the basic rules are the same.

The old Adam in us.

Not many crimes of violence. Knifings in some low saloon; robbery by force and violence; now and then a murder, a city brawl or some farmer paying off an old grudge; a tortured mind cracks. Petty thievings; some embezzlements; fraud, deceit, crooked dealings. We can be a crafty people when we go wrong. Most of our sins are of lustful bodies. Not much is said about who is grassing who. The flesh is weak, and yet the spirit may be strong; he and she are likely to settle down later on. And if they don't; well, then, they aren't worth talking and worrying over. Every city has its prostitutes; every town its willing girls—that is as it always has been and always will be. About every decade a town has a case of flagrant incest, but it doesn't always get into the courts. Making a fuss might cause more pain than good.

This country can't be classified.

There are too many ways of living and doings things. Going to church on Sunday and hiring the kind of minister folks want and keeping him or getting rid of him. No state or national board or bishop tells a New England town what sort of shepherd it pays for. A congregation is more than so many separate people. It is the town worshiping.

Doing your best to get ahead. Tight as the bark on a tree; got the first dollar you ever earned. Making your wife and kids work as hard as you do. Paying out money if it's good economy to do so. A thoroughbred herd sire, good farm machinery, a new silo; these are wise investments. But pretty clothes and a sled and new furniture do not pay dividends.

Making your business bring you in good returns. Sending your children to college. Giving your wife a maid and the house she wants. Florida in the winter as you grow old. Don't waste money but don't let it rule you.

Voting the straight Republican ticket. "I wouldn't vote for my own brother if he was a Democrat." Don't ask why the Party is sacred; just uphold it.

To hell with these mossbacks! Vote for Hurley for Governor and McGuire as Mayor. They're for the common man; they'll see to it that the boys are taken care of.

Supporting the big church with the cross. Bowing to the Father as he walks by. Bringing up the children to be good Catholics. Only misery and suffering come when young people marry out of the faith.

Remembering that you are Polish, French, Irish, Croat, Serb, Italian, Portuguese, Finn, Russian, Scandinavian. Thinking that you are better than those dirty foreigners next door. Voting for the man with the right name. Or staying a Slav or Celt or Latin and yet putting in John Moseley as First Selectman because maybe he'll run the town better than Jim O'Hara or Pierre Labert.

Going to grammar and high school and then for a year at the state college. Back home to the old farm. Marrying the girl you went to school with. Taking over your father's place in the church and Grange. Raising a family. Sending them off to college if they want to go. The middle boy wants to be a farmer. The oldest girl marries a farmer, too. That is the way a town keeps going.

Or finishing Yale and coming back to the family store on Main Street, into the bank or the insurance office. The good old home city is the best place after all. Boosting for the high-school teams. Being an Elk and Mason, a Rotarian. In the Chamber of Commerce. You and your wife part of the Younger Business Set, Anglo-Saxon, Republican, and Cocktails at Five. She goes shopping in Hartford; the two of you run down to New York twice a year for shows. *The New Yorker* on the living-room table.

Seventy-five years old this fall. Second richest man in the city. Old and well-off enough to do as you damn-well please. Hire a gardener to grow all the roses you want. Always did love roses but never had time for them until a year or two ago. To hell with the newfangled societies like the Rotary. Dropping in now and then on old friends, that's being sociable in the right way. Taking a snifter of Old Overholt with Ed Congdon or somebody like him. Too old to drive a car. Truth is, never really learned how. Always scared of the hell-blamed things. Felt safer with a horse and buggy. If "she" wants to go anywhere, let her call the man to back out the Buick and take her. As for him, he'll stay with his roses.

Growing old like an old-style New England banker. Never did much that was startling, but then again maybe he helped keep the country on an even keel. That crew in the White House! Oh well, his bank is sound, and that *Gloire de Dijon* rose lived through the winter. He always did like that name. His boy saw a rose garden in Dijon in France. Wrote home about it. Then he went on up to the front. Never wrote again. Only child, too.

That means the name dies out pretty soon. Some cousins out West—in Ohio or Indiana—but nobody in these parts. Well, that's the way things went. There have been Tillinghasts 'round here since long before the Revolution. Sort of funny, knowing you're the last one. Wonder if maybe he shouldn't ask one of the Ohio, or is it Indiana, cousins to come here. If he was a bright young fellow he could be pushed ahead in the bank, not too fast of course, but so he'd be at least assistant cashier by the time he was forty. Probably the fellow would have a lot of children— those westerners always do—so there would be Tillinghasts in the city for a long time to come.

But no, he guessed that sort of thing wouldn't do. Probably it could be worked out all right, but that wasn't the way folks like him handled their affairs. They didn't ask for help from outsiders, and any man from Ohio or Indiana or wherever it was, was an outsider no matter if he was a Tillinghast and a cousin. That was New England for you. Independent as a hog on ice. Rather let an old family die out than call for help. But he guessed it wasn't such a bad spirit after all. Look at where New England stood to-day. So if it had to be, it had to be. Sometimes a man couldn't help himself; he obeyed the rules of his people who had gone before him.

In Town Meeting Country there are many people doing many different things, but two common folkways unite them, two in-clusive and powerful patterns of behavior hold them together, First, these men and women are individuals. They are people working in one business or on one farm for themselves and their families. Second, they are folks who can come together in town meeting and act for the good of the community.

Those are the common denominators of this country. We are free men and women, doing as we please. We can also act as the town demands, for we are bound by its old and wise customs. That is why we can vote in the main wisely in town meeting. You have to be free before you can endure being bound by society; and you must be bound before you can build a society in which you can be free.

Index

243